THE SEXUAL POLITICS OF GENDERED VIOLENCE AND WOMEN'S CITIZENSHIP

Suzanne Franzway

Nicole Moulding

Sarah Wendt

Carole Zufferey

Donna Chung

First published in Great Britain in 2019 by

Policy Press
University of Bristol
1-9 Old Park Hill
Bristol
BS2 8BB
UK
t: +44 (0)117 954 5940
pp-info@bristol.ac.uk
www.policypress.co.uk

North America office:
Policy Press
c/o The University of Chicago Press
1427 East 60th Street
Chicago, IL 60637, USA
t: +1 773 702 7700
f: +1 773-702-9756
sales@press.uchicago.edu
www.press.uchicago.edu

British Library Cataloguing in Publication Data
A catalogue record for this book is available from the British Library

Library of Congress Cataloging-in-Publication Data
A catalog record for this book has been requested

ISBN 978-1-4473-3779-9 paperback
ISBN 978-1-4473-3778-2 hardcover
ISBN 978-1-4473-3781-2 ePub
ISBN 978-1-4473-3782-9 Mobi
ISBN 978-1-4473-3780-5 ePdf

The right of Suzanne Franzway, Nicole Moulding, Sarah Wendt, Carole Zufferey and Donna Chung to be identified as authors of this work has been asserted by them in accordance with the Copyright, Designs and Patents Act 1988.

Cover design by Policy Press
Front cover image: Miracles of Each Moment kindly supplied by Kazuaki Tanahashi
Printed and bound in Great Britain by CPI Group (UK) Ltd, Croydon, CR0 4YY
Policy Press uses environmentally responsible print partners

Contents

List of tables and figures

Tables

Figures

Notes on authors

Suzanne Franzway is Emeritus Professor of Sociology and Gender Studies at the University of South Australia. Her research focuses on sexual politics, greedy institutions, gendered violence and citizenship, and epistemologies of ignorance. She is a scholar activist in the area of women, work and social movements, serving on non-governmental organisations and is founding member of the UNESCO Women's Studies and Gender Research Network. Her publications include *Challenging knowledge, sex and power: Gender, work and engineering* (2013); *Making feminist politics: Transnational alliances between women and labor* (2011); *Sexual politics and greedy institutions: Union women, commitments and conflicts in public and in private* (2001) and *Staking a claim: Feminism, bureaucracy and the state* (1989).

Nicole Moulding is Associate Professor of Social Work at the University of South Australia. Her research and teaching interests are gendered violence and mental health. Her work has contributed to the development of a social perspective on mental health and wellbeing that acknowledges gender and other social power relations, and challenges pathologising discourses and practices. Her publications include *Gendered violence, mental health and recovery in everyday lives: Beyond trauma* (2016) and *Contemporary feminisms in social work practice* (2016) with Sarah Wendt.

Sarah Wendt is Professor of Social Work at Flinders University and has researched and published on violence against women and social work practice for over a decade. Her work focuses on gender power relations and domestic violence, and engaging men to address domestic violence. In particular, Sarah has been researching rural Australian women's experiences of domestic violence and more recently how domestic violence work shapes social workers living and working in rural communities. Her publications include *Domestic violence in rural Australia* (2009) and *Domestic violence in diverse contexts: A re-examination of gender* (2015).

Carole Zufferey is Senior Lecturer of Social Work at the University of South Australia. She has been researching gendered violence and homelessness for over two decades. Her research projects include exploring intersectionality and social work responses to gendered violence and homelessness. She has examined notions of home and homelessness as they relate to gender, age, cultural diversity, migration, sexuality and class relations. Her publications include *Homelessness and social work: An intersectional approach* (2016) and *Faces of homelessness in the Asia Pacific* (2017).

Donna Chung is Professor of Social Work at Curtin University. Her research interest in gendered violence has spanned over 20 years and involved a number of national studies in Australia as well as research in the UK. Donna's research has examined various facets of gendered violence including domestic violence-related homelessness for women, young people and dating violence, interventions for men who perpetrate domestic and sexual violence, and employment and economic abuse for women experiencing intimate partner violence. Her publications include 'Domestic violence: UK and Australian developments' in T. Evans and F. Keating (eds) *Policy and social work practice* (2015) and *Domestic violence: Working with men. Research, practice experiences and integrated responses* (2009).

Acknowledgements

We came together in our dismay at the persistence of the damning rates of violence against women. As feminists and researchers we have worked for gender equality and taken heart from the gains women have made in legislation, public policy and social conditions. Gendered violence is no longer invisible. However, there are very few signs that women have less cause to fear sexual abuse, harassment and even damaging long-term violence. The publicity given to extreme acts of violence and carefully worded national policies are clearly not enough. In pooling our knowledge and understanding, we asked what do we need to develop a more useful and effective approach that could contribute to substantive change. This book is one outcome of these efforts.

We began the project with the support of the University of South Australia and funding from the Australian Research Council, Project No: DP1130104437 titled *Gendered violence and citizenship: The complex effects of intimate partner violence on mental health, housing and employment.* We also thank Curtin University and Flinders University for their support over the course of the whole project. We were very fortunate in being joined by Dr Alison Elder as our Research Associate during a major period when we were designing and undertaking the empirical research on which the book is grounded. Associate Professor Janet Bryan gave us excellent advice on the statistical aspects of our research. Dr Claire Nettle provided timely research assistance in the later stages and Dr Sam Franzway gave fine editing support.

We would like to thank and acknowledge all the women who participated in the research for their courage, thoughtfulness and generosity.

We also give thanks to the artist, Kazuaki Tanahashi for allowing the use of his image, Zen Circle, for the cover design. Finally, we each thank our loved ones for their support and care throughout this endeavour.

ONE

The sexual politics of gendered violence and women's citizenship

Introduction

Gendered violence is now such a major problem globally that the United Nations has named it as a significant violation of women's human rights and freedoms. However, men's violence against women persists even in those societies where women have formal and equal citizenship. Citizens expect their rights and freedoms to be protected and supported by the state, but statistics report that instances of gendered violence, particularly domestic violence, remain alarmingly high. In 2005, the World Health Organization (WHO) established that violence against women caused more death and disabilities among women aged 15 to 44 than cancer, malaria, traffic accidents and war combined (de Silva de Alwis, 2012). Public debates about the causes of gendered violence and the possible solutions to it are fiercely contested in both the popular media and the research and policy communities.

Studies across the world consistently show that domestic violence in the form of intimate partner violence (IPV) is largely perpetrated by male partners against female partners (Alhabib et al., 2010; Akyüz et al., 2012; Manjoo, 2014; Cox, 2015). As True (2012: 10) points out, we cannot ignore the global evidence that women and girls are more likely to be killed or injured by male partners than by any other class of individuals. Feminist perspectives on domestic violence have developed more nuanced and inclusive approaches to the problem that enhance the provision of specialist services and the efforts to eliminate or reduce violence against women (Murray, 2002). These developments have encouraged more diverse groups of women to speak about their experiences of violence, experiences which contribute to local, national and international policy and service systems (Laing and Humphreys, 2013).

Sexual politics

The view that domestic violence is closely connected with gender inequality has gained ground and is to be celebrated. However, the politics of gender inequality, and therefore of gendered violence, tends to be side-stepped. We draw on the term 'sexual politics', originated by Kate Millett (1969), to bring the contested arena of gender and power onto the field. We then propose the argument that sexual politics is at the centre of the refusal to challenge the political implications of the argument that gendered violence is integrally connected to gender inequality (Franzway, 2016).

In this contribution to feminist theorising we argue that sexual politics is present in all aspects of our lives, including gendered violence, the state and citizenship. Sexual politics opens up new possibilities for understanding the persistent effects of domestic violence by shifting attention to the politics of gender relations. This shift away from the binary category of gender as men/women to the active and relational dynamics of sexual politics undercuts assumptions that gendered violence is natural or inevitable, or that violence is only caused by individuals. Sexual politics has material and discursive effects and offers an understanding of how the gendered dynamics of domestic violence and its long-term consequences have remained largely hidden from view. We argue that the persistence of violence against women is implicated in the sexual politics of citizenship and the state. Hence, the challenge of violence against women is recognised as an issue for the state, citizenship and society.

Reformers seek to work around the problem of gender and power when constructing strategies to persuade governments and policy makers to endorse measures and reforms in support of women experiencing violence. Rather than confronting the problem as based on the sexual politics of unequal gendered power or of deeply embedded patterns of gender inequality, an apparently successful approach in western societies is to frame the violence in terms of individual women's experiences. Incidents of IPV may incite public interest and dismay when a particularly gruesome story can be told of a woman's death at the hands of her partner who 'snapped'. However, this view of IPV as a matter of separate and isolated incidents, perpetrated by individual men, effectively deflects attention from the sexual politics of gendered violence and gender inequality. Campaigners against gendered violence adopt this focus on individuals as a strategy that seeks to win state support for policies aimed at the prevention of violence against women without seriously challenging the prevailing male-dominated gender regime. In contrast, we argue for an approach centred on the sexual politics of gendered violence and its impact on women's citizenship rights and responsibilities.

Support for women experiencing gendered violence has been won in terms of changes in community attitudes as well as in the legal, policy and service areas. However, feminists who have agitated for decades to win these changes must continue to contest contemporary sexual politics in order to keep the focus on domestic violence as a social, economic and political concern (Walby, 1990; Wendt and Zannettino, 2015). In addition, when gendered violence is understood as isolated events, a widespread ignorance prevails about the discriminatory impact it has on the millions of women who are negotiating, surviving or leaving violent partners every day. Further, there is a pervasive lack of awareness that domestic violence invades all areas of women's lives (Kwesiga et al., 2007; Staggs et al., 2007; Devaney, 2008). Women affected by domestic violence are faced with high levels of housing stress, threats to their employment and income stability, and undermined health, particularly their mental health (Chung et al., 2000; Franzway et al., 2009; Wendt and Hornosty, 2010; Moulding, 2016). One of the more significant yet invisible effects of domestic violence is that it serves to curtail women's ability to move freely in public and private spaces.

Citizenship

The aim of this book is to focus on the sexual politics of the substantial impact that domestic violence has on women's lives and their rights as citizens. We are concerned with the far-reaching effects of domestic violence on women's rights and so we draw on a historical definition of one's membership in a community: 'It is comprised of an indivisible and interrelated set of rights and it demands a corresponding obligation on States to respect, protect and fulfil rights' (Manjoo, 2014: 4).

The feminist scholar Ruth Lister refers to citizenship as a set of social and political relationships, practices and identities that can together be described as a sense of belonging (Lister, 2007). Others have described it as a 'momentum concept' which demands continuous development of its egalitarian potential (Hoffman, 2004: 138). Certainly, citizenship is a concept which signals a society that endorses justice, equality, freedom, dignity and a sense of belonging (Franzway, 2016). Paradoxically, gender inequalities persist, as do class and race inequalities among the citizens of all contemporary modern states. We take the feminist view that gender inequality and gendered violence are interconnected through the dynamics of everyday sexual politics and we argue that the material and discursive effects of the state of male-dominated sexual politics works to obstruct all women from exercising their full rights as citizens.

Framing domestic violence as an erosion of women's citizenship can offer greater understanding of the complex and long-term consequences long after the incidents of violence have ceased. Citizenship also enables us to explore the corresponding obligations of the state to enable, respect and protect women's rights as well as to develop understandings about why domestic violence persists at such disturbing rates. We therefore mobilise the concept of citizenship to investigate the impact of domestic violence on key dimensions of the everyday life of women citizens, specifically their housing, employment, mental health and social participation and engagement. Examining the impact of domestic violence on these dimensions helps us make sense of the specific and interconnected ways in which gendered violence undermines women's citizenship. Furthermore, citizenship turns our attention to women's agency and their capabilities in navigating their rights and responsibilities in relation to the state's policies and responses.

Combined capabilities

We understand these key dimensions of everyday life in the light of Nussbaum's 10 central capabilities, which form a minimum threshold for a decent political order for all citizens. These capabilities are defined by Nussbaum and Amartya Sen as 'a set of (usually interrelated) opportunities to choose and to act' (Nussbaum, 2011: 20). Nussbaum expands on the 10 capabilities as follows:
First, and perhaps foremost, is the capability of the citizen to live a normal life span and not die prematurely.

Second is the capacity to have good health, including reproductive health, adequate nourishment, and shelter.

Third is bodily integrity, which involves the ability to move freely from place to place, to be secure against violent assault, including sexual assault and domestic violence, having opportunities for sexual satisfaction, and choice in the matter of reproduction.

Fourth is sense, imagination and thought and means being able to use the senses, including imagination, thought and reason, cultivated by adequate education.

Fifth is emotions, that is, citizens are able to have attachments to things and people outside themselves, to love, and not have one's emotions blighted by fear and anxiety.

Sixth is practical reason and being able to form a conception of the good (in the light of the liberty of conscience and religious observance) and to engage in critical reflection about the planning of one's life.

Seventh is affiliation, which refers to being able to live with and toward others, to recognise and show concern for other human beings, to engage in various forms of social interaction and to imagine the situation of another. It also includes having the social bases of self-respect and non-humiliation, being treated as a dignified being whose worth is equal to that of others. Affiliation entails non-discrimination based on race, sex, sexual orientation, ethnicity, caste, religion and national origin.

Eighth is being able to live with concern for and in relation to animals, plants and the world of nature.

Ninth is being able to play, to laugh, and enjoy recreational activities.

Finally, Nussbaum names control over one's environment as the tenth capability, that is, the political and material environment. This is being able to participate effectively in political choices that govern one's life, being able to hold property and have property rights on an equal basis with others, and having the right to seek employment on an equal basis with others (Nussbaum, 2011: 33-34). We recognise that the impact of capabilities are complicated by the effects of the intersectionality of class and race as well as gender (Crenshaw, 1994).

We draw on the connections between these 10 capabilities and citizenship in our argument about the impact of gendered violence on women's citizenship. Nussbaum's 10 capabilities enable social and political relationships, practices and identities, as well as dignity and belonging; in other words, citizenship. Domestic violence is an ongoing threat that interferes with every major capability in a woman's life (Nussbaum, 2005). Fear and humiliation created by violent perpetrators compromise women's capabilities, limiting their opportunities and crippling imagination, thought, senses and emotions. This erodes women's active participation in many social and political activities. Domestic violence affects social and physical mobility, independence and control over one's environment, such as enjoying a rewarding working life, property, leisure, and play (Nussbaum, 2005: 173). However, it is important to note that capabilities are not simply internal to each individual, and thus solutions to domestic violence cannot reside in the individual abilities of women to manage, escape, survive and recover.

As we discuss in more detail in Chapter Four, Nussbaum (2011) develops the concept of combined capabilities to connect personal abilities and freedoms or opportunities with political, social and economic environments. The concept of these combined capabilities directs attention to the significant and central role of the state in shaping those environments. If domestic violence undermines a person's combined capabilities, we need to ask what part does the state play in the prevention and protection of those capabilities if a decent political order is to be sustained? We therefore argue that the extent of violence against women depends on the state, rather than simply on the actions of individual violent men or on the individual initiatives of women themselves.

We examine the protracted effects of domestic violence on women's lives through investigating housing, employment, mental health and social participation as important, combined capabilities of women who have experienced domestic violence. Researchers, activists and policy makers have paid close attention to the damaging impact of domestic violence on each of these areas. For example, the women's shelter movement recognises the specific needs of women escaping from violence with frightened children and few resources. Research has established domestic violence as one of the major reasons for women's homelessness (Netto et al., 2009; Baker et al., 2010; Ponic et al., 2011). Domestic violence also affects women's access to and availability for employment and their performance while at work (Jackson, 2007; Abraham, 2010; Pollack et al., 2010). Similarly, domestic violence is found to result in both short- and long-term physical, mental and sexual health problems, and can lead to some women increasing their use of drugs and alcohol as a means of coping (Fischbach and Herbert, 1997; Montero et al., 2011).

What is less well observed is that the harm caused by violence has effects which are interconnected across all dimensions of lived experience; for example, flight to a women's shelter can make it difficult to meet employment commitments, such as having access to work clothes, as well as maintaining a healthy sense of self and community. By examining the debilitating consequences of domestic violence on women's lives, we demonstrate the interconnected and often long-term erosion of women's material and emotional wellbeing, and argue that domestic violence has dire consequences for women's citizenship. Nussbaum's combined capabilities provide a useful conceptual framework within which to analyse these interconnected and multiple adversities experienced as the result of domestic violence.

Outline of the book

In the following chapter, we draw together these theoretical perspectives in developing our argument about gendered violence and women's citizenship. We suggest that the state's role in securing, enabling and maintaining the rights of citizens plays an important part in how violence is perpetrated and challenged. The apparent failure of the state to protect women as citizens from persistent violence is examined, with particular attention to the sexual politics of power and violence, and the interconnections of material conditions, discourses and subjectivities in the everyday life of the citizen. The chapter proposes that the persistence of domestic violence is implicated in the sexual politics of citizenship. In addition, the discursive impact of a politics of ignorance serves to deny or obscure how women's inequality, materially and discursively, is produced and reproduced in everyday life.

Our argument is grounded in the empirical data from a large-scale national study we conducted across Australia. The respondents were generous in their responses, providing a good deal of written and verbal commentary about their experiences of IPV. In Chapter Three, on the challenges of researching gendered violence, we present the empirical foundation and design of the study, which included a major survey, in-depth interviews and constructed life histories, and consider some of the challenges faced when conducting and participating in gendered violence research in the context of the politics of ignorance and sexual politics.

Chapter Four on living the connected effects of violence situates our argument that domestic violence reverberates across women's lives and erodes their citizenship. Our data analysis reveals the effects of IPV on the material, emotional and social aspects of women's lives, and how such violence disrupts and restricts their combined capabilities to participate in everyday life, very often for lengthy periods. We offer insights into how women's experiences are shaped by a range of factors, such as state legislation and policy, the resilience or hostility of their own families and communities, and the availability of opportunities to gain and maintain employment. We find that women who have experienced violence rarely regain their place on their original life course. The quality of their housing, employment, mental health and social participation is generally diminished.

We devote Chapter Five to questions about why IPV is understood in terms of its psychological impact on individual women. We suggest alternative ways that the serious psychological and emotional impact of IPV might be understood and addressed so that policy and practice may be more beneficial. The notion of coercive control has become an important explanatory concept, exposing how IPV is almost always experienced as repeated, patterned violence, intimidation, isolation and fear. Our data shows how gendered discourses, practices and power relations that are embedded in domestic violence erode women's sense of themselves as persons, and hence their capabilities to exercise their citizenship.

Perhaps one of the most important outcomes of our focus on the impact of violence on women's citizenship is the light it throws on the issues of participation and engagement in society. Women's opportunity to move and engage as freely as men is always a site of contention, and of sexual politics. The prevention of women from driving in Saudi Arabia is just one, admittedly extreme, example of constraints on women's freedom of movement. (The recent decision to allow women limited freedom to drive is something for which Saudi feminists have long campaigned (Zoepf, 2017).) Recognising that domestic violence, especially in the form of coercive control, is likely to damage women's ability to move freely from place to place, we asked participants about their social participation and whether it was compromised by the deleterious material effects of domestic violence. In Chapter Six, on re-engaging lives, we examine how the sexual politics of domestic violence gives rise to stigma and shame, eroding women's confidence and trust in others. We identify the ways that IPV isolates women and effectively limits their social participation, autonomy and agency. Our discussion also turns to how women overcome these limitations.

In Chapter Seven, we step back to take a larger view that acknowledges the effort required to reach the point where gendered violence in all its forms has become a visible political issue. We track the feminist struggles and campaigns to name domestic violence as a significant social, economic, cultural, and health problem that brings enormous costs to women, children and the wider community. At the same time, we remind the wider movement against gendered violence that it is a feminist claim that domestic violence is a political problem, a problem of sexual politics, and this claim continues to be strongly contested by those who oppose gender equality.

We write this book to expose the long-term and interconnected consequences of gendered violence on women's citizenship. In doing so, we contribute to the ongoing contestation of sexual politics by challenging the ignorance which seeks to deny connections between gender inequality, violence and the role of the state. Since the state is central to the political, social and civil rights of equal citizenship, it plays a key role in the struggle against domestic violence which undermines those rights. It is the state which has the obligation to protect women's rights to safety, housing, mental health, employment and social connection from men's violence, and it is the state's betrayal of those rights that needs to be exposed. The lens of sexual politics spotlights the gendered conflict integral to the struggle in the elimination of domestic violence, but also draws attention to the valuable sources of agency and the practices of citizenship that have already produced the gains we discuss in the following chapters.

This book contributes to feminist politics that aims to promote gender equality and to end violence against women. We investigate how domestic violence affects women's citizenship and we take an innovative and original approach which involves three distinctive foci. First, we demonstrate the effects of domestic violence across interconnected combined capabilities. Second, we show how these interconnections play out over time in complex and diverse ways in women's lives. Third, we understand domestic violence as arising out of the conflict, denial and struggle of sexual politics in families, communities and states. Awareness of the complexities as well as the material and discursive conditions of sexual politics is vital if we are to make real progress in stopping the appalling damage caused by domestic violence.

TWO

Problems of citizenship, violence and gender

Introduction

Violence against women seems to pervade all societies, even those societies where women have won formal equality with men. Women may have achieved full legal citizenship in most societies, but their rights continue to be damaged by the persistence of violence against them. The first waves of feminists fought hard and for decades to win full citizenship rights for women at the levels of the nation state and of international institutions such as the United Nations (UN). Although gains have been made and gender-based violence has become a visible problem of social and political concern, women do not yet have the substantial equal rights envisaged by the suffragists. In our research, we have puzzled over the apparent failure of women's citizenship rights to protect them from violent male citizens. Together with victims of violence, women in social justice movements, social workers and other support workers, and policy makers, we confront the question of how to tackle the problem of violence against women effectively, in particular its persistent and ubiquitous nature.

In our focus on the impact of violence against women, we recognise citizenship as a site of contested gender relations where there is an 'on-going struggle with no stopping point' (Hoffman, 2004: 13). Rather than searching for reasons for gender-based violence within individual psychologies or gendered biologies, we explore the connections between violence, citizenship and gender. While there is no doubt that individuals have unique life stories that contribute to their propensity for engaging in violence or abuse, violence against women is a social, political and cultural phenomenon. We recognise in our own significant data set, as well as in the research literature, that there are clear patterns to the perpetration of violence, its effects on women's rights, and the public and private responses to gender-based violence. These patterns cannot be understood in terms of individual actions, since there is no equivalence between men's violence and women's violence in terms of cause, context, effect or response. And yet, in societies premised on full and equal citizenship for all, it is assumed that all citizens enjoy their rights equally.

In order to argue that violence undermines women's rights as citizens, our attention needs to shift to questions of gender and citizenship, and therefore to the state which is integral to both citizenship and equal rights. In doing so we draw on long standing arguments that the power of the state is interconnected with the control of violence (Gerth and Mills, 1948; Walby, 2009), and therefore is central to challenging the persistence of violence in society as well as to ameliorating its effects on individuals and communities. The state's power relies on its control of violence, institutionalised in the state's control of the military and the police. It is the state which enables, supports and secures citizenship. In this chapter, we tackle these debates around citizenship and gender, and draw on Franzway (2016) to argue that the concept of sexual politics provides a useful lens to analyse violence, the state and citizenship.

Citizenship

Many scholars and practitioners in the field of violence against women have paid close attention to the question of rights in order to ground campaigns around prevention, support and change (Keck and Sikkink, 1998; Kelly, 2013; UN Women, 2017). Citizenship has become a valuable sign of modernity and of justice, freedom, equality, dignity and integrity of the self, seen as 'inflected by identity, social positioning, cultural assumptions, institutional practices and a sense of belonging' (Yuval-Davis and Werbner, 1999: 4). At a global level, the UN General Assembly adopted the Universal Declaration of Human Rights in 1948 (Article 25), which states that everyone has the right to a standard of living that is adequate for their health and wellbeing, including access to food, clothing, housing and medical care.

The 1993 UN Declaration on the Elimination of Violence against Women was premised on the affirmation 'that violence against women constitutes a violation of the rights and fundamental freedoms of women and impairs or nullifies their enjoyment of those rights and freedoms, and [that it was] concerned about the long-standing failure to protect and promote those rights and freedoms in the case of violence against women'. The declaration was an outcome of lengthy and extensive feminist campaigns framed in terms of a rights discourse. Some twenty years later a Note by the UN Secretary-General (2014: 4/21) observed that violence against women plays an important, if overlooked role, in 'obstructing the realization of women's citizenship rights'. Arguing for the value of utilising a 'citizenship lens' in the campaign to eliminate such violence, the Note proposed that citizenship highlights the importance of women being able to participate as full citizens. This reveals the ways that violence impedes women's capacity to exercise their citizenship rights, and importantly, emphasises the need for states to fulfil their responsibilities to prevent violence against women. Along similar lines, the UN report by the special rapporteur on violence against women, Rashida Manjoo, promotes the need for state intervention to work towards eliminating gender-based violence in public and private spheres (Manjoo, 2014: 4).

The UN defines citizenship in terms of the state and the citizen's mutual rights and obligations, while being careful to include a broad notion of belonging to community without being limited by nationality. Nevertheless, citizenship and the state are closely intertwined; the rights, duties and freedoms of citizenship depend on a structured and ordered power, while disorder and chaos undermine the status and practices of citizenship, as we see in any community torn by war.

Both the scholarly and the everyday meanings of citizenship are highly contested (Mann, 1987; Hall and Held, 1990; Walby, 1994; Lister, 1997, 2003; Turner, 1997; Hearn et al., 2010). Gender–neutral language tends to be employed. For example, citizenship is defined as 'the passive and active membership of individuals within a nation–state with universalistic rights and obligations at specified levels of equality' (Janoski and Gran, 2002: 3). Debates on definitions of citizenship focus on questions of the universal rights of individuals, but, we note, fail to examine the effects of conceptualising individuals as gender–neutral. Some writers argue that framing rights as universal may have the strategic benefit of winning greater legitimacy and discursive leverage in legislatures and the courts than specific group rights are likely to (Kymlicka, 1995). Others argue against universality since 'there are assumptions within the broad concept of citizenship of universality, that citizenship status transcends "particularity and difference"' (Young, 1989: 250). Ruth Lister suggests that citizenship can incorporate both meanings (Lister, 2002) while Chantal Mouffe (1992: 375) prefers that 'sexual difference' becomes irrelevant when it relies on 'women's so-called specific tasks'. The problem is that such arguments fail to recognise gender as historical, dynamic and social, rather treating it as a static category that needs to be simply made visible or, at worst, added on as a concept.

When gender is invisible and the citizen is understood as gender–neutral, the problems of women's citizenship reverts to a focus on women rather than onto the politics of gender and citizenship, and therefore onto the role of the state in relation to women's citizenship issues. An important strategy aimed at countering such effects is adopted by Jeff Hearn who proposes to name 'men as men' to break '[t]he silence that has persisted on the category of men [as gendered actors] in both theory and practice around citizenship' (Hearn, 2002: 246). As is typical, in this argument when men are seen as gendered actors, the category includes the assumption that men are always advantaged in relation to women. Naming men as men rather than as merely gender-neutral citizens, in this case, means naming their unequal power, a progressive move in arguments for gender equality. However, it is the unequal power that needs to be addressed if progressive change is to be achieved.

Gender and sexual politics

Gender is a multi-dimensional concept. Yet it has become a one-dimensional way to signal the presence of women. A survey is seen to be gendered if it collects information from women as well as from men, a union membership list is gendered if it distinguishes members into the categories men and women, and citizenship is gendered only if it overtly refers to women as well as to men. Even among feminists the meaning of gender tends to be taken for granted, referring to (heterosexual) women as a social category, or to relations between women and men, or less often, to a diversity of sexualities. In this book, gender is conceptualised as sexual politics, based on Franzway's (2001; 2016) reworking of Kate Millet's term. Millett originally argued that the sexes, in parallel with races, castes and classes, should be understood as well-defined and coherent groups and thus subject to politics. Sexual politics understands gender

> as fluid and relational, and centrally, that gender relations are continually being contested. ... contested gender relations are dynamic and therefore open to change, including transformative challenges to women's disadvantage. Sexual politics is not simply a matter of women in conflict with men, but recognises the wide and mobile diversities of gendered identities. (Franzway, 2016: 19)

Thus all men may benefit from male dominance, but not exhaustively; for example, non-heterosexual men have a history of being subjected to a most intense subordination (Seidman, 1997; Browne et al., 2007; Tiemeyer, 2013). In capitalist societies, working-class men do not enjoy the same privileges of male dominance as elite men do (Connell, 1995).

Sexual politics comprise complex gender relationships of power that may produce domination, resistance, alliances and/or pleasures, noting that relations of power are not entirely matters of oppression, but can and do involve desire and satisfaction. The politics of gender relations are complex also because they are shaped by historical shifts in the interconnected meanings of race, class, age, ableism, sexuality and theories of their intersectionality. Sexual politics is not restricted to relations between women and men, but includes the wide range of diversity between and among all genders. This is illustrated, for example, by Wendt and Zannettino who identify the limitations of four main theoretical approaches that have been proposed to explain abuse within same-sex relationships, including perpetrators' personality disorders, socio-political oppression of at-risk populations (and its patriarchal version in the case of lesbian partnerships), and the negative effects of internal and external stressors of discrimination and internalised homophobia (Wendt and Zannettino, 2015: 172). By contrast, we argue that the dominant discourses and practices of sexual politics shape and influence how LGBTIQ (lesbian, gay, bisexual, transgender, intersex and queer) relationships are positioned in the context of gendered violence.

The value of the term 'sexual politics' is that it draws attention to both the sexual and the political, in contrast to the way in which gender has become a binary and descriptive category. The focus of sexual politics on the political in gender lays stress on the changeability of gender relations through the contestations of power in contrast to the stability of gender as a binary category. It allows for an integrated understanding of gender as diverse in contrast to a model where multiple genders are simply added on to the main binary. In sexual politics, male dominance must be continually re-won and reaffirmed against challenges from the shifts in, and changes to, the meanings and effects of power, masculinities, femininities, bodies, and material, social and political contexts. Sexual politics exposes the struggles around the dominance of masculine heterosexuality and the effort required to maintain (heterosexual) men's power in contemporary society. Hence, the state of play in the sexual politics of gender relations, whether patriarchal or egalitarian, at any particular time and place is the result of that contest.

Sexual politics shapes transnational and global organisations such as the UN. For example, the UN Universal Declaration of Human Rights fails to include the specific rights of women (Yuval-Davis and Werbner, 1999) or, rather, it occludes women's rights into an apparent gender-neutrality. Munday (2009: 260) observes that 'issues of bodily integrity and intimate violence are often ignored and not seen as legitimate grounds for granting [women] refugee status'. Similarly, sexual politics plays out through issues of migration, including legal and illegal economic migration as well as movements of refugees and asylum seekers (Pettman, 1996; Ehrenreich and Hochschild, 2002).

In this theorising of gender, relations of gender are never settled, although the apparent universality of male dominance and gender inequality gives that impression (Okin, 1991). If the sexual politics of relations of gender were fixed, the considerable and constant efforts to enforce and maintain male dominance would not be needed (Connell, 1987; Walby, 2009; Bradley, 2013). For example, the thin representations of women's sports in the media and the equally thin pay packets women receive in contrast to men in sport are largely accepted as simply the way things are. Likewise, sexual politics is central to the wilful ignorance and denial about the causes of the systemic inequalities integral to the sexual division of labour (Franzway et al., 2009a). Although gender inequality is either denied or taken for granted, efforts to challenge male dominance and its effects are often met with considerable antagonism. For examples, articles in the mainstream media which seek to draw attention to the extent of violence against women are met with extreme hostility. Even the usually popular First Dog on the Moon (a cartoon strip published in Australia) aroused an unusually large and rancorous commentary for a strip titled 'A how not to guide on men's violence. Thanks Donald Trump' (First Dog on the Moon, 2016), responses that were in sharp contrast to the more usual feedback to the cartoonist's work.

Sexual politics does not see women's inequality as inevitable. With its stress on politics, the term stands against the common depoliticising of the term 'gendered' and the implication that women's disadvantage is normal and impossible to change. It challenges the assumption that when a concept or condition is recognised as gendered, women are likely to be disadvantaged relative to men, particularly heterosexual white men. Such assumptions obscure the enormous changes to the dynamics of gender relations, and everyday lived experience, as well as the histories of material and discursive struggles over gender and power. Gender relations are seen to have the potential to be configured in multiple different ways and not as inevitably patriarchal.

Sexual politics allows us to ask how women's inequality is produced and reproduced, both materially and discursively. The dynamic and changing conditions of sexual politics help to explain inequalities in the everyday life of public and civic power, wealth and income, status and authority, independence and mobility, while opening up spaces for political action. This approach avoids static understandings of gender which tend to default to the category 'woman'. Such a category ignores the diversity and fluidity of gender, and effectively hides the workings of gendered power. In sum, sexual politics recognises that gender was, and is, integral to the state, citizenship and society in general, whether or not women themselves are directly involved.

Citizenship and gender

We argue that citizenship has always been defined, understood and practised in terms of gender. Sexual politics recognises that gender has been neither excluded nor ignored. Rather, the sexual politics of contested gender relations has produced the historical changes in the meanings of citizenship since it originated in the Athenian city-state and on through feudal states to the democratic nation state. Traditional historians agree that only (free born) men could be Athenian citizens and they '... secured [the] leisure for politics and culture largely at the expense of their wives, of aliens who had no share in the government, and of slaves who had no rights whatever' (Childe, 1954: 207). Feminist scholar Ann Towns describes the Athenian state, as '...an alleged pillar of Western civilization ... [that] was a slave state in which women were subordinated and isolated in the home, away from the cherished public life of equal citizens' (Towns, 2016: 83).

Gender was not ignored, rather it was an active and specific criterion for inclusion or exclusion, which was the result of a sexual politics aimed at ensuring certain men's dominance of city-state power. When the Roman Empire later extended citizenship beyond the city to the vast majority of its imperial subjects, it was granted only to the free men (Nicolet 1988 cited in Janoski and Gran, 2002: fn 2, 54). Over the following centuries, the sexual politics of gender was and continues to be a central feature of the continuing and changing construction of the category of citizen (Pateman, 1992; Walby, 1994; Lister, 2003; Lombardo and Verloo, 2009).

The substantial changes to the meanings of citizenship resulting from the deployment of material levers and discursive strategies in these historical struggles have seen the state change from small city-states, to feudal regimes, colonial empires and to contemporary capitalist nation states (Isin and Turner, 2002). Citizenship did not develop in a direct, progressive line through these changing forms of state power. In feudal states, a small elite of monarchs reigned over subjects whose rights as citizens had largely disappeared. Likewise, male dominance has taken diverse forms in the face of changing configurations of sexual politics,

17

shifting from patriarchal rule (of the fathers) to the apparently more egalitarian fraternal sexual contracts or rule of the brothers, as Pateman describes it (1988). A major paradox in the history of citizenship is that women have been either excluded or included on the basis of the very same capacities and attributes (Pateman, 1992). At times, women were granted a degree of inclusion as citizens, based on their capacity for motherhood, yet remained subordinated to men. Nineteenth-century feminists argued that women's duty to the state undertaken through their roles as mothers should entitle them to full and equal rights of citizens (see for example Ehrenreich and English, 1978).

Citizenship has long roots extending into the histories of the BCE world, but in contemporary social and political theory the theoretical starting point is generally located in T.H. Marshall's work, encapsulated in his 1949 lectures and subsequent essays (Marshall, 1950). Marshall drew on earlier thinkers, but was also heavily influenced by the effects on the populace, markets and state institutions of the Great Depression of the 1930s and the upheavals of post World War 2 social and economic change. His model of the citizen was 'an advanced construct of a man [sic] who could operate with dignity free from want and enforced idleness' (Murray, 2007: 225). His most influential contribution was to divide citizenship into three aspects: civil, political and social. Marshall defines civil rights as 'necessary for individual freedom, … [including] the right to defend and assert all one's rights on terms of equality with others and by due process of law'; political rights as the right to participate in 'the exercise of political power' and social rights to include economic security and the ability to 'live the life of a civilised being'. Importantly, he goes on to identify the institutions most closely associated with civil rights as the courts of justice; parliament and councils of local government correspond with political rights and the institutions most closely connected with social rights are the educational system and the social services (Marshall, 1950: 10-11).

Marshall's historical analysis of citizenship rights connects their emergence in their contemporary forms with the rise of capitalism and the nation state since the 17th century. For Marshall, civil rights were accumulated, politics rights were actively gained and social rights were originally associated with membership of viable local communities and functional associations. However, he fails to recognise the extent to which citizenship rights were actively achieved through struggles in and around the state and the market. For example, social rights were won by labour movement struggles for 'collective bargaining over wages and working conditions, insurance against unemployment and ill-health and the guarantee of minimum standards of housing, employment and health care' (Murray, 2007: 228). Walby (1994) cautions that Marshall, and later Mann (1987) and Turner (1997), fail to recognise that women won their citizenship rights in a different historical sequence from men. However, it is worth noting that Marshall at least did recognise that women's citizenship history was not the same as men's.

> The story of civil rights ... is one of gradual addition of new rights to a status that was held to appertain to all adult members of the community – or perhaps one should say to all male members, since the status of women, or at least of married women, was in some important respects peculiar. (Marshall, 1950: 18)

Just what was peculiar about married women is left unexplored. Walby, among others, reminds us that in the US and the UK women did not have the equal political right to vote until much later than men (1920 and 1928 respectively). Married women did not have the 'right to justice' in that they had no right to refuse their husband's sexual intercourse (Walby, 1994: 381). More recently, at times of national independence from colonial powers in many developing countries, women have won the franchise together with men (Walby, 1994: 384; see also Nash, 2001). Nation states have diverse histories of formation and so the histories of their citizenship are similarly diverse.

Feminists and others concerned with social justice have paid a great deal of attention to questions and debates around the meanings and effects of citizenship rights, particularly as developed in Marshall's model. What tends to be overlooked however, is the significance of the associated agencies and institutions without which citizenship rights would be merely abstractions. The capacity to exercise and enjoy full civil, political and social citizenship depends on the agencies and institutions of the courts, parliaments and social services, and in turn they are very much part of the modern state. The state is therefore critical to the development and meaning of citizenship. The citizenry for its part has responsibilities, duties and obligations to the state, including taking up and exercising its rights (Pateman, 1992, 2011).

Marshall believed that equality was a principle inherent in the concept of citizenship, but it contradicted what he saw as the necessary inequality of the class system for the capitalist market. '... in the twentieth century, citizenship and the capitalist class system have been at war' (Marshall, 1950: 29). The problem was how the state could provide the necessary support for citizens to exercise their equal rights while also providing the equally necessary support for the capitalist market. He sought to resolve the problem with the argument that civil rights are indispensable for the capitalist market, that political rights could be exercised peacefully and that social rights could benefit capital more directly (p 33). More recent commentators point to the resulting permanent tension between the principles of equality that underpin democracy and the de facto inequalities of wealth and income that characterise the capitalist market (Jessop, 1978; Mann, 1987; Murray, 2007). Such tensions are further complicated by the intersectionalities of the constructs and effects of race and ethnicity as well as caste and status within modern states (Yuval-Davis, 1997).

Subsequent changes to the connections between the state and the capitalist market have occurred with the growing strength of neoliberal policies aimed at enhancing the market at the expense of the principles of citizenship equality (Turner, 2001; Wacquant, 2012). The combination of material cutbacks and discursive attacks on the agencies and institutions of citizenship has effectively undermined the values of equality and public, state-based services. This shift has the 'clear intention to alter the social distribution of wealth, and the dismantling of Marshall's trinity of rights', and results in 'the consistent weakening of human bonds resulting from the interrelated processes of deregulation, privatization and individualisation' (Bauman, 2005: 22). The roles and functions of nation states have also been modified by processes of globalisation with their concomitant effects on citizenship (Turner, 1990; Hobson and Lister, 2001). For some scholars and policy advocates, when the state's value as a meaningful concept is reduced, the possibility of global citizenship is suggested as a viable alternative in alignment with the changing social and political environment. The idea has strong advocates for whom the growth in international transport and trade is creating quite different modes of social interaction, work and ways of being (Urry, 2007).

Nevertheless, the issue of equal access and enjoyment of civil, political and social rights remains. Or rather, how are the agencies and institutions necessary for the achievement of such rights to be structured and supported? What global powers and institutions are sufficient to enable and support citizenship rights? A good deal of political capital is certainly invested in establishing international rights conventions and covenants, international criminal courts, world trade organisations and agreements, and peace-keeping forces and treaties. However, and importantly for our argument, such proposals either sideline or neglect the prevailing male dominance of sexual politics at international as well as local levels. Hence, women are more likely to be disadvantaged as global citizens in comparison to men.

Public and private citizens

The problem of the sexual politics of citizenship and the state has led feminists to question liberal theories of the public/private spheres where the public–political sphere was defined as the realm of liberty and equality and central to classical formulations of citizenship. The private sphere, dubbed the 'woman's sphere', was positioned as lesser than the public sphere. The rigid separation drawn between the two spheres served to disguise the reality of women's subordination and has prevented women from gaining access to the public and hence to full citizenship (Lister, 1997; 2003; Bussemaker and Voet, 1998; Prokhovnik, 1998; Longo, 2001; Nash, 2001; Lombardo and Verloo, 2009). Feminist scholarship on citizenship and human rights (Hobson and Lister, 2001; García-Del Moral and Dersnah, 2014) has documented the pervasive role of the public/private divide in structuring the relationship between women and the state in ways that have (re)produced gender inequality. These effects are constructed by the dynamics of sexual politics in which the public/private functions as a gendered mechanism of exclusion that intersects with other areas of difference to prevent women from becoming full subjects of citizenship and human rights (Young, 1989; Lister, 1997; Yuval-Davis, 1997). In Okin's terms, both the separate spheres and the radically unequal conception of the household that it presupposed are clear outcomes of a politics of gender (Okin, 1991).

Pateman and Grosz (1986a) identify such contestations of sexual politics as producing divisive gendered inequalities. Their argument proposes that the masculine, public world and its claims for the universalities of individualism, rights, contract, reason, freedom, equality, impartial law and citizenship 'gains its meaning and significance only in contrast with, and in opposition to, the private world of particularity, natural subjection, inequality, emotion, love, partiality – and women and femininity' (Pateman and Grosz, 1986a: 6). We note that, historically, feminist demands for equality of citizenship have not been based on an all-inclusive concept of equality, and at times ran campaigns that ignored women of colour or women without property. Political strategies for women's citizenship have tended to calculate that success is likely either if the claim is made for gender-neutral citizenship rights or if based on women's specific capacities, talents, needs and concerns. In the latter case, the expression of their citizenship would be differentiated from that of men (Pateman, 1992: 197). Women's citizenship concerns may demand specific laws and policies about rape and abortion, child-care policies, allocation of welfare benefits (Pateman, 1989: 131), and more recently, those that deal with violence against women. These demands do not overcome the problems of the public/private divide, but they do rely on the permeability if not the variability of the public/private spheres as social constructs that are open to contestation and change (Okin, 1991; Lister, 2011).

Feminists have worked to dismantle the entrenched public/private divide and its damaging impact on epistemologies of women (Okin, 1991). Over many decades of theorising and campaigning, the private sphere has been brought into the political domain, effectively challenging the gender-neutrality of the public sphere; it has made it possible to create possibilities for reconfiguring women's citizenship in its national and transnational dimensions (García-Del Moral and Dersnah, 2014: 663). This strategy has been central to feminist critiques of the exclusionary character of citizenship with its limitations of membership to the public sphere.

It has also been crucial to the moves to challenge beliefs, policies and practices that have hidden violence against women within the private sphere, and hence beyond the reach of the state. The point is well made by Garcia-Del Moral and Dersnah: 'The gendered politics of the public/private divide underlying this historical depoliticisation of violence against women has shielded the state from addressing it' (2014: 661). The success of feminist advocacy that violence against women should be a matter of public concern and recognised as a question of human rights has seen it taken up by agencies of the UN and its member states (see for example, Keck and Sikkink, 1998; Joachim, 2007). In effect, the private sphere has been politicised as the issue of violence and women's citizenship rights are brought into the public sphere, with the result that nation states and transnational agencies are argued to have responsibilities towards the private sphere as much as to the public.

The body of the citizen

When the body gained visibility in feminist and social theory more broadly, some feminists mounted critiques of the concept of the citizen as bodiless, rational and reasonable, unhampered by the emotional, leaky and irrational body. In this conceptualisation, only male individuals could be '... deemed capable of transcending the body; women as sexual beings and bearers of children were not' (Lister, 2002: 7). By contrast they argued, as Lister does for example: 'In both the liberal and republican traditions, the citizen has stood as the abstract *disembodied,* individual of reason and rationality' (Lister, 2002: 7, italics in original; see also Benhabib and Cornell, 1987; Gatens, 1996). In addition, the citizen is not only capable of reason, but also capable of action in the interests of the state, in particular to take up arms in its defence. Women's bodies were deemed weak and dependent on the protection of the male citizen. Thus, it was not so much a bodiless reason and rationality that would protect women, but the material capacity of the male body that may safeguard them. It is important here to challenge the assumption that this material capacity is natural to the male body and recognise that it is a 'body that has been formally or informally trained which can then be deployed as a weapon' (Walby, 2009: 198). Women's bodies are equally able to achieve capacities of strength and resilience, as demonstrated by their historical participation in everyday life as well as in war. Bacchi and Beasley focus on how it is the capacity to control the body which constitutes full citizenship:

> Political subjects who are deemed not to exercise this control, who are considered to be controlled by or subject to their bodies, do not measure up on the citizenship scale; hence, their activities can be regulated in ways deemed inappropriate for full citizens. (Bacchi and Beasley, 2002: 334)

In the sexual politics of the body and citizenship, it is claimed that only men 'could attain the impersonal, rational and disembodied practices of the model citizen' (Yeatman, 1994: 84). But we argue that the concept of the rational, controlled citizen is contradictory. Citizenship is fundamentally a relationship between the individual and the state, in which it is the ultimate duty of the citizen to die for the state, to the extent that the state may kill its own citizens who refuse to bear arms in its defence. The citizen is required to become the embodied soldier, yet in the histories of states and their defence, the embodied soldier is frequently in conflict with disembodied rationality. For example, Joan Beaumont's (2013) excellent study of Australia's World War One (*Broken nation*) provides graphic and detailed evidence of the huge efforts required to ensure that the soldier's body did not refuse its obligations to kill and be killed in the service of the state. But it was groups of citizens who campaigned against the state's demand for soldiers' bodies, framing their protests on the rational repudiation of the relentless destruction of that most irrational enterprise.

The kind of political action taken by these anti-war campaigners is indicative of the dynamic nature of citizenship rights, as Marshall's history of the shifts and changes in political, social and civil rights also demonstrates. The citizen has slowly achieved a degree of choice over how they undertake their responsibilities and obligations to the state. Such choice, however, is not the same for every citizen. Rather, 'the extent of citizenship rights and obligations is directly connected to the level of the individual's independence' (Janoski and Gran, 2002: 47). The individual citizen's independence relies on the state and its demands and supports.

As we observed in Chapter One, the components of individual independence may also be characterised by Martha Nussbaum's 10 capabilities for a decent life. We propose that the citizen's independence is contingent on these capabilities. In this project we have focused on the broad domains of health, education, employment and housing as critical for full citizenship. Hence, state support for these domains, legally, materially and discursively, is essential to citizenship. As Nussbaum (2011: 65) argues, '[f]undamental rights are only words unless and until they are made real by government action'. We note that where the market replaces the state in provision and access to these domains, individual capabilities and consequently citizenship are put at risk. An extreme example is in the state's refusal to provide access to these supports for asylum seekers and refugees. In Australia, current policies deny access for both asylum seekers and refugees who are formally recognised by the United Nations High Commissioner for Refugees to independence of movement and only provide the most rudimentary access to housing, education, work and health services (Procter et al., 2013; James, 2014; Welch, 2014).

The conceptualisation of the independent citizen may appear to be abstract and disembodied if understood as separate from private concerns (Beasley and Bacchi, 2000: 350), but the private sphere clearly encompasses individual capacities and capabilities and these are integral to that independence. Susan James' notion of 'citizenly independence' precedes Nussbaum's capabilities, but is similar in arguing for physical independence and freedom 'from bodily violation or the threat of it' (1992: 60). As Sylvia Walby (2009: 209) observes, 'women's dependency in marriage is correlated with violence: among women with high marital dependency … the rate of severe violence was much higher'. This kind of freedom has an obvious connection to the concerns of this book about the impact of domestic violence on women's citizenship. Less obviously but equally important is the freedom identified by James that citizens need to be able to express their political views (that is, to participate as citizens) without running the risk of either destitution or slavery. In the case of women experiencing violence, their capacity to exercise their political rights is at risk directly in the immediate sense as well as indirectly over the longer term. We expand on this point in later chapters. Here it is important to note the role of the state in defending these freedoms, which are traditionally secured by individual rights to life, liberty and property.

From the perspective of sexual politics, citizenly independence is not only affected by violence against women. Gendered inequalities that limit women's capabilities overall must also be taken into account. As Mary Gardiner (2004) argues, political rights count for little without the capacity to exercise them free from sexist barriers. Such barriers are constituted not only by material obstacles, such as limited education, unequal health and labour conditions, but also by the undermining effects of sexism on a woman's sense of self. 'To be able to voice one's own opinions in the polity one must esteem one*self*, as one is, rather than believing that some of one's characteristics – one's gender, colour or class, for example – disqualify one from participation' (James, 1992: 63, italics in original). In James' terms, self-esteem is important to emotional independence; in a similar vein, Nussbaum lists emotions that are not blighted by fear and anxiety as a core capability of human dignity.

In this argument, the independence of the body of the citizen depends on whether capacities and capabilities are enabled, weakened or denied. We argue that it is the citizenship relationship between the state and the individual which is critical. The state has both power and force to secure citizenly independence, or, in Nussbaum's terms, to secure the capabilities of human dignity. And it is this power of the state that connects citizenship and violence.

Violence, the state and citizenship

Public awareness and to a lesser extent concerns about personal, intimate or domestic violence and abuse has grown in some contemporary western countries over recent decades. Thirty years ago, Franzway and her colleagues were able to note that some degree of force could still be used by parents against their children, by husbands against their wives, and by the population in general against gay men (Franzway et al., 1989: 37). Although public dismay is often expressed when instances of such violence come to light, the story of violence has become much more complex. For example, the Australian novel *The Slap* by Christos Tsiolkas aroused intense debates among readers who either loathed or loved it; certainly there was enough interest to create a successful TV series (2011), sold to the UK and Europe, and remade for the US. Ostensibly, *The Slap* raised the question of whether other adults can physically punish a child, rather than whether anyone should be able to hit a child. We note that to date only 29 countries have banned corporal punishment altogether (Isaacs, 2011: 491). For some, the book was less about violence as such and mounted a much more useful challenge to assumptions about the emerging complexities of relationships between family and friends in such a way as to 'queer mainstream suburban Australia' (Treagus, 2012). An equivalent sense of moral ambivalence about violence is at work in Helen Garner's recent book, *This House of Grief* (2014), which canvasses the shock, dismay and confusion commonly expressed when separated fathers kill their children. Violence against gay men and lesbians is much less visible in the public sphere, although the recent emergence of public bullying of transgender individuals has placed a spotlight on the issue; nevertheless, up to a third of the LGBTIQ community still encounter violence, and mostly in public (Altman, 2013: 47).

In recent years, the state has initiated quite extensive actions designed to uncover the nature and extent of violence previously hidden beyond its reach, whether within institutions such as the Church or the military, or behind the closed doors of the family and custom.[1] Some lead to legislative change or the development of policies aimed at prevention as well as effective response. One such example is the 1993 Declaration on the Elimination of Violence against Women by the UN General Assembly, which called on member states to 'condemn violence against women' and that they 'should not invoke any custom, tradition or religious consideration to avoid their obligations with respect to its elimination. States should pursue by all appropriate means and without delay a policy of eliminating violence against women…'. In addition, we have seen a real shift described by De Silva de Alwis (2012: 177) as the

> concept of state responsibility [to include] accountability for acts of private individuals is an integral part of the definition of domestic violence as a human rights violation. The

---

[1]   See for example, The Royal Commission into Institutional Responses to Child Sexual Abuse established in 2013; Independent Inquiry into Child Sexual Abuse (England and Wales) established in 2015; The Council of Europe Task Force to Combat Violence against Women, including Domestic Violence set up in 2005; The Chicago Taskforce on Violence Against Girls & Young Women established in 2009.

concept of state responsibility has expanded to not only direct state action but also a state's systematic failure to act.

Yet violence against women has not declined. We are suggesting that the persistence of violence against women may be best understood in terms of the dynamics of sexual politics. When sexual politics produces unequal gender relations, or gender inequality, gendered violence is very much part of the mix. The subordination of women is based on the threat and more of gendered violence. But violence and the control of violence comes within the purview of the state. Weber's influential definition of the state describes it as 'a human community that (successfully) claims *the monopoly of the legitimate use of physical force* within a given territory' (Gerth and Mills, 1948: 77, italics in original). It is the state which controls violence. However, Weber goes on to say that '… the right to use physical force is ascribed to other institutions *or to individuals* only to the extent to which the state permits it. The state is considered the sole source of the 'right' to use violence' (Gerth and Mills, 1948: italics added). We argue that the phrase 'the extent to which the state permits it' is key to our understanding of the persistence of violence against women.

We recognise that individuals do perpetrate violence against each other, and that more men experience violence than do women. However, we also recognise that such violence occurs under different conditions, with violence against men occurring in the public domain while that against women occurs mainly in private. Importantly, the state and society respond to such violence in different ways. The sexual politics in play is clear when we observe that public male violence is treated by the state as a crime, qualified to varying degrees by class and race politics, whereas violence against women is dealt with as resulting from a complex psychosocial phenonomen or as a form of self-harm, with the woman seen as inciting the violence. In parallel with other feminists, Sylvia Walby (2009) argues that the state lacks a monopoly on the legitimate use for force, and fails to definitively criminalise interpersonal violence. The state generally does not permit individual public male violence, but in effect it does permit domestic and interpersonal violence against women. (In practice, public male violence still occurs, and the contemporary state makes some attempts to prevent domestic violence against women.)

Before feminists began to pose questions about the sexual politics of the family, the state's refusal to intervene in family violence was accepted as an appropriate aspect of the social and legal divisions between the public and private domains. (That state and/or church power was always integral to the family as an institution is yet one more aspect of the complications of this deeply ideological debate). One of the most useful achievements of feminist theorising has been the unpicking of divisions between public and private domains. It allowed for the recognition that the state is not the only site of power, since the family is an important site of power relations and therefore of force and violence (Barrett and McIntosh, 1982; Franzway et al., 1989). The sexual politics of the heterosexual western family has become relatively unstable with the power of the male patriarch challenged by the gains won in recognition of the rights of women and children. Feminists have also directed light onto the family as a site of violence, particularly in forms of intimate partner violence, child abuse and the broad category of domestic violence (Stark, 2009; Wendt and Zannettino, 2015). Instability of gender relations compounded by the continued inequalities embedded in feminine and masculine family positions have somewhat paradoxically become a common rationale for men's violent exercise of power. It is argued that men are threatened by their apparent loss of power in the family, and so they 'naturally' defend themselves against their women partners who are becoming less feminine, dutiful and submissive (Wendt and Zannettino, 2015).

Violence against women has become more visible among policy makers and in the community more generally, but, as we show in our extensive data and survey of the research literature, the incidence and extent of violence persists; some even suggest that it is increasing (Walby et al., 2016). Perhaps just knowing that this violence occurs is not enough to create effective change at policy, cultural and personal levels. In a move designed to underline the significance of violence and therefore to be taken seriously, Walby proposes that violence should be granted equivalent importance to the economy, the polity and civil society in our theorising and understanding of society. Violence is both an instrument of power as well as 'constitutive of social relations' (Walby, 2009: 20). Walby's proposal points to the centrality of violence in our argument about how it is deeply interwoven with citizenship and gender. Gendered inequality in citizenship is intensified by violence.

Citizenship, sexual politics and ignorance

The persistence of violence against women is implicated in the sexual politics of citizenship. If women were citizens on equal terms with men, their access to the power of the state, and to their political, social and civil rights would ensure effective and equitable responses to IPV. The incidence and consequences of such violence would no longer be denied or ignored by perpetrators, families, communities or state agencies.

The effects of violence against women and the inadequate responses by the state, and society more generally, are shaped by the conditions of sexual politics. As we have argued, male dominance of sexual politics is achieved to an important extent by the threat of physical force and its manifestations as rape, sexual assault and domestic violence (Dobash and Dobash, 1980; True, 2012; Wendt and Zannettino, 2015). Male dominance disadvantages women's capacities as citizens through legal, political and social processes of exclusion and subordination, and, equally effectively, by discourses and practices that inhibit women's independence and the capabilities that enable their full citizenship.

However, this comes up against a key aspect of contemporary citizenship in western democratic states, which is its constitution within discourses of equality. Citizens are, by definition, equal within their particular state. In this sense, citizenship works as a powerful discourse that obscures differences, including those of class, race and gender. More explicitly, citizenship effectively conceals inequality, including the subordination of women. It is the discourse of citizenship equality that allows the denial of gender inequality, that is, the denial of men's unequal advantage (Eveline, 1998). The discourses and related practices of citizenship take the form of a politics of ignorance, which refuses to know about the systemic and discursive gendered inequalities in citizenship. The politics of ignorance actively and persistently works to deny the unequal effects of a sexual politics in which male dominance prevails (Franzway et al., 2009a). In Nancy Tuana's (2006: 13) typology, this form of ignorance is described as 'knowing that we do not know, but not caring to know', although such knowledge does exist and continues to be articulated from personal experience and produced by research.

We argue that ignorance constituted by sexual politics has significant impacts on the incidence, the consequences and the responses to violence against women. It is striking how virulent and frequent are the denials of the complexities of the practices and discourses of this violence by individual male perpetrators, as well as by those at more organised levels. Women's evident personal experience of violence may be denied; women (and children) are discounted as liars and the risk that male perpetrators of violence may murder their partners and their own children is rarely accepted. In Tuana's terms, the politics of ignorance includes the category, 'not caring to know', which has become all too common in spite of the increased visibility of interpersonal violence. The distressing result is that many women find that their experiences of violence are rejected and ignored by their families and communities, and by the institutions and agencies of the state. In our research, many women report rejection and hostility from their own families, from police and courts, from colleagues and employers, and from health and service providers (see also Jasinski, 2010; Rowntree, 2010; Ailwood et al., 2012; Drigo et al., 2012). As Franzway observed, 'denial is the cause, betrayal is the experience' (2016: 23).

The effect of the politics of ignorance about the already gendered meaning of citizenship not only seeks to deny that sexual politics involves dynamic struggles, but also makes it difficult to recognise that such conflicts are constant. Gender inequality is thus registered as both invisible and inevitable. Critically, the politics of ignorance constructs specific categories of people as 'epistemically disadvantaged identities' by knowledge practices imbued with prejudices about their character, intellectual capacity, body and nature (Mills et al., 2013). In these terms, women are constructed as having less capacity, credibility and knowledge to be active citizens than almost any man. For example, women must always overcome assumptions that they lack the requisite capabilities whenever they seek leading citizenship roles in the public domains of the state, business or bureaucratic administration. While a successful politics of ignorance allows the denial of gendered inequality in citizenship, domestic violence exacerbates women's epistemic disadvantage in part because of the long-term consequences on women's capabilities including their health, housing, employment and social participation, and in part because of inadequate responses by the state and the community.

Sexual politics has shaped the history of citizenship in which male dominance has claimed the power of the state. Women were deliberately excluded from citizenship, but nevertheless always had an integral role in the state. Women were and continue to be necessary to the material and social reproduction of citizens. Without their incorporation into the construction of citizenship, that is, without their bodily inclusion, the state and citizenship would be short-lived. Not only do women reproduce new members, they also contribute to the social, material and cultural reproduction of essential aspects of the state. Historically, deeply embedded and socially constructed divisions based on sex differences mean that women's contributions remain generally different from men's. Feminists have therefore argued that women's difference be recognised and valued, but this demand is not sufficient to end citizenship inequality. Recognising these limits of a feminist campaign based on difference, Pateman (1992: 29) proposes that if women's citizenship is to be 'worth the same as men's, patriarchal social and sexual relations have to be transformed into free relations'. In the terms we are arguing here we understand this move as a call to challenge the prevailing sexual politics of citizenship.

However, women's struggles have won some measure of equality. We recognise that struggles for citizenship have become a fruitful source of political agency and activism. The long and bitterly fought struggle for suffrage opened up legal and electoral citizenship to women. 'The success of the women's suffrage movement was the largest single step ever accomplished in the democratisation of state structures' (Franzway et al., 1989: 38). Struggles to recognise the sexual politics of violence are becoming valuable sources of agency and activism across the whole community, as evidenced by current national campaigns, as well as the White Ribbon organisation (True, 2012), the UN's 16 Days of Activism against Gender-based Violence, and trade union moves to incorporate measures to counter domestic violence into industrial awards (Elger and Parker, 2007; McFerran, 2011). We therefore endorse the view of women in Bombay who responded to Srilathla Batliwala (2013: xxii) when she asked "Don't you have problems like domestic violence, sexual harassment, things like that?" "Oh yes," they said, "but these are not women's issues, they are community issues – they have to be solved by the whole community."

THREE

Challenges of researching gendered violence

Introduction

Investigating gendered violence involves a host of challenges, from safety concerns to the ethical questions associated with asking women to recall, relate and relive experiences that often remain highly distressing for many years after. Accordingly, it is imperative that research is designed well so that women and researchers feel and remain safe, emotional distress is minimised and the benefits of participation outweigh the costs. In this chapter, we elaborate on the design of the study, linking this with the conceptual framework for the research that was laid out in the previous chapter. We also consider some of the challenges we faced, such as recruitment issues, dealing with interdisciplinary differences in the team and managing vicarious trauma for research staff. We then consider some of the strengths of the methodology and methods used, as well as some of the limitations.

Conducting and participating in gendered violence research

Taking part in research into gendered violence might be thought of as inevitably upsetting for women who have had these experiences. While some women did experience distress at recounting the impact of violence on their lives, many women also reported that they found participation helpful and even therapeutic. UK sexual violence researcher Liz Kelly (1988) reported similar experiences from the women who participated in her seminal research into sexual assault. Women described as acknowledging and reassuring the opportunity to tell their stories and the experience of being listened to by someone who was supportive but not charged with 'helping' them. This aspect of doing research into gendered violence is sometimes overlooked. As discussed in the previous chapter, intimate partner violence (IPV) and its impact on women's lives occurs within a politics of ignorance (Tuana, 2006). Many women experience denial and lack of acknowledgement of violence and its effects from partners, family and friends, with some women even blamed for their partners' behaviour. In this context, being invited to tell one's story to help increase understanding and improve community responses to violence can be affirming and validating. Many women were not only motivated for themselves, but also by the desire to help other women, challenging assumptions of women in IPV as powerless victims.

Given the risks that can flow from participating in and conducting research into gendered violence, it was particularly vital that the study was tightly conceptualised and methodologically sound, so that the benefits of participation by contributing to the development of new knowledge clearly outweighed any risks. As argued in the previous chapter, it is our contention that violence against women is implicated in the sexual politics of citizenship, and that denial of this violence and its gendered dimensions is borne of, and perpetuates, gender inequality. The research study we undertook aimed to reveal the breadth and interconnected nature of the impact of IPV on women's citizenship as part of challenging wilful ignorance about violence and its relationship to gender inequality. As such, this research was an inherently political project that involved balancing a number of key considerations.

First, as feminist researchers, we sought to acknowledge and do justice to women's experiences, but also to maintain a level of analytic detachment. The research therefore involved both inductive and deductive elements through its attention to lived experience alongside the application of feminist theories of violence, citizenship and gender inequality. Second, we sought to balance attention to the material gender power relations that structure women's experiences of violence with awareness of the ways in which discourse shapes narratives of gender, violence and the impact of violence (McNay, 2004). For example, many women described IPV as having a serious negative impact on their psychological wellbeing, with some drawing on medical discourses about mental illness to explain their distress. Use of these discourses can help to underscore the severity of violence-related emotional distress and can be politically powerful in drawing attention to the negative material effects of IPV on women's capacity to live, work, maintain housing and exercise citizenship. However, medical discourses and practices of diagnosis also pathologise women who struggle psychologically and emotionally as a result of IPV. A medical diagnosis of mental illness rests on longstanding western Enlightenment ideas about rationality and self-control, where mentally ill individuals are constructed as less rational and self-controlled, and therefore less agentic and credible, than other people (Moulding, 2003). In our approach to data analysis, we sought to both demonstrate the severity of emotional distress related to IPV, but also retain a critical perspective on the discourses available to women to explain this distress and the potential effects of these.

Third, while the research project was concerned with identifying the negative impact of IPV on women's citizenship, we also attended to how women had rebuilt their lives and overcome not only the direct effects of violence, but also the lack of support and acknowledgement – the wilful ignorance – that so often goes hand-in-hand with it. The study therefore focused on women's agency and resistance as part of the sexual politics of IPV, as well as the oppressive impact of IPV on citizenship.

Last, while we sought a level of analytic detachment in approaching the research and analysing data, we also endeavoured to be reflexive in our approach in terms of understanding how our own social located-ness might have affected our perspectives and understandings. We are five Australian women working as mid- and late-career teaching–research academics in Australian universities. We might be described as 'middle class' now, but none of us was born into middle-class families of origin. Three of us come from rural farming families of relatively modest means, while two are from working-class urban backgrounds. Our ethnic heritages are diverse: two Anglo-Celtic, one Chinese-Australian, one Swiss-French and one German-Australian. Four of us are over 50 years of age; our movement from urban working class or rural farming backgrounds to the educated urban middle class reflects the fact that most of us are 'baby-boomers' who were fortunate enough to experience the most significant period of upward social mobility in Australian history. While none of us suffers socioeconomic disadvantage any longer, our relatively modest backgrounds certainly bring some experience of social inequality. One of us also has lived experience of racial prejudice while two live with chronic health conditions that can involve levels of disability. Moreover, as women, we all bring experiences of gender discrimination, gender inequality and, in at least one case, gendered violence.

Designing the research

The research study was concerned with theorising how IPV erodes women's citizenship with an initial focus on mental health, housing and employment as three key domains of citizenship. We included the impact of IPV on women's social participation as a further area of investigation because of its relevance to citizenship. As the study progressed and we began to engage with our data, we observed that the impact of IPV on women's social participation was even more significant than we had originally envisioned. In response to this, we decided to reconceptualise social participation as a fourth key dimension of citizenship. In the previous chapters, we outline the theoretical perspectives that informed this research. To recap, the study was informed by feminist concepts of sexual politics (Franzway, 2016) and by Nussbaum's (2011) theory of capabilities for citizenship. As noted above, the research was also premised on the understanding that the discursive and material gender inequalities which enable and maintain gendered violence are fundamentally intertwined and that while they reinforce and reproduce each other, they are also open to contestation and change.

The specific stated aims of our research study were to:

1. Provide a detailed understanding of how IPV erodes women's citizenship.
2. Generate empirical data on women's experiences of IPV across their life course.
3. Develop a critical analysis of the impact of IPV on the interconnected domains of mental health, housing, employment and social participation.
4. Generate new theoretical explanations of how citizenship is a central concept for the analysis of women's oppression through IPV.

As the research was concerned with the long-term impact of IPV on citizenship, it was necessary to design a study that could capture women's lived experiences over time across a sizeable and diverse community-based sample. However, so that we could better theorise the interconnections between the different domains of citizenship, it was also necessary to include methods that produced more detailed, in-depth data. In-depth data was also fundamental to gaining rich insights into the gender discourses, practices and material power relations framing and constituting women's experiences of IPV and gender inequality, and their impact on citizenship.

With these multiple purposes in mind, we designed a mixed methods study that included both quantitative and qualitative elements. Our specific methods included an online national survey and in-depth life history interviews. The mixed methods approach enabled us to capture the breadth and frequency of women's experiences and the impact of IPV on their lives alongside increased understanding of how the effects of IPV are interconnected and framed by discursive and material gender power relations. Both the survey and life history interview method sought to gain an understanding of the impact of IPV over time, that is, prior to the experience of IPV, while women were living with their violent partners, and since separating. Unlike previous research that focuses on specific incidents of IPV or single effects, this methodological approach enabled an understanding of how partner violence is experienced, how it interacts with different dimensions of women's lives, and how the effects unfold and compound each other over time. This is a more complex and multifaceted approach than those previously used in research into gendered violence.

The survey

The online survey was concerned with assessing the impact of IPV on the four key domains over the life course, as well as identifying the interconnections between these. The survey collected both quantitative and qualitative data, the former mainly focused on specific measures of impact within the key domains, and the latter providing opportunities for women to describe the effects of IPV in greater detail. We planned to obtain a community sample to provide broad-based understandings of the impact of IPV on the four domains of citizenship. Much existing research into IPV draws on samples from domestic violence services rather than the general community. Selection criteria for women participating in the survey were that they be over 18 years of age; live in Australia, either permanently or temporarily; self-identify a history of IPV; and have sufficient English to enable completion of the survey. We aimed for a sample size large enough to enable comparisons between different sub-groups of women, such as women from Indigenous backgrounds, culturally and linguistically diverse backgrounds, different socioeconomic groups, city and rural women, older and younger women, and women with and without children.

A total of 755 respondents completed the survey. Of these, 729 were women. Those who commenced but did not complete essential parts of the survey were excluded. The total sample therefore comprised 658 women. We sought a level of diversity across the sample in relation to socioeconomic background, age, Indigenous status, women with and without children, ethnicity, ability/disability, and the city/rural divide. Hence, while the study was primarily concerned with researching and theorising the relationship between gender inequality and the interconnected impact of IPV on women's citizenship across four life domains, the analysis of data also attended to how this was intersected by other key social positionings. Figure 1 below shows the age distribution of women who participated in the study. As can be seen, most women

(61%) were aged between 35 and 54 years but younger and older women were also represented. It is relatively unusual to have such strong representation of older women in domestic violence studies.

Figure 1: Age of participants

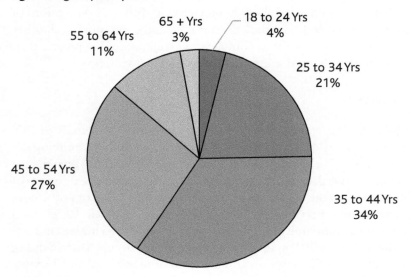

Source: Authors' calculations

The sample of women included 2.9% from Aboriginal or Torres Strait Islander backgrounds, which is slightly higher than the proportion of Indigenous people in the wider Australian population (2.8%) (ABS, 2016a). The relatively strong participation of women from Indigenous backgrounds most likely reflects the high prevalence of family and domestic violence in Aboriginal communities (Lumby and Farrelly, 2009). More than 40% of the women reported that they live with ongoing physical conditions, impairments or disabilities (43.2%). We also asked about sexual identity in the survey because we did not assume that women who are, or have been, in relationships with men are exclusively heterosexual. We recognise that sexualities can be fluid and changing rather than fixed and singular. Most women reported that they were heterosexual (94.5%), with 1.4% reporting as lesbian, 3.2% as bisexual and 0.2% as transsexual.

Categorising women by social class is not straightforward because dominant conceptualisations fail to account for gendered divisions of labour (Acker, 2006). In some respects, our sample reflects how women's lives do not fit easily into common conceptualisations of social class because the majority (52.6%) had completed post-secondary school but most were represented in the low-income ranges; 40% earned under $30,000pa, 14% earned $30,000-$39,000pa, and 10% earned $40,000-$49,000pa.[1]

The sample was diverse in relation to location of residence. Figure 2 below shows that while 66% of women resided in the city, 34% were located in rural locations. The city/rural divide is a significant factor in virtually all social problems and inequalities in Australia, including women's experiences of domestic violence (Wendt, 2009).

Figure 2: Location of residence

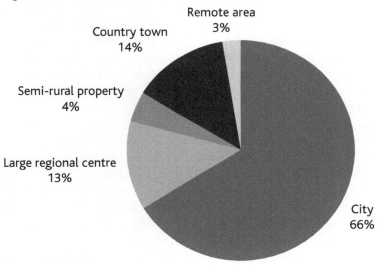

Source: Authors' calculations

Most respondents were born in Australia (81.2%), with 6.1% born in non–English-speaking countries. This is much lower than the wider population prevalence of 17.9% of Australians born in non–English-speaking countries (ABS, 2016a). Most women indicated that they considered their cultural identity to be Australian (78.7%), with 6.3% indicating non–English-speaking cultural identities. The majority of women considered themselves to be either non–religious (50.2%) or Christian (40.0%). The relatively low numbers of women born in non–English-speaking countries and women indicating non–English-speaking cultural identities may reflect the survey method and its reliance on English language skills as well as potential cultural barriers

---

[1]   Income ranges are in Australian dollars.

around acknowledging IPV in some cultural groups. Later in the book, we consider the scope for further research into IPV and citizenship among women from diverse cultural backgrounds.

The survey was implemented online and manually, and involved both closed and open-ended questions. The first section was designed to collect women's demographic information, including age, gender, marital status, education levels, income levels, cultural background, number of children and location. The second section focused specifically on the type and duration of women's experiences of IPV. The remaining sections asked about the impact of IPV on women's mental health, housing, employment and social participation. Women were asked to report their experiences before, during and after the violence within each domain to gain some understanding of the impact of IPV on citizenship over time. At the end of the survey, women were asked to indicate their willingness to participate in an in-depth, face-to-face interview and to provide a first name and appropriate contact details if they wished to take part. The survey was open for a period of six months.

Analysis of quantitative survey data involved obtaining frequencies by using demographic filters (such as age, location, income, care of children). Thematic analysis of qualitative survey responses sought to identify commonalities and differences in women's experiences of the impact of IPV in the different dimensions of citizenship. This multi-faceted analysis helped to build a broad, preliminary picture of the interconnected impact of IPV across the dimensions of citizenship and the complexities of this across a large community-based sample. In reporting the quantitative survey results in following chapters, percentage figures are based on the number of women who responded to any given question, although the numbers who missed certain questions were not large. Qualitative survey data is reported thematically alongside or after quantitative survey data to elaborate findings at a greater level of depth.

Life history interviews

Qualitative data was obtained from semi-structured life history interviews drawing on the work of Connell (1995), Riessman (2008) and Plummer (2001). The aim of the face-to-face semi-structured life history interviews was to investigate in greater depth and complexity the impact of IPV across the four interconnected dimensions of women's citizenship over time and women's agency in negotiating this. Life history interviews are a widely used and versatile social research method. They provide insights that are highly personal but also reflect broader social dynamics and, most importantly, attend to diverse and complex experiences. An important feature of the life history interview is that it encourages participants to recount their stories about the unfolding of events in relation to time (Riessman, 2008). This does not assume that the impact of IPV across the dimensions is temporally linear. Rather, it enables analysis of how events are relationally linked across and through time, including in cyclic and compounding ways. This was crucial to understanding and explaining the interconnections between mental health, housing, employment and social participation.

This emphasis on experiences over time distinguishes a life history interview from a more structured, thematic interview that focuses on each key dimension separately and categorises them accordingly, and was therefore appropriate to the aims of this study. The questions were developed with reference to survey responses, with the broad areas of inquiry including: individual participants' experiences of IPV; its immediate impact on mental health, housing, employment and social participation; the interconnected and continuing impact of IPV across the four dimensions over time; any support received and its effects on the different dimensions; suggestions about the kind of support that might have better addressed their needs and the compounding effects of IPV in their lives; strategies women use in their everyday lives to maintain their mental health, housing, employment and social participation; and how women negotiate their citizenship rights within and across the four dimensions over time.

An important aspect of the life history method was that while interviews followed the same overall structure, we planned for flexibility within each interview (Connell, 1995). This enabled recognition and exploration of the diverse ways in which IPV affected the key life domains, and of the particular ways the women negotiated their citizenship over time in this context. Research team members, rather than a research assistant, conducted the interviews because of this need for flexibility. Interviews of between one and one-and-a-half hours duration were conducted with 17 women, and were digitally recorded and transcribed. A large number of women from the survey volunteered for interviews, and we chose as wide a range of women as possible from this wider group in relation to all the characteristics specified for the survey.

The life history interview transcripts were analysed through thematic analysis and narrative analysis. While thematic analysis identifies thematic categories across the data set, narrative analysis involves keeping individual accounts intact and plotting the themes and causal connections within them (Riessman, 2008). Thematic analysis involved categorising data across the interviews to identify dominant themes and their relationships to sub-themes. For the narrative analysis, we adopted a method drawn from Connell (1995) that combines a close focus on individual women's experiences of IPV with broad questions of social dynamics, discourses and practices relevant to gendered citizenship. This allowed us to theorise at a more detailed level the complex interconnections between the four dimensions and their impact on citizenship over time. The narrative analysis specifically attended to (a) the sequence of events, (b) the impact of IPV within the four dimensions of citizenship over time, (c) the complex interconnections between the four dimensions, and (d) women's agency in negotiating the four dimensions of citizenship.

Constructing life histories

The next phase of the research involved combining survey and interview data for the women who participated in interviews to create detailed histories of women's experiences of IPV and its impact within and across the four dimensions of citizenship. These histories enabled mapping of the interconnections between the four domains using both sources of data. Interestingly, sometimes the qualitative survey data included a level of disclosure and detailed descriptions of the nature of emotional distress that were not always present in the interview data, perhaps because the survey was anonymous and a researcher was not present. As such, there was no pressure to avoid shame and maintain composure, as there is in face-to-face interactions (Budden, 2010). On the other hand, the interviews were able to access a greater level of complexity in tracing how the impact of IPV played out across the domains of citizenship over time. The combination of these two types of data therefore enabled breadth, richness and complexity in the analysis.

This phase of the research involved undertaking a theoretical analysis of the survey and life history data to identify and map the complex ways that IPV impacts across the selected dimensions of citizenship, including how this varies for different groups of women and in relation to different socio-historical contexts (Connell,1995; Riessman, 2008). The findings of the life history analysis are particularly drawn on when we tease out how the impact of IPV is interconnected across the four dimensions of citizenship. We present six short case studies within the following three chapters to specifically demonstrate how these interconnections played out in individual life histories. While we present extracts from the survey and interview data to demonstrate the impact IPV has on women's lives, our prime concern does not lie with documenting women's lived experiences as such. As noted earlier, the theoretical analysis was informed by the understanding of IPV as an aspect of sexual politics that erodes women's citizenship but it also acknowledged how women use agency in their attempts to negotiate their lived citizenship in this context. Without eliding the importance of women's testimonies, our premier goal is to reveal how sexual politics is not only bound up with IPV itself but also plays a central role in reproducing the gender inequalities that perpetuate IPV by reducing women's capacities to exercise citizenship into the long term. We also show how sexual politics is implicated in the continued wilful denial of IPV and how this compounds the negative impact on women's citizenship. Last, we examine how individual women have resisted and challenged community denial of IPV and the associated lack of support and protection from the state, as well as consider how feminist politics can continue to build global and local momentum for change.

Doing the research

When research is documented in books, journal articles or reports, it invariably appears as if it unfolded in a relatively straightforward, planned and logical way. The act of explaining and justifying research perhaps inevitably leads to a somewhat linear account that irons out the creases. This era of enhanced competition between researchers and research metrics most likely contributes to this ironing out process so that research often seems to have progressed quite smoothly. However, all researchers know that research is a fundamentally iterative, collaborative, messy and intersubjective process; this reality was widely acknowledged and recognised in the past, before the current age of research monitoring and metrics (see, for example, Roberts, 1981). And so it was with our study. While many of the key concepts were in place from the outset, such as gender inequality, IPV and citizenship, other concepts such as sexual politics, male privilege and the politics of ignorance, were woven into the study as it progressed. In the following section, we consider some of the specific challenges we encountered in undertaking the study and how we managed them. These include the challenges of recruitment, challenges associated with working in an interdisciplinary team of feminist researchers, and the issue of managing vicarious trauma.

Recruiting the women

One of the major challenges in undertaking this study lay in obtaining a robust sample. Survey participants were initially recruited through advertisements in newspapers around Australia, media releases and through contacts in national and local IPV and housing services. The sample grew slowly in response to these strategies, reaching some 200 women after a few weeks. At that point, our research associate, Dr Alison Elder, made contact with a colleague who is a journalist with marketing expertise. He rewrote the media release into a newsworthy story reporting on the initial findings from a preliminary analysis of the data. The story was uploaded to a well-known, popular online Australian news site (news.com.au) complete with a link to the online questionnaire. The story and link were picked up quickly by other online and paper-based news outlets around the country. Domestic violence advocacy organisations such as White Ribbon Australia, which aims to stop violence against women, also picked up the story and link, sharing them on Facebook, from where they were reshared many times afterwards. The sample grew rapidly from this point onwards, from 200 to the final total sample size of 658 completed surveys by women in just three days.

The timing of the study also coincided with a series of brutal, widely reported public killings of women and children by men who had histories of domestic violence. Among these was the horrifying murder of Rosie Batty's young son by his father at a children's sports training session; Rosie Batty went on to become Australian of the Year in 2015 for her high profile advocacy work in the area of domestic and family violence. We were therefore recruiting for our study at a point in time when public awareness of domestic violence was arguably higher than usual. At one point, we received 50 completed questionnaires in one hour. Obtaining such a large sample is also testimony to the value of electronic media – both news and social media – as a recruitment strategy. But it no doubt also speaks to a strong desire among women who have lived through domestic violence to have their experiences acknowledged and heard. One limitation of a reliance on electronic recruitment is that it may attract lower numbers of women who are uncomfortable with digital technology or who do not have access to computers. This might in part explain why the sample included fewer women from ethnic communities than we had hoped for. However, the sample did include a substantial number of older women, a group also generally seen as less digitally engaged. The large numbers of older women is a distinctive aspect of our sample because it is relatively unusual in domestic violence research and at least in part reflects our focus on the effects of IPV over the long term.

Differences of opinion

Interdisciplinary research is promoted by universities and across much of academia as the preferred approach (Mills, et al., 2011). Research team members on this study were united by a shared feminist knowledge of IPV and its relationship to gender inequality, but we also came from a variety of academic disciplines. Hence, one team member was a sociologist, two team members were from academic social work, one team member had a background in gender studies, policy studies and social work, and the fifth team member had a background across gender studies, public health and social work. While this mix might be thought of as only mildly interdisciplinary because all these disciplines sit within the social sciences, we nonetheless experienced a number of interesting differences in 'knowledge practices' (Mills et al., 2011) that required ongoing acknowledgement, discussion and resolution. First, there were differences of emphasis in relation to the practices of inductive and deductive data analysis. Feminist social work research tends to focus on women's lived experience and on exploring themes that are not necessarily predicted or expected in the data (Gringeri, et al., 2010). Feminist sociological research can be more detached and analytic, and driven by theoretical frameworks that are highly developed and refined prior to, or very early in, the research process (Fonow and Cook, 1991; Stanley, 2013). As a team, we needed to find a comfortable middle ground where women's lived experiences were respected and acknowledged, but the analysis remained true to its focus on the social context and sexual politics of IPV and citizenship. In reality, we had all moved backwards and forwards between inductive and more deductive analytic approaches in our previous research work, but we needed to explicitly lay out our approach in this study to ensure we all worked in a similar way when undertaking analysis.

Another area of difference related to perceptions of the benefits and risks of quantitative data analysis. Some team members were concerned that quantitative findings could be used to misconstrue IPV. For example, the analysis revealed that some women had a pre-existing diagnosis of mental illness prior to IPV. It could be argued that the negative impact of IPV on their lives was due to mental illness rather than the IPV. Many debates were had about the risks of findings that can be used to inadvertently universalise women's experiences or to victim-blame in a wider context of sexual politics and wilful ignorance.

Where we report quantitative data, we are careful to emphasise the social context, meaning of the findings and their limits. For example, we contextualise women's experiences in the wider context of gendered violence by pointing out that women with pre-existing mental health problems very often have histories of child sexual abuse and adult rape prior to IPV (Herman, 1997; Cantón-Cortés and Cantón, 2010; Trickett et al., 2011). By contextualising our findings in this way, we situate them in intersubjective and structural gender power relations rather than within individual women and thereby challenge the potential for misrepresentation. Our quantitative findings actually revealed that the vast majority of women who experience IPV have no pre-existing history of mental health problems, helping to challenge and dispel myths that only 'vulnerable' women enter relationships with male perpetrators.

Another challenge lay in managing the qualitative data analysis because it was complex and multidimensional rather than singular in focus. The analysis required us to keep many balls in the air in relation to women's lived experience: the material effects of IPV; the structure of women's narratives over time; the discourses women used to explain their lives; the discourses at work in women's social environments – that is, not simply women's use of explanatory discourses but the discourses at work in the gendered social practices surrounding IPV, including wilful ignorance and neoliberal state responses to IPV; and, finally, the interconnections between the different life domains and the impact on citizenship. Managing these multiple perspectives was demanding but has hopefully contributed a multifaceted understanding of the impact of IPV on women's citizenship.

Finally, the team members managed heavy academic workloads, including significant teaching loads, as well as leadership responsibilities over the life of the project. While it might have been prudent in terms of furthering academic careers to focus more single-mindedly on the production of a large number of journal articles about different aspects of our findings, we chose instead to capture the complexity of IPV's impact on women's citizenship through this book. As such, the book should be thought of as our practice of sexual politics. We have chosen to contribute to widening the debate about IPV through this medium because it enables deeper engagement with, and fuller consideration of, IPV and women's citizenship and the directions for feminist politics into the future.

Handling vicarious trauma

The term 'vicarious trauma' (VT) refers to harmful changes that can occur as a result of exposure to others' traumatic experiences (Baird and Kracen, 2006), and is also sometimes referred to as 'compassion fatigue' (Bride et al, 2007). VT is commonly reported by social workers and other helping professionals who work in the area of domestic violence (Baird and Jenkins, 2003). More recently, there has been growing awareness that VT can also be experienced by researchers who study traumatic experiences (Cole et al., 2014). In undertaking this research study, managing the impact of listening to women's traumatic experiences was an intrinsic part of the data collection phase, as was ensuring that women were referred to appropriate sources of help if they needed it. However, managing our exposure to women's traumatic experiences did not pertain only to the face-to-face interviews.

As mentioned earlier, women's written responses to survey questions were sometimes more heartfelt and unguarded than their spoken responses in face-to-face interviews. Hence, reading through qualitative survey responses for the purposes of thematic coding could also be a quite a challenging experience at an emotional level. Emotional reactions were not only in the form of sadness or stress, though, but also included anger. Women's descriptions of the kinds of abuse they had endured at the hands of violent male partners often inspired anger. These included both the mundane and the more extreme acts of cruelty and control, ranging from criticisms about physical appearance, housework and child-rearing practices to the monitoring of women's whereabouts through digital surveillance, sexual assault and extreme physical violence that endangered the lives of women and their children. It was unavoidable that team members would feel anger in response to stories of this mistreatment. We debriefed as much as possible during team meetings throughout the data collection and analysis phases of the study. While this was not the first time team members had heard women's stories of violence, the experience of engaging with so many women's experiences was particularly sobering and arguably strengthened our resolve to extend understandings of the impact of IPV on women's citizenship.

Undertaking research into gendered violence, or any activity that involves 'going public' on gendered violence, also involves the risk of being targeted by men who react negatively to such efforts. Over the life of this study, there were two incidents of this nature. In the first, a male student at our university contacted our research associate by telephone to complain about the study and about "women like us". A threat of harm was made, so we called in the university security staff who dealt with the matter appropriately, but it was nevertheless stressful for the research team member. In the second incident, an article based on the research and written by one of the research team members was published in the Australian online academic forum, The Conversation. The comments section at the bottom of the article had to be closed down because of inappropriate and abusive comments from men.

Examples of hostility and attempts at silencing experienced by our research team reach beyond this project. In past research studies into domestic violence conducted by other members of the team, male perpetrators have come on to the university campus to accost researchers face-to-face. Members of a so-called men's movement group wrote a disparaging letter to the then-vice chancellor complaining about one of the team member's research into domestic violence and accusing the lead researcher of 'unethical' practice. Hostility from men towards feminist researchers, scholars and commentators is not only reserved for the area of gendered violence, either. Another team member has witnessed attempts to silence women critical of the patriarchal structure and practices of Buddhist institutions in a well-known Buddhist magazine. Feminists are well-aware that their work is likely to attract abuse from men who are challenged when the realities of gendered violence, gender inequality and male privilege are pointed out. It is also arguable that online forums and media have provided such men with easier and more protected pathways to perpetrate their abuse, with many feminists, including MPs and journalists, now experiencing unprecedented levels of hostility and vitriol, including threats of rape and death. We understand the phenomenon of abusing women who speak up about gender inequality and gendered violence as a form of sexual politics, where the intent is to disparage their credibility and to frighten them into silence. Researchers into domestic violence are cognisant that there is a real risk of being targeted by such individuals and men's groups, and it has been important for us to learn to plan for the management of these incidents.

Conducting research into gendered violence occurs in the context of a wider gender order based on male privilege, where women are disadvantaged both symbolically and materially. Actively acknowledging this context has implications for the design of research because it brings particularly high levels of complexity to the research process. Hence, our study aimed to attend to both the discursive and material bases of women's oppression through IPV over the long term, drawing on a mixed methods methodology that was capable of showing the breadth of this impact across a wide cross-section of women, as well as the complex interrelationships between the impact on mental health, housing, employment and social participation as key dimensions of citizenship. Central to our analysis of the impact of IPV on women's citizenship has been the concept of sexual politics, which understands gender and gender relations as fluid, relational and continually contested (Franzway, 2016). In the following chapters, we present the findings from our study, identifying the complex and diverse ways in which IPV undermines women's capabilities for citizenship. We also show the ways in which many women rebuild their lives after IPV in spite of wilful ignorance among family, friends and the wider community. Last, we consider the implications for a transformative sexual politics into the future that engages with the need to redress symbolic and material gender inequalities as central to challenging gendered violence.

FOUR

Living the connected effects of violence

Violence is a social phenomenon, not reducible to psychological traits, hormones, emotions, or individual pathology. Violence constitutes a social system, an institutional domain, that is parallel to those of economy, polity, and civil society. When complex inequalities are brought into focus, the range of phenomena visible as violence is extended beyond the traditional focus on war and criminal violence to include non-criminalized forms of inter-personal and group violence. (Walby, 2009: 191)

'It destroyed my family, career and community; it wreaked havoc on my credit rating and my ability to do the work I'm professionally trained to do. Even more than 10 years since the abuser finally disappeared from our lives, there is really no part of my life that is not still affected.' (Fran)

Introduction

Much of the public attention on domestic violence goes to the horrors of specific incidents. The more severe incidences such as murder, and physical and sexual assault are criminalised, but not all acts of domestic violence are treated as seriously or attract media attention. More importantly, intimate partner violence (IPV) in all its forms is not contextualised within the broad regimes of gender inequality, which are given no attention in traditional state responses (Walby, 2009). As Sylvia Walby points out , when complex inequalities are brought into focus, our understanding of violence extends beyond war and its already criminalised forms. In this study of the impact of certain forms of gendered violence, we recognise that the complex social circumstances that maintain and reproduce inequalities of gender are critical to our understanding and argument. One means by which we illustrate these complexities of inequality is by drawing attention to the long-lasting and interrelated effects of domestic violence on women and how this compounds existing inequalities for women post separation.

The evidence of substantial and complex inequalities of gender is well-established worldwide, across diverse societies. Although much of the international data relies on the simple binary, women/men, it nevertheless points to decisive evidence of the persistence of such inequality. For example, the Global Gender Gap Index includes over 90% of the world's population from 144 countries. It reports on the gap between women and men on health, education, economic and political indicators. The 2016 report finds that progress towards parity in the key economic pillar has slowed dramatically with the gap, standing at 59%, now larger than at any point since 2008 and no country in the world has yet achieved gender equality (Leopold et al., 2016). Inequality between men and women has been exposed in relation to paid work, modes of production and reproduction, patriarchal relations in the state, and other institutions such as the family (Nussbaum, 2000; Walby et al., 2017). Despite some progress in decreasing women's inequalities, it is well recognised that violence against women remains one of the greatest challenges facing all our communities.

Perhaps one of the most significant advances is the growing awareness that gendered violence and domestic violence in particular is not merely an episodic, individual problem but is embedded in wider social, economic, organisational and cultural factors, resulting in enormous social and economic costs to women, children, and the wider community (Chappell and Di Martino, 2006). The findings from the study that we discuss in this book are framed in these terms by focusing attention on the interconnected effects of the sexual politics of violence across key areas of housing, employment, mental health and social participation. This standpoint allows the development of a methodology that produced data that encompasses the long-term consequences of domestic violence on women's lives. The extract above from Fran, one of the participants, captures this impact in graphic terms.

Capabilities and interconnected domains

It is telling therefore that Nussbaum opens her recent book on 'creating capabilities' with a lengthy story of domestic violence experienced by Vasanti, a woman living in north-western India, and her successful struggles against its effects. Nussbaum returns to this story a number of times in order to underline the centrality of her list of 10 capabilities in answer to the question: what does a life worthy of human dignity require? (Nussbaum, 2011: 32). For Nussbaum, and Sen before her, a capability is a kind of freedom: 'the substantive freedom to achieve alternative functioning combinations' (Sen cited in Nussbaum, 2011:

20). Capabilities are not simply a set of personal abilities, but rather are 'the freedoms or opportunities created by a combination of personal abilities and [importantly for our argument], the political, social and economic environment' (p 20). These are substantial freedoms or opportunities which Nussbaum refers to as 'combined capabilities'. In the Indian woman's story, her combined capabilities are 'the totality of the opportunities she has for choice and action in her specific political, social and economic situation' (p 21).

A key aspect of Nussbaum's argument about the significance of combined capabilities is the attention to the importance of 'substantial freedoms', a term she derives from Sen who defines them as 'a set of (usually interrelated) opportunities to choose and to act' (Nussbaum, 2011: 20-1). Both Sen and Nussbaum are concerned to distinguish between personal internal abilities and the external political, social and economic environment. But importantly for our argument, internal abilities and the external environment are interdependent. The term 'combined capabilities' refers to the necessary connections between the conditions that produce the substantial freedoms and characteristics of the person: personality traits, intellectual and emotional capacities, states of bodily fitness and health, internalised learning, skills of perception and movement (Nussbaum, 2011: 21). Such characteristics are not innate to the person, but are traits and abilities that are trained or developed through interaction with social, political and material conditions. Nussbaum offers the example of affiliation, a capability that involves 'being able to live with and toward others…' Affiliation is enabled and protected by 'institutions that constitute and nourish such forms of affiliation, and also protect[s] the freedom of assembly and political speech' as well as by 'provisions of non-discrimination on the basis of race, sex, sexual orientation, ethnicity, caste, religion, national origin' (Nussbaum, 2011: 34). It is these combined capabilities that enable, support and allow the individual to live with human dignity.

Nussbaum's argument has parallels with T.H. Marshall's analysis of the necessary connections between political, civil and social rights, and their related institutions that, in contemporary societies, depend on the state. As Alexander (2014: 425) observes, Nussbaum makes

> a broad range of civil and political rights as well as property rights as part of the list of basic capabilities. Civil and political rights create the required social and political institutions that would enhance the development of people's innate powers and capacities.

Although rights are not the same as capabilities, without some basic capabilities it would not be possible to make effective use of already existing rights. The most important human capabilities can only be developed through systems of education, resources to enhance physical and emotional health, support for family care and viability, and security. For Nussbaum (2011: 32) some capabilities are clearly central, and she cites the worldwide consensus on the importance of primary and secondary education, (although we note that certain societies still reject – or perhaps refuse – the value of education for their girls). Nussbaum goes on to observe that it has taken centuries for some societies to recognise the value of some capabilities, and lists the long delay in the recognition that a woman's right to refuse her husband's demand for sexual intercourse was a crucial right of bodily integrity.

It is our argument that the historical process through which women gained this right was shaped by sexual politics involving the contest of ideas and arguments about liberty and human dignity. While we endorse Nussbaum's (2011: 32) view that 'vague intuitive appeals to the idea of dignity all by itself' are not enough, we are less persuaded that 'it is the quality of the argument, not the number of supporters, that is crucial'. Certainly, the relationship of women's bodily integrity to their full citizenship is central to the case, but it can only be won (and re-won) through the contestation of sexual politics. It is not only a matter of winning the argument, but also of making gains for women's bodily integrity through changing and developing supportive institutions, for example, in health systems and the law around sexual assault and marriage. As we discuss in more detail in Chapter Eight, it took the persistence of social movements making feminist politics to achieve these changes. These reforms, although hard won, are never immutable. This has been highlighted in recent times where some nation states have repealed laws, policies and programmes that undermine women's rights, such as the Trump administration's ban on US foreign aid to any agencies that mention or promote abortion, or the Russian parliament's recent decriminalisation of domestic violence whereby a first offence of such violence that did not result in hospitalisation would not be treated as a criminal offence. These examples highlight the role of contemporary nation states in the control of women's bodies and men's entitlement over women's bodies which undermine and violate women's human dignity.

We argue that sexual politics has constructed and continues to shape the ways the interconnected and mutual responsibilities of citizens and the state are producing the combined capabilities, which are necessary for a life of human dignity. Although Nussbaum declares that all citizens deserve equal respect from laws and institutions, she readily points out that human dignity may be denied or violated in different ways. Social, political, familial and economic conditions may thwart people's capabilities, but so too can the actions or inactions of citizens towards each other undermine them. In this argument we follow Nussbaum's emphasis on respect as particularly important, recognising that the meaning of respect and its significance to human dignity is created and challenged through the dynamics of sexual politics. In Nussbaum's example, 'rape can be said to violate a woman's dignity because it invades her internal life of thought and emotion, changing her relationship to herself' (2011: 31). In a similar way, our study of the impact of gendered violence on women's citizenship finds that IPV damages women's capabilities to be employed, to enjoy mental health and to have access to good quality, safe housing. Further, IPV limits freedom and opportunities to engage and participate as citizens of society.

In our study, we have selected housing, employment, mental health and social participation as significant and interconnected elements of these substantial freedoms. These elements or domains of everyday life are connected in multiple ways. For example, adequate housing depends on sufficient income derived from steady employment of at least one member of a household, while the ability to sustain employment and housing depends on reliable mental health – none of which is possible to maintain in isolation from the other domains. Nor is it possible to sustain the complex of domains in complete isolation from one's fellow citizens or from political, social and economic institutions and agencies, (usually) enabled by the state. It is the domain of social participation and its interconnections with the other domains as well as its significance to the meaning of citizenship that emerged in our study as a capability that was particularly damaged by IPV. In the following sections, we discuss our findings in terms of the sexual politics of the immediate and long term effects on the combined capabilities of women who have experienced IPV.

Housing

Housing, or in Nussbaum's terms, 'adequate shelter', is a core capability, which depends on social/political/economic conditions if citizens are to be able to have the choice and freedom to achieve it. In turn, health and wellbeing are affected by housing quality, while employment options are interdependent on the location, cost and condition of the citizen's shelter. As our study shows, it is much more difficult to engage in the labour market and to participate in the community, including sustaining family life, without safe and reliable housing. Nussbaum also points to the significance of housing as a form of property, an instance of material control over one's environment particularly 'the right to hold property on an equal basis with others' (2011, 34). In many societies, women have only gained this right in recent decades, although many are yet to have the combined capabilities to fully exercise this right. In other societies, women's access to adequate shelter, let alone the right to control it, is yet to be achieved.

Home ownership is constructed as part of the 'Australian dream' and the experiences of purchasing and owning a home often feature in Australian media and political debates regarding affordability and opportunity for first home buyers. In Australia, women are slightly more likely to be homeowners than men (62% compared with 59% of men), and women who are homeowners predominantly live in coupled families with children (45%) rather than in couples without children (38%) (ABS, 2016b). In this study, while living with a violent partner, 42% of the women jointly owned a house, which is lower than the general population. The impact of IPV can particularly be seen when examining rates of sole female home ownership, because after leaving violent partners 21% of the women were currently sole home owners, which is also considerably lower than the general population. In Australia, home ownership is lower for female sole parents (41%) than male sole parents (50%) but much higher than for the women in this study (ABS, 2016b). These findings illustrate how the effects of IPV further exacerbate gendered housing inequalities and women's ability to exercise their economic and social citizenship rights.

Perhaps one of the most troubling and far-reaching effects of IPV is that the violent perpetrator (frequently) remains in control of the home and causes severe housing disruption for women and children subjected to his violence. Imagine the utter immensity of the task faced by women cut adrift from their home base: "I left with no possessions and had to re-establish everything" (Natasha). Women who experience IPV encounter multiple systemic barriers to accessing safe and appropriate housing, often placing them and their children at risk of further exposure to violence (Clough et al., 2014). Other research has found that housing problems are worse among women who experienced severe violence, who contact fewer formal systems, have less informational support, and reported receiving a negative response from formal welfare services (Baker et al., 2003, 2010).

Housing involves much more than whether it provides adequate shelter. In many societies, the house is discursively understood as the home, the site of the intimate partnership, and the discourses and practices of the family. One woman described the effects of IPV on her home as

'I felt a prohibitive and controlling sense of insecurity and instability. Being single, and suffering anxiety, and poverty, has meant exposure to stigmatisation, discrimination and exclusion from many rental properties, which has meant numerous moves and an inability to ever know a "home."'(Emilia)

The discourse of the family home constructs it as private, situated outside the public domains of the state, politics and the economic world. Given these discursive and material conditions of housing, IPV in its many forms causes a great deal of havoc that can have long-term consequences for all members of the household. During and following separation from a violent partner, women and their children are likely to experience significant income loss, financial hardship and housing instability, particularly for those women who were at least partially financially dependent on their partners since they are at risk of not being able to meet rent or mortgage payments (Pavao et al., 2007). Women's opportunities to choose their housing are severely constrained.

'I'm contemplating leaving, but have no job and the rental market is so expensive – contemplating moving to a regional location or the country to afford housing but am scared of being isolated and not providing my children with good schooling and life. All family and friend support [are] in Sydney, but it is so expensive. So here I am staying with my partner.' (Jayne)

'I had to leave my home. ... I was told by police that I had to leave, not him, even though he is the person being violent. Now I cannot stay in the house alone. It's not recommended since he was served with an intervention order. This has affected my living arrangements and life.' (Scarlet)

At the time of completing the survey, the majority of women who answered the question about housing during IPV were either living alone with children (39%) or living alone (18%). As female single-headed households, these women are among the most disadvantaged households in Australia (Baker and Tually, 2008), which is exacerbated by their experience of domestic violence.

Table 1 presents women's housing circumstances over time: from when they were living with a violent partner, immediately on separating from him, and their current arrangements. The housing patterns of the women reveal definite shifts over time. While living with a violent partner, the majority of women jointly owned a house (42%) or were in a private rental property (36%). On separation the women most often left the home/property, of whom one third went to stay with friends or family while a small group (10%) accessed a women's shelter. Just over a quarter were able to secure a private rental property (27%), although the quality of this housing was rarely satisfactory. Nearly 70% of the women reported that their housing costs increased on separation, with 10% reporting a decrease in their housing costs.

Table 1: Living arrangements during IPV, straight after leaving, and currently

Living arrangements	During IPV		After IPV		Current	
	n	%	n	%	n	%
Remained in family home	NA	NA	55	8.40	0	0
Sole owner	47	7.10	40	6.10	136	20.70
Jointly owned with violent partner	278	42.20	39	5.90	43	6.50
Jointly owned with others (family)	10	1.50	9	1.40	65	9.90
Private rental	240	36.50	176	26.70	265	40.30
Public rental/housing trust	45	6.80	27	4.10	51	7.80
Caravan	2	0.30	8	1.20	1	0.20
Lodging/boarding house	1	0.20	5	0.80	4	0.60
Staying with friends or family	25	3.80	217	33.00	45	6.80
Women's assisted shelter	NA	NA	64	9.70	4	0.60
Improvised dwellings (e.g. car)	4	0.60	12	1.80	4	0.60

Source: Authors' calculations

As the sexual politics of violence in relation to the capability of adequate shelter plays out, the women who left found that their options were limited and costly. What this data shows is that even though women were able to ultimately secure housing post IPV, the journey to achieving home ownership or secure rental was not straightforward. It required planning, staying with family and taking on an increased financial burden. The most common housing pathway outcomes were private rental accommodation and sole ownership of a house.

Whether it was through mortgage or rental payments, most women experienced increased financial stress from meeting their housing costs on their sole incomes.

> 'I was financially worse off than before we bought a house together. After I left I lived with my parents [with our daughter]. It took me three years to save enough money for a deposit and my parents assisted me and I bought much further away from the city as that is all I could afford.' (Becky)

> 'I had to borrow money to buy a house and furniture and had to downsize to what I could afford for my sons and myself. I had to live with my mum for nearly two years and share a room with my youngest son.' (Eileen)

Like many of the women, Becky and Eileen were able to rely on family support in order to resolve their disrupted housing situation, which was compounded by inadequate income. Overall, women are disadvantaged by incomes which are generally lower than men's and this is further exacerbated by experiences of IPV. When women have disrupted work histories – as is common with IPV (Raphael, 2001) – they consequently tend to have paid work with lower wages and poorer conditions, such as being employed on a casual basis without many of the entitlements that are available to others, for example sick leave and holidays. The gender pay gap in Australia is currently averaging 18% (Workplace Gender Equality Agency, 2016) and women's employment pathways following domestic violence highlight how this gap is likely to continue. Those women with dependent children are likely to have relatively low incomes due to interrupted work histories and child-care demands and costs. The combined effects of unequal pay, and inadequate or costly child-care support in addition to the disruptions caused by IPV limit women's capability to accessing adequate income and housing. They responded by moving to cheaper housing areas or renting smaller properties.

> 'I had to relocate three times to distance myself from domestic violence, which is disruptive, destabilising, expensive and stressful.' (Camilla)

> 'I am under extreme financial stress due to refinancing the house loan solely in my name after settlement. This was

done to keep kids in the family home to help them cope. I have 100% care of the kids and thus financial costs are high due to little financial help from my ex-partner.' (Elenor)

The usual costs associated with moving house were exacerbated by domestic violence. Women needed to find safe and secure housing, with 42% reporting that they had to make a significant geographical move. In addition, some women had to bear the consequences of their partner's damage to the property in the course of the violence, which meant that they did not receive their rental bonds on leaving the property or good references from agents or landlords in order to secure future private rental housing. They were also likely to be burdened with their ex-partner's debts, and debts from legal fees associated with separation. This form of abuse has long-term consequences for women's financial recovery, which affects their opportunities to secure permanent housing. The fear for their safety also had an impact on women's housing following separation. Some women described extensive arrangements to gain security in their home: "I had a lot of extra security put on my home: roller shutters, sensor lights, window locks and security doors" (Nina). Others listed the direct costs of the violence:

'He broke in and damaged my rental property while me and my kids were home. Unsafe and afraid to return there I had to eventually break the lease. My bond was retained, and because we had to change our names, we could not supply accurate references to new agents. I was ... threatened to be blacklisted as a tenant for breaking the lease, causing extreme stress whilst I tried to obtain a home for me and my children when we fled interstate.' (Susie)

Many women described their grief at having to move away from their home and what was familiar to them and their children. The desire to achieve a home in which to sustain a family became even weightier as women fled the violence while trying to care for children and themselves. Our study shows that the majority do navigate the housing market with a degree of success, that is, they secure home ownership or a rental property in re-establishing their lives after IPV. However, for some women, achieving adequate shelter can take years because of difficulties in gathering sufficient finances while often being forced to accept lower standards of housing. Eventually, just over 37% returned to home ownership compared to the 51% during the period of the violent partnership.

The combined capabilities involved in achieving adequate shelter include safety, reasonable health and the material conditions sufficient to create the possibility of making a home for the woman herself and her children. While this was generally achieved, the long-term consequences of the impact of domestic violence meant that the quality of women's housing rarely returned to the levels they had experienced before the violence disrupted their lives. This is very well summed up by Rena in her response to the question about the impact of the violence on her housing.

> 'I have felt "invaded", under siege, at every house I have been in, including the shelters, where he was able to "charm" the addresses out of the children ... I set up a series of safe and happy households, where the children could live, play and have visitors ... I have found that my capacity to have or maintain good/high quality housing has diminished, exponentially, as my age and disabilities from the violence have negatively affected my ability to "get things done". I stopped being able to bounce back anywhere near as far as I had fallen, which is why I moved to the country. This house and my relationship to it is a daily litmus test of my physical and mental health, but even on my worst days it is still mine – my safe place.' (Rena)

Securing housing where one can feel safe, connected with family, friends or community, is an important capability that contributes to women's mental health and wellbeing and is interdependent on reliable and sufficient income.

Work (and education)

Income in western societies is generally derived from paid work and/or from social security benefits provided by the state. Nussbaum (2011: 34) includes income within the capability she characterises as 'the right to seek employment on an equal basis with others' that she defines under the heading of 'control over one's environment'. Equal employment opportunities are an important right of citizenship, as we argue in Chapter Two. It is the state's responsibility to ensure that citizens can access the institutions and agencies of education systems and social services which are necessary to enable this right. However, the interplay of sexual politics on employment legislation, policies and regulations creates barriers to gender equality around work conditions, including wages, workplace safety and educational and career opportunities (see, for example, Peetz and Murray, 2017). The distribution of women across the labour market is uneven; they predominate in casual, low-paid fields of work and their work is less valued. Men continue to exercise much of society's institutional power and also to occupy the higher paid positions across all fields (Pocock, 2003; Franzway et al., 2009a).

We argue that violence against women, particularly in the form of IPV exacerbates women's employment inequality. International and national research shows that domestic violence has a severe impact on women's paid employment (Brush, 2003; Swanberg and Logan, 2007; Hughes and Brush, 2015). In Australia, it is estimated that 55% to 70% of women who have experienced some form of violence, including stalking, harassment, physical assault and threat, sexual assault, violence by current and previous partners, are working full or part time (ABS, 2006). This shows that women are continuing to work while coping with the effects of domestic violence, but that domestic violence is likely to have negative impacts on their experiences of work.

The first Australian empirical study of the links between women's employment and domestic violence found that employers and co-workers, and, to some extent, women's services tend to view domestic violence as a 'private' issue (Franzway et al., 2009b). Our study is framed in recognition that the material, social and personal effects of IPV go well beyond the private domain. We therefore asked a series of questions of the women about their work experiences and were given strong evidence that IPV exacerbated their already existing gender inequality in the labour market.

Our study found that IPV erodes women's position in the workforce. The majority of women in our sample who answered the question about education had completed a level beyond secondary high school, with 34% completing a Bachelor degree or higher degree such as Master's and/or Doctorates. However, the reported current incomes indicate that the women are most frequently represented in the low-income ranges with 40% earning under $30,000pa, 14% earning $30,000-$39,000pa, and 10% earning $40,000-$49,000pa. Yet, we note that at approximately the same time as we collected our data, the Australian Bureau of Statistics reported, 'While average wages and salaries income for all Australia (persons) in 2010-11 was $51,923, males recorded a higher average of $62,699 compared with $40,312 for females' (ABS, 2013a). The low incomes of the women in our study are linked to the shift to part-time or casual paid work, or full-time caring roles, post domestic violence. This indicates that after domestic violence, it may be that women are much more likely to experience changes in their employment status, decreasing their chances of earning a significant wage to support themselves and their children, with compounding negative effects on their incomes across the life course. The effects of domestic violence on loss of employment affects women's abilities to access housing and intersects with the effects on mental health and wellbeing. This has long-term negative effects on their incomes, access to housing and social participation across the life course.

As noted earlier, Australian women workers are disadvantaged by a substantial gender pay gap in spite of overall equal access to education. Their incomes are also affected by structural sexual divisions in the labour market and that they are more likely to be employed part time (56%) than full time (44%) (ABS, 2014a), while a larger proportion of women are in casual jobs, without leave and other entitlements. In November 2013, 27% of female employees were in casual jobs compared with 21% of male employees (Charlesworth and Macdonald, 2015: 367). The workplace participation rates of the women in this study were similar to the larger population before they experienced IPV. However, at the time of completing the survey, this had dropped, with less than a third of participants in full-time employment (29.6%), and over 16% who described themselves as 'unemployed not seeking work' (see Table 2).

In addition, as outlined in Figure 3, women's employment was dramatically affected.

Table 2: Annual gross income and main income source*

Source of income	Employee	Self-employed	Income Support	Dependent on partner	Other	Total
Under $30,000	52	9	157	35	12	265
$30,000 - $39,000	60	4	23	2	1	90
$40,000 - $49,000	54	6	2	1	2	65
$50,000 - $59,000	53	3	3	0	1	60
$60,000 - $69,000	52	2	0	1	2	57
$70,000 - $79,000	36	0	0	0	0	36
$80,000 - $89,000	22	1	0	0	2	25
$90,000 and above	45	6	0	0	2	53
Total	374	31	185	39	22	651

*7 missing values

Source: Authors' calculations

Figure 3: Employment status prior to relationship and currently

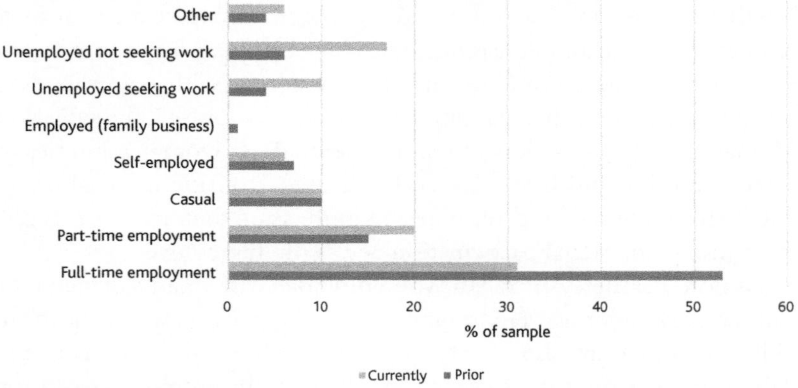

% of sample

■ Currently ■ Prior

Source: Authors' calculations

Although most women did not change their occupation over the period from before the IPV began to when they came to complete the survey, their patterns of employment participation, work trajectories and conditions underwent considerable change. Over half (60%) experienced significant changes to their hours, work locations and job levels while the majority (67%) reported that they had not remained in the same place of employment since the violence started. Approximately one third moved for safety reasons (30%), or because they felt they could not perform at work (27%) and/or were embarrassed by their situation (30%). The demands of the care needs of others, usually children, affected the employment of a fifth of participants (20%) while the lack of stable accommodation or transport affected a smaller number (11%). When asked in the survey, 9% of the women reported job loss after experiencing domestic violence, a proportion that is almost double the overall Australian women's unemployment rate of approximately 5% (ABS, 2014c).

These findings show that women's capabilities in terms of the freedom and opportunity to participate in employment and education is severely affected by domestic violence. Similarly, a 2009 report found that '[w]omen experiencing or escaping domestic violence can be the most vulnerable people in the labour market' (Franzway et al., 2009b: 45). The issues around how domestic violence has these effects are complex and complicated, ranging from its impact on self-confidence and the visible effects on the body, to external factors of workplace safety and employers' perspectives. We argue that the women's labour market vulnerability is not just a consequence of the immediate experience of IPV; it is a vulnerability which stretches into the future.

Our discussion of the impact of domestic violence must now turn to the complexities of the sexual politics of the workplace in relation to gendered violence. The workplace can become an opportunistic site of violence for the woman herself as well as for her co-workers, employers and the public with far-reaching consequences. The effects are compounded by gender inequality and discourses of ignorance which deny or refuse women's equal rights to the necessary combined capabilities to equal and dignified work. It is only recently being recognised that the workplace (and/or educational institutions) offers many possibilities for causing hurt, trouble and fear (Franzway et al., 2009b), even though it lies outside the purview of the violent partner, except where both partners are employed at the same place.

Violent partners themselves take the violence into this domain. Most obviously, domestic violence causes physical injuries that can prevent or limit women's employment capabilities, but it can take many forms, and these include harassment and violence before, during and after work with perpetrators interfering and sabotaging women's work through stalking, abusive and persistent phone calls and emails, harassment of colleagues, keeping women awake all night, monitoring the amount of time they take to get home after work, and verbal insults about their work abilities. Partners were reported as interfering directly with the woman's access to employment, for example by creating obstacles that prevented her mobility: "When our son was a toddler, he put an 18 inch screwdriver into my radiator so I couldn't drive my car. He also pierced my tyres so I couldn't get to work" (Mimi).

Many women had partners who were strongly opposed to their participating in the labour market, or who were concerned to ensure that the women only worked under specific conditions, such as only weekend shifts, or only daytime hours: "My violent partner did not want me to work and insisted I give up my full-time job" (Mindy). Clearly, perpetrators are intending to exercise coercive control of women by limiting, undermining or even destroying their freedom to choose their employment options. The workplace is also targeted by perpetrators as a place where the woman can be located after separation (Murray and Powell, 2009): "He was able to stalk me through colleagues that either didn't know what was happening or didn't understand. This caused me to feel unsafe and isolated at work" (Selene).

However, the sexual politics of gendered violence continues to see the woman blamed, ignored or punished for her violent partner's actions. Women described employers and co-workers who were suspicious or critical of the disruptions caused by violence, whether by the perpetrator directly or through its impact on the woman as a worker. Many of the women resorted to using secrecy to hide their circumstances in their job applications, avoid criticism by management and co-workers, or even prevent the loss of the job itself. The experience of intolerance for their circumstances was not uncommon for the women.

'I experienced a lack of support from HR [human resources]. Employers need to be aware that an employee who had an AVO [Apprehended Violence Order] needs support rather than judgement and/or secrecy at work.' (Gabby)

'[You are] forever defending your own experience to people who can't believe "such a great guy" would do that.' (Andrea)

'People are not supportive in the workplace. [There is] no support from government when you leave this situation.' (Emma)

The women's employment experiences indicate that employers, as well as state agencies and services, as Emma observed, generally remain unaware of the possibility that domestic violence may have an impact on their workplaces. Perpetrators who cause disruptions in the workplace are affecting the broader enterprise or organisation and may also be committing criminal acts (Franzway et al., 2009b: 11). Australian employers are required to maintain a safe workplace for all employees under occupational health, safety and welfare legislation and are tasked with the responsibility to develop policies and procedures designed to respond to workers who may be victims of violence (Department of Social Services, 2016). Just how effective such changes are proving to be will be discussed in more detail in Chapter Seven. Some of the women did report that their employers and co-workers were both understanding and supportive: "My boss was aware of the abuse and supported me to seek counselling. She understood that I had to take steps to apply for a restraint order" (Marilyn).

These women benefited from the material support provided by their employer, supports such as enabling them to have flexible work hours, as well as the emotional support from the trust and encouragement they received. When adequate supports are in place, the workplace is an important site for women to escape from the constraints of a violent partnership.

'My workplace at the time was my place of refuge with supportive workmates.' (Isobel)

'Work became my haven, my safety net. There he couldn't hurt me.' (Yolanda)

Work can simply be a place of safety, but it can also become a springboard for women to escape from the violence. In Nussbaum's book (2011), the woman, Vasanti found an escape option through the initial support of a brother who gave her a job. For most of the women in our study, however, the obstacles to accessing employment created by the violence and the lack of safety at the workplace were compounded by the impact of IPV on their mental health and well-being.

'[I experienced] lack of concentration, crying all the time, feeling scared and not being able to tell anyone. Shame on the days I went with black eyes, shame for lying that I was drunk and fell off my bike. I feel like fellow employees lost trust in me because of my decision to be with him. I was tired and drained, irritable and not a happy person to be around. Management got upset as to why I couldn't attend night meetings and it was part of my job description to attend. Training sessions I couldn't attend unless in work hours, then I was scared he would find out, as he would expect me to refuse, otherwise I could be up to no good.' (Kylie)

For many women like Kylie, it is common to feel trapped between the expectations of co-workers and managers about the demeanour and availability of the functioning employee, and the frightening likelihood of abuse from a controlling and violent partner. Their feelings of fear and shame caused by IPV contribute to a sense of powerlessness. Many women in our study described how their own emotional wellbeing affected their abilities to undertake work tasks, demonstrating the interconnections between how mental health and wellbeing influence performance and functioning at work. If IPV has negative effects on women's emotional and psychological wellbeing, it will therefore have an impact on their employment experiences. Wellbeing underlies the capacity to train and study, to seek employment and to perform and maintain paid work, but can be eroded by IPV. In our study, the women's opportunities to access the capabilities of a rewarding working life were tainted or interrupted by IPV.

Mental health and emotional wellbeing

As the employment options of women who experience domestic violence are diminished by reduced emotional well-being, the resulting financial instability compromises their housing security, which affects their employment choices and so on. The consequences are far-reaching for the women, as well as for their children, as the violence disrupts the interconnections between these domains and reduces their capabilities to pursue a decent and flourishing life.

> 'I am not the same person. I fear life now and feel stuck in a horrible black rut. I had to rent and then bought a much cheaper house in the outer suburbs where I have felt completely isolated and fell into depression. I have changed and this has affected my ability to work. I have lost friendships and have become alienated further from my family.' (Elise)

In Nussbaum's list of 10 capabilities, we find mental health and emotional wellbeing under several headings, including 'senses, imagination and thought', 'affiliation' ('being able to live with and toward others … to engage in various forms of social interaction') and 'control over one's environment' ('entering into meaningful relationships of mutual recognition') (Nussbaum, 2011: 34). Importantly, these several capabilities are protected by guarantees of freedom and 'not having one's emotional development blighted by fear and anxiety' (p 34). The problem is that sexual politics which contributes to unequal gender relations undermines the guarantees of women's equal freedom. Women who experience violence at the hands of their partners are not sufficiently protected by their citizenship rights from suffering damage to their emotional wellbeing.

We argue that mental health and emotional wellbeing are interdependent on the discursive and material environment, rather than being a matter of individual psychological conditions. One of the more corrosive, if nevertheless widespread, views about the connections between mental health and IPV is that women bring the violence onto themselves, as we discuss in the following chapter. Women are not uncommonly assumed to have psychological issues resulting from childhood abuse, low self-esteem and masochistic tendencies which lead them into relationships with abusive men, repeatedly. In this discourse, the problem of violence becomes the problem of the victimised woman. This discourse affects women themselves, who feel shame and guilt around their experiences of domestic violence. It also modifies the interpretations of domestic violence by the medical, social and legal services that are charged with responding to the multiple consequences of violence. When the victim is regarded as the cause of her own suffering, her opportunities for attaining the capabilities to flourish as a full citizen are weakened.

People who are subjected to personal violence, in whatever form, are likely to experience stress from the emotional pain as much as from any physical damage it may cause. In the area of violence caused by a loved one, an intimate partner, the shock and disturbance to beliefs about relationships and family can be profound: "I never thought it would happen to me. My ex-husband looked like a nice guy to everyone [but] behind the closed doors would be a Jekyll and Hyde." Western societies strongly endorse intimate partnerships between heterosexual couples. They are assumed to be the cornerstones of family life, and above all, are assumed to be grounded in romantic love. The key institutions of political, civil and social rights – including parliaments, courts and schools – work to ensure that intimate partnerships are sustained and valued. Freely chosen loving partnerships are the normative ideal. Not surprisingly, violence within these partnerships confronts deeply held beliefs and values which can prove very destabilising for those under attack.

The damage to mental health and wellbeing is compounded by the ways that gendered violence is reported. Reviewing media coverage in Italy, for example, Claudia Torrisi (2017) observes that

> [the violent partner] is usually described by neighbors or relatives as a good man, a lovely dad, a great husband. ... For instance: On 28 October 2014, Franco Sorgenti stabbed his partner, Laura Livi, to death in their house ... in central Italy ... a local newspaper quoted neighbours describing the man as 'respectable and distinguished ... very attentive to self-care' and as a 'loving dad, like so many others'.

We discuss the feminist campaigns that seek to overturn the victim-blaming inherent in these representations in Chapter Seven. Here, we draw attention to this aspect of the experience of domestic violence as an important aspect of sexual politics that is likely to exacerbate the difficulties women face in overcoming the direct effects of the violence.

Not surprisingly, women's mental health is often heavily compromised. In our study, just over half (52%) of the women who answered the question about mental illness reported that they were diagnosed with a mental health problem during or after they escaped the IPV. It is noteworthy that only 13% had any reported mental health issues before IPV; most received a diagnosis of mental illness either during (43%) or after (44%) experiencing domestic violence. The most common issues were depression (44%) and anxiety (41%), including post-traumatic stress disorder and panic disorder. Only very small numbers of women reported bipolar disorder, personality or psychotic disorders. Just over a third of the women reporting a mental illness (34%) identified multiple mental health problems, mainly anxiety and depression.

A significant proportion of women answered the question that asked them to rate their psychological and mental health before, during and after domestic violence. Almost three quarters of this group (70%) indicated good psychological and emotional wellbeing before domestic violence, while 90% reported poor psychological and emotional wellbeing during violence and 65% reported poor mental health afterwards. Our data show that many women do not consider themselves to have bounced back in terms emotional wellbeing, even though they had left the violent relationship. Most of the women (84%) reported that they had had contact with a professional about their psychological and emotional wellbeing. In spite of many women reporting poorer mental health as a result of domestic violence, many nonetheless reported feeling hopeful about their future (44.8%) or not discouraged about their future (17%). However, 18% reported that they feel discouraged about the future, and a further 13% reported that they do not expect things to work out and that the future is hopeless and will get worse. The women themselves described the impact of domestic violence in quite graphic terms: "It absolutely shattered me"; "I live hourly with the impacts of anxiety, feelings of worthlessness and depression." The anxiety and depression continue to be part of their everyday lives long after they manage to move away from the violence: "I am tired of having to live this way, but have come to realise that I will never be free of the emotional and physical effects of my married life." The women's mental health conditions seem perfectly predictable, for example finding they have post traumatic stress disorder (PTSD) even after leaving the relationship: "where he was actively searching for me and 'hunting me down' promising to find and kill me". For many however, the traumatic stress continues to be part of their lives, even after they have separated from the violent partner; they continue to feel fear, unsafe, and describe themselves as needing to be always on high alert.

This is particularly the case for those who have children who they feel are also under threat from the violent partner, either directly or indirectly.

'I am hyper-vigilant in my parenting and my work practice. The anxiety is overwhelming when I have to deal with him … I am highly motivated to protect my son but feel "let down" and confused by the family court system, and despite our history of IPV being documented on their system or that during my son's lifetime, four women in two states had AVOs (Apprehended Violence Orders) against him. The court system observes my son has not come to any harm, but they don't acknowledge it is because I have repeatedly protected him at expense of my own physical, financial and emotional wellbeing. The fear of him having that little boy alone petrifies me.' (Rosalie)

'[I am] permanently in a hyper-vigilant state for myself and my children. Never feeling safe. I am scared to use social networking (like everyone else) in case we are found. The kids have had mobile phones since a very early age to get to and from school. I drummed personal safety message into them since very young. I am no longer confident personally and professionally. I used to be a tax accountant with a comfortable income. Now the children and I live in poverty – the guilt that I can't provide for them is overwhelming.' (Ilene)

The children in the women's lives cause grave worries, and can be victims themselves, but they can also become a source of support, comfort and in Nussbaum's terms, offer very real opportunities of affiliation: "I was extremely suicidal for a long time, and only survived for the sake of my children." Children can be powerful influences on the wellbeing of those who experience IPV. In discursive terms, children are constituted as integral to family life, but are also highly significant to women's sense of identity, something we explore in more depth in the following chapter.

Women frequently reported that domestic violence caused loss of confidence in their internal capabilities, which, when it was combined with severe anxiety and depression, served to disrupt their employment (and education) and reduce their housing options: "I had no confidence, lost respect in my field due to absences therefore not considered for promotion or salary increases" (Meg). The loss of income and employment, frequent housing moves and low levels of income support in a residual welfare state can plunge women into poverty. IPV not only increases the risk of housing instability and poverty, but also aggravates loss of belonging to place, family and community (Murray, S., 2008). A woman's ability to secure adequate housing has ongoing implications for her employment and her emotional wellbeing, which are all seriously violated when domestic violence occurs (Paglione, 2006).

These interconnected effects could set in train a maelstrom of problems and dilemmas that the women described as a 'black hole'. Navigating through in the vulnerable craft of their own identity while suffering unpredictable violence and not always reliable support from family and state agencies has left many women with reduced capabilities and options. While some women managed to regain their wellbeing, very few reported their current mental health as 'good' or 'very good'. A very small number described themselves as gaining in strength from the experience, but most continued to grapple with the internal and external consequences.

> 'The truth of the situation broke every friendship and family relationship I had and I lost my two best friends, three brothers completely and all others have been strained since from that time. I don't discuss the domestic violence with new people and have been isolated socially being a single woman, everyone is partnered – I have not been to dinner at anyone's home for 10 years, no catch ups in the evening with couples, just coffees with other school mums. I have been incredibly lonely.' (Trista)

These are stories of loss, not only of the material conditions of home, adequate shelter and employment, but also of the combined capabilities necessary for a decent and flourishing life. These are stories of the impact of domestic violence on women, the results of a sexual politics which gives a certain licence to men in heterosexual relationships to resort to multiple forms of violence and control. The damage to the women is compounded by the refusal and rejection of family, friends and the inadequacies of the labour market and state institutions. We characterise these effects as outcomes of a politics of ignorance which works to deny the implications of gender inequalities on our understandings of gendered violence. Domestic violence is constituted through a sexual politics in which men's violence against women remains largely accepted as isolated incidents, jointly caused by both partners, or perhaps even instigated by the woman herself. 'The truth of the situation', as Trista describes it, confronts the preferred denial buttressed in the discourses and practices of gendered violence, which results in the breakdown of social and family relationships. If women's political, social and civil rights as citizens were given equal weight to men's, by the state and by society, domestic violence would be commensurate with – and punished in equal measure – the violence between men.

Social participation

Our perspective on citizenship rights gives weight to the citizen's responsibilities. In order to undertake their responsibilities, citizens need to have a threshold level of Nussbaum's central capabilities. In this chapter we have discussed the damage domestic violence does to the capabilities associated with adequate shelter, employment and emotional wellbeing. What has also emerged in our study is the corrosive effect of IPV on women's freedom and opportunities for social participation, which is a critical element of the citizens' responsibilities. Domestic and sexual violence researcher Liz Kelly (2003) has proffered the idea of 'space for action' as a way of understanding how women rebuild their lives after IPV. She draws on Eva Lundgren's (1998) original concept of 'space for regulative action', arguing that 'agency is exercised in context, and contexts are always more or less constrained by material and other factors' and that 'gender violence decreases women's space for action, while simultaneously increasing men's' (Kelly, 2003: 144). Social participation, engagement and involvement are foundational to being able to enjoy citizenship. Citizenship represents dignity shaped by cultural assumptions, institutional practices and a sense of belonging (Franzway, 2016). When sufficient income derived from steady employment is disrupted by domestic violence, and housing and mental health become compromised because of the associated fear, trauma and stress, together these compounding effects also erode women's capability to actively participate in many social and political activities. Domestic violence immobilises women's ability to more freely from place to place (Sharp-Jeffs et al., 2018). The fear, surveillance, monitoring and control perpetrated by an intimate partner halts freedom to imagine, think, attach, love, laugh and have fun; this has long-lasting effects: "I felt overwhelmed and unable to cope because of the continual state of fear" (Nadia).

The General Social Survey (GSS) in the Australian context provides an understanding of people's opportunities to participate fully in society, recognising that strong social capital is linked to increased individual and community wellbeing (ABS, 2014d). The GSS therefore includes elements such as community support, social participation, civic participation, network size, trust and trustworthiness, and an ability to have a level of control of issues important to the individual. However, we found that these elements are compromised by domestic violence.

In our study, 94% of women reported social abuse as a tactic of domestic violence. Social abuse is a term used to describe how a perpetrator controls their victim through forms of surveillance and monitoring, for example, where she goes, who she sees, and what she wears. It also includes perpetrators isolating victims from family and friends by convincing them that they do not need anyone else, or by sabotaging relationships, or making contact with victims difficult (Wendt, 2016). The results of a sexual politics have conferred long, deeply held assumptions and social constructions that women are home-makers and their primary role in society is to raise children. This has produced a politics of ignorance or denial that women have every right to participate freely in public realms and seek a sense of belonging outside institutional practices of family. For example, Cat explained in her survey response the social abuse she endured and how this had an impact on her social networks, emotional wellbeing, and material security:

> 'I always had to do everything to do with the kids and the home so could never make my own friends at uni. I had no time or money to do what I wanted and he would make me feel guilty as he had the job and I did nothing.' (Cat)

Domestic violence does not just affect women as wives and mothers, but as citizens with rights and responsibilities in public spaces. Social abuse erodes opportunities to participate fully in society, shrinks women's social, civic and political networks, and muddles women's sense of trust and trustworthiness. Even after fleeing domestic violence, it can take years for women to repair or build new relationships and networks as well as to feel safe, comfortable, and willing to trust others again.

> 'Have lost a lot of trust in people. Have become quite isolated.' (Lisette)

'Finding it difficult to trust even friends, feel isolated even when with people, don't want to disclose anything personal.' (Lily)

'I lost all confidence during, and find difficulty regaining confidence after DV [domestic violence] to participate. It's hard work to get involved again and challenge those feelings.' (Abigail)

Volunteering is considered one indicator of community support and civic participation in the Australian context. Volunteering is understood as people willingly providing unpaid help in the form of time, service or skills through an organisation or group. In 2014, the Australian Bureau of Statistics reported that there were 5.8 million people in Australia (31%) who had volunteered in the previous 12 months. Women are more likely to participate in voluntary work than men (34% compared to 29%, respectively) (ABS, 2014d). Volunteering is reported as highest for people in the 35-44 year age group, which most likely reflects parents providing assistance to groups in which their children are involved such as sport, school, church, and other hobbies. However, our study found that women's participation in all these activities decreased significantly during domestic violence. Women also reported that their participation in volunteering, hobbies, sport and church activities did not recover to the levels before domestic violence. Domestic violence severley impacts women's levels of involvement in activities connecting them to their broader community, and therefore shapes and erodes how women interact with the community outside their households.

'It [he] crushed my soul, made me not believe in myself. Lost my potential of what I could have achieved in my life if I had not met him. Had to fight to keep my self-confidence in a world where that already is hard to attain for a woman.' (Bethany)

Women's personal abilities, together with the freedoms and opportunities that come from political, social and economic environments, that is, their combined capabilities, are continually compromised in IPV. Combined capabilities are central to citizenship and allow individuals to live with human dignity. Yet sexual politics works to deny the negative interconnected impact of this violence on housing, employment, mental health and social participation. As

Blanche explains, domestic violence has long-term, compounding impacts, infiltrating all aspects of her life.

> 'Sometimes I don't get involved in activities because I am exhausted, depressed and/or financially drained. Sometimes it is just too hard to put myself out there. A lot of activities these days have some sort of cost attached as well. Even though I have a good income, the cost of legal bills, psychology, GP visits due to stress–related illnesses makes it hard.' (Blanche)

Eroding women's citizenship

We have begun to unpack the breadth and depth of IPV's impact on women's citizenship through a specific focus on the life domains of housing, work, mental health and social participation. In particular, we have shown how the impact in one domain reverberates through the others. We conclude this chapter by presenting two case studies from the life history analysis which clearly illustrate the interconnected nature of this impact.

Amaya is aged 25-34 years and has two children under 10 years of age. Amaya is from a South East Asian background. She lives in a rural area with her children and has an income under $30,000 from Centrelink government social security benefits. She has a university degree. Amaya experienced violence for 10-15 years. She lived in a jointly owned house with her partner pre-separation. She went to a refuge on leaving and then stayed with friends or family. She then went into her own very basic private rental, but later experienced a period of homelessness for a year where she was between a friend's place and her car, with her children living with grandparents. Amaya was a full-time student before violence and she was also in full-time professional employment. She had to resign from her job to move away because of the IPV and safety concerns. She now describes herself as in full-time home duties and is not seeking work. She was forced to quit a good job to move to a rural location to be safe from her ex-partner, and this was experienced as a major loss of identity and life satisfaction. It also led to a loss of social networks. Amaya was prevented from seeing friends and family during IPV. She has lost friends and is estranged from family because she kept trying to make the relationship work. She has kept away from people because she doesn't want them to know about the IPV. Amaya described her mental health as poor during and immediately after IPV, but as good now. She was diagnosed with depression during IPV and still has difficult times. Her ex-partner has moved into the same town and sees the children, so he is back in her life, prompting her to observe that "you never can get away".

The effects of a geographical move were significant for Amaya because it meant leaving her job and losing what was a safe haven, income and a social network. The loss of her job also emerges as a key factor, which led to inadequate rental housing because of lack of funds. Amaya was also prevented from seeing friends and family during IPV, and has now lost friends and is estranged from family. Her mental health has improved, but has not rebounded to pre–IPV levels. Amaya's narrative shows clearly how the impact of IPV in one domain flowed through to impacts in others in a compounding way.

Lizzie is aged 45-54 years of age. She has three children over 16 years of age. Her income is over $90,000. She has a university diploma. She experienced IPV for five years. Lizzie lived in a jointly owned home when in the violent relationship. She is living with a new partner and has full custody of her children. She initially retained the family home, but it was eventually sold and she was able to buy another smaller house from the proceeds as sole owner. Her housing costs have increased greatly since she moved. The new home is in a neighborhood near to her old house and she is positive about the house and the area. Her ex-partner does not pay child support but her father has helped her financially and this has enabled her to purchase and keep her house. Lizzie works full time in senior administrative work and has been able to retain her job because IPV is understood by her employer and there are flexible hours, a carers policy and counselling. However, she has had to be careful not to let IPV affect her performance at work because this would not be tolerated by her boss. Her self-confidence at work has been negatively affected by IPV. Her ex-partner socially isolated her and controlled her contact with her female friends, and verbally attacked her family. She chose not to say much about the IPV to her friends and one rejected her for this, but she nonetheless says she has good friendships. Lizzie says that her mental health was poor during and straight after leaving IPV, but is good now, although her energy levels are much lower. Lizzie has never had a diagnosis of mental illness but has sought help for psychological wellbeing, and, while not diagnosed with PTSD, she believes she has experienced it. Lizzie spoke of trying to access state-funded medical, financial and housing services for herself and her children to leave and recover from IPV, but reported that she could not obtain any help because of her income and assets; she was therefore entirely reliant on her own and her family's resources.

Lizzie survived IPV better than many women in our study because of a well-paid, flexible job that included employee counselling services and flexible hours, as well as some understanding of IPV in the organisation. The marital home was also of a reasonably high value and the settlement was important to Lizzie re-establishing herself, as was financial support from her family. Lizzie's narrative serves as a useful contrast to those of other women, including Amaya, who did not have well-paid work, jointly owned homes or financial support from families to help manage increased housing costs. Nonetheless, Lizzie had to manage a challenging transition alone, and she particularly emphasised the difficulty of accessing state-funded mental health support for herself and her children.

Each of these life histories reveals how IPV exacerbates and compounds gender inequality through its interconnected impacts on housing, work, mental health and social participation. The life histories also reveal intersections of class and how the failure of the state to provide adequate support for women leaving IPV has particularly serious effects on women who have reduced means because their employment is low paid or non-existent, or because they do not own homes or have family support. However, even where women do have these cushions, as in the case of Lizzie, the impact of IPV remains significant and women's personal, social and material resources are seriously stretched in the effort to meet their own and their children's needs. In the following two chapters, we explore in greater detail how IPV affects mental health and social participation, and explore the implications for women's citizenship.

FIVE

Gendered violence and the self

Introduction

As one of us sagely observed when we were planning this chapter, it would be more remarkable if a woman did *not* experience mental health problems as a result of intimate partner violence (IPV) rather than if she did. It is hardly earth-shattering to point out that intimate partner violence has a serious deleterious effect on women's mental health and wellbeing. What is more noteworthy is the finding from our research that this negative impact often endures for many years afterwards. Unlike our own study, most research into IPV and mental health does not include women who left violent male partners many years ago, so there is usually a focus on the more immediate impact. Most existing research in this area is also concerned with establishing the links between IPV and mental illnesses such as anxiety, depression and post-traumatic stress disorder (PTSD). In so doing, a psycho-medical discourse of mental illness is implicitly adopted, most clearly demonstrated in the use of the language and definitions of the *Diagnostic and statistical manual of mental disorders* (APA, 2013), the diagnostic tool of psychiatry, medicine and psychology. Hence, while it is generally understood within this research that abuse is the primary cause of women's mental health problems in domestic violence, their psychological states are nonetheless tacitly defined as symptomatic of abnormal functioning or psychopathology. A host of potential consequences flows from this uncritical adoption of a psychiatric illness framework for the types of health and support services available to women who have experienced IPV.

Research linking IPV with the development of certain mental health conditions can be important – for example, it is useful in making the case for increased support services – but its dominance means that there is little attention paid to the phenomenology of women's distress and the impact of IPV on sense of self and identity. While psycho-medical constructions of women's mental health in IPV may not be as deeply pathologising as those applied to women who were abused in childhood, this narrow understanding does mean that, in practice, state-sponsored support for the mental health care of women who have experienced IPV is extremely limited, narrow in its orientation and focused only on one-to-one intervention. Both research and practice in this area, then, largely concerns itself only with the psychological impact of individual men's violence on individual women. What we aim to do, instead, is critically explore how IPV and mental health have come to be understood in largely individualistic, psychological terms and how this, in turn, links to particular approaches to policy and practice that are supported by the state. Rather than asking about the impact of IPV on women's mental health, instead we query why the relationship between IPV and women's mental health is approached only in particular ways. We also ask, what other ways might the psychological and emotional impact of IPV be understood and addressed so that policy and practice more usefully support women's capabilities and citizenship?

In our study, some women resisted medicalised approaches to their distress, but still others drew on dominant psychological and medical understandings of anxiety, depression and PTSD to validate and establish the seriousness of IPV and its impact on their lives. Women therefore drew on available discourses to understand and explain what had happened to them. While acknowledging this, our goal is to situate women's psychological distress squarely within the sexual politics of IPV and coercive control. In doing so, we demonstrate how gender discourses, practices and power relations harnessed in IPV systematically erode women's sense of themselves as persons and selves, and by extension, their capabilities to exercise their rights and entitlements as citizens. The fact that this erosion of selfhood and citizenship rights extends well into the long-term is specifically important to broadening understandings and responses to IPV-related emotional distress beyond psycho-medical perspectives. The long shadow of IPV has not been widely considered in policy or practice, and points to interconnections between the impact of IPV on women's mental health and its impact on other domains of work, housing and social relationships over time, hence the long-term negative consequences for women's citizenship. We explore how a politics of ignorance concerning IPV and its effects contribute to the prevailing psycho-medical approach to IPV and mental health which works to compound gender inequalities.

Looking beyond the individual woman

Common mental health problems such as anxiety, depression and PTSD are known to be some two to three times higher in women than men across the Australian population as a whole (ABS, 2007), which is comparable with most countries around the world. Through quantitative analysis of national IPV and mental health data in the UK, Walby and Allen (2004) have shown that this gender asymmetry can be largely attributed to IPV. Their work challenges historical and contemporary discourses that explain observed gender differences in mental health by pointing to women's supposedly innate psychological and hormonal vulnerabilities (Ussher, 2010). While the World Health Organization has long acknowledged the centrality of violence against women to improving women's mental health worldwide (WHO, 2005), the Australian government's National Mental Health Policy (Australian Health Ministers Conference, 2009) makes not one mention of it. At the national level in this country, there is still a significant disconnect between policy on mental health and policy on violence against women.

As noted, most of the research into IPV and mental health is undertaken within psychology and medicine and is focused on measuring associations between IPV and specific mental illnesses. This research tends to use quantitative violence scales to measure IPV, such as the Conflict Tactics Scale (for example, Nixon et al., 2004) and psychological assessment tools such as the Hospital Anxiety and Depression scale, to assess the types and severity of mental disorder (for example, Clark et al., 2014). Such measures generally fail to capture the complexity and nuanced character of IPV and its impact on women (Kimmel, 2002). As noted earlier, psycho-medical approaches also assume and adopt a medicalised understanding of, and approach to, mental illness as real and definable 'disorders' that inhabit an individual body and are reflective of psychopathology in that body (Moulding, 2016). More recent psychological and psychiatric research and practice in this area adopts a trauma framework where women struggling with their mental health during or after IPV are often understood to have developed PTSD (Goldenson et al., 2007). However, even for those conditions where external experiences are acknowledged, such as PTSD, psychological disorder remains effectively located in, and contained by, the individual's body rather than the social body. Within such conceptualisations, traumatising events become unfortunate experiences that happen to some unlucky individuals; the social texture and gendered pattern of IPV and its impact on women's lives and on wider society is rendered invisible. Moreover, trauma approaches tend to prioritise fear above all other emotions and collapse all traumas together, irrespective of whether they arise from war, accidents, natural disasters or interpersonal violence and abuse. Trauma models do not account very well for other types of gendered violence and abuse that do not necessarily involve direct physical violence and fear, such as psychological, emotional, financial, social and spiritual abuse, as well as sexual coercion. It is these less physical forms of abuse that are known to be most strongly associated with poor mental health (Stoltenborgh et al., 2012; AIHW, 2014), although clearly fear of physical harm and death is also of great importance.

Feminist scholars and researchers have historically questioned the wisdom of psycho-medical approaches to mental illness for women, particularly for abused women. Feminists have shown how these place women (rather than men or society) at the centre of a medical gaze that fails to account for the gendered discourses and practices that construct subjectivities or the gender power relations that make these possible (Reavey, 2003; Warner, 2009). While there is a robust feminist critique of psycho-medical approaches to women's mental health more generally, and specifically in relation to child sexual abuse, feminist theory and research into IPV and mental health remains quite thin on the ground. Indeed, historically, feminist scholars and activists have been hesitant to focus on women's mental health in the context of gendered violence and abuse for fear of shifting attention to questions about what is wrong with women, with all the risks of victim-blaming that can ensue, and away from questions about violent men's responsibilities and gender power relations (Breckenridge, 1999). Nonetheless, some feminist researchers have brought a feminist perspective to examinations of IPV and mental health, with distinctive differences from conventional psycho-medical approaches.

Feminist research into the impact of IPV on mental health is primarily qualitative and focuses on women's lived experience, avoiding psycho-medical language and interpretation. For example, feminist researchers in Sweden found that women who leave IPV commonly feel fear, uncertainty, shame and guilt, with psychological and sexual abuse causing the deepest and longer-term problems (Scheffer Lindgren and Renck, 2008). Many of the women in this study regarded themselves as strong people before IPV, which made the violence and abuse particularly shocking. With a similar emphasis on the non-physical aspects of IPV, an Australian study found that it was the controlling nature of the relationship and the ongoing knocks to self-esteem that women experienced as leading to depression, panic attacks, PTSD, insomnia and suicidal actions. The experience of panic and anxiety were directly linked in this research to women's feelings of relative powerlessness and inequality in relation to their partners (Laing and Toivonen, 2010). Both these studies reveal how women centre non-physical violence and control as key to feelings of low self-esteem, shame and guilt.

In a UK study, women drew a direct, causal relationship between domestic violence and their mental health problems. One woman's comment to the researchers was particularly illustrative when she said, "you call it symptoms of mental illness, I call it the symptoms of domestic violence" (Humphreys and Thiara, 2003: 213); the term 'symptoms' was being used somewhat ironically here. Similarly to the other feminist studies above, women described losing their confidence and self-worth through being worn down by abuse and being made to believe that they were inferior to their partners. Humphreys and Thiara (2003) illustrate the extreme control exerted on women by their violent partners, borrowing Johnson and Ferraro (2000)'s concept of 'intimate terrorism' to suggest that violent men seek to 'eradicate the women's sense of self and create instead a "puppet woman" subject to their authority' (Humphreys and Thiara, 2003: 215). They argue that male control such as this is the contextual frame for the suicide attempts described by some of the women in their study. We pick up on this theme of coercive control as an attempt to eradicate sense of self later in discussion of our own findings.

Feminist research into the impact of IPV on mental health focuses on women's lived experiences and eschews psycho-pathologising discourses that position women as mentally ill. Feminist researchers have challenged the idea that women's psychological and emotional distress means that they are, by definition, irrational, out of control and therefore not credible witnesses to their own experiences. Feminist research and practice approaches have therefore sought to normalise women's responses to abuse by problematising men's behaviour and the gender power differences that produce it, rather than intra-psychic processes in women. They have also sought to give voice to the meaning of women's distress as well as the negative impact of medicalisation itself on women's mental health and wellbeing. Feminist research has specifically demonstrated the negative effects of medicalising abuse-related distress and how women's experiences of IPV often go unheard in traditional health care settings (Laing and Toivonen, 2010). Feminist research uses everyday understandings of psychological distress rather than psychiatric language and labels, and this is important in understanding women's lived difficulties. But existing feminist research also focuses on mental health in isolation from the other challenges women face, and tends to focus on the immediate effects of violence rather than on the long term. It also focuses on documenting the details of individual women's experiences rather than broader questions about the socio-cultural discourses framing practices of IPV and their impact on women, the state's role and responsibilities, and the implications for women's citizenship.

As part of challenging medicalised understandings, we show how the impact of IPV on women's emotional wellbeing is far more complex than allowed by the diagnostic labels of psycho-medicine, or even common-sense feminist approaches. We want to take analysis a step further by showing how the nature of women's emotional distress directly reflects the gender discourses, practices and power relations that constitute IPV itself. This brings sexual politics to the fore in understanding both IPV and its psycho-emotional impact. Rather than a simple 'violence = mental illness' equation, or even 'violence = emotional distress', both of which fail to unpack the gendered emotional dynamics of violence and abuse, we explore how the typology of gendered violence is itself embedded in the phenomenology of women's embodied psycho-emotional responses. The aim of doing this is to situate women's experiences within gendered social power relations and sexual politics, challenging the individualising and pathologising discourses and practices in the mental health field that contribute to wilful ignorance about the impact of IPV.

Many women in our study characterised the psychological and emotional impact of IPV as an assault on their very personhood or selfhood, which is the basis of citizenship. We aim to demonstrate how this assault on selfhood and, by extension, citizenship is intimately connected with, and helps to reinforce, the undermining of women's capabilities, rights and the exercise of citizenship in the other life domains of housing, work and social participation, and vice versa. We will argue that dominant psycho-medical conceptualisations and treatment approaches encountered by many women, and supported by the state, are enabled by and contribute to the wider politics of ignorance about the gender inequalities that structure IPV and its impact on women. We argue that a simple violence = mental illness equation should be understood as part and parcel of a sexual politics that minimises, objectifies and diminishes women as persons and citizens at the same time as it obscures the male privilege and unequal gender power relations that enable and maintain IPV.

Coercive control, sexual politics and mental health

The following analysis shows how the specific nature of the distress described by the women in our study connects directly to the gender discourses and power dynamics that structure the practices of IPV itself, particularly coercive control. Stark (2012: 7) defines coercive control as

> an ongoing pattern of domination by which male abusive partners primarily interweave repeated physical and sexual violence with intimidation, sexual degradation, isolation and control. The primary outcome of coercive control is a condition of entrapment that can be hostage-like in the harms it inflicts on dignity, liberty, autonomy and personhood as well as to physical and psychological integrity.

Most of the women in our sample who struggled with mental health after IPV described coercive control in addition to physical abuse from their male partners. For many women, the threat of physical violence hung over these control tactics and was central to their enforcement, even if it was not always enacted (Stark, 2007). As one woman explained with heavy sarcasm, "I experienced only occasional violence because I was very obedient and didn't need much beyond a threat to refocus me."

A central feature of coercive control is the imposition of social isolation in order to increase control over women (Stark, 2007). Many women in our study described being prevented from seeing or contacting friends or family. One woman who had migrated from overseas said, "He was trying to isolate me . . . he started saying, 'Oh you cannot Skype your family.'" In the extract below, constant movement from place to place instigated by a woman's violent partner ensures that there are no friends for her to rely on.

> 'The first thing he did was isolate me. So he got me away from the family and every time I would make friends in a new town we would move. ... I would make friends, we would move. I'd make friends, we'd move. I'd make friends, we'd move.' (May)

Another woman spoke about her partner monitoring who she socialised with, driven by extreme jealousy and fear that she might be seeing other men.

> 'He didn't let me have friends, he would get jealous and, very jealous. One occasion where I went to see a movie with some friends from Uni, just two girls, later when I

mentioned I'd seen the movie he was like "Oh yeah, who did you go with again?" Jealous.' (Freya)

The above examples constitute what is often defined as social abuse in the IPV literature (Wendt and Zannettino, 2015). Control tactics focused on the management of women's appearance, weight and sexualities were also depicted as motivated by male partners' extreme jealousy and their fears that women might be seeing other men.

> 'I didn't even realise just how bad things were actually getting because it was so gradual. Like in the beginning it was "Oh you can't wear that because it makes you a slut. Why do you have make up on? Who are you trying to impress?" And things were just so gradual that by the end I wasn't allowed to see any friends, wasn't allowed to go anywhere, do anything without him accusing me of cheating ... you don't even realise it's happening.' (Felicia)

Jealousy and fear that women will attract the interest of other men was also understood by the women as driving practices of extreme monitoring through phone calls and accusations of infidelity, including after women had left the violent relationship.

> 'He kept phoning me at first and saying that I've got another boyfriend, that I'm pregnant to someone else, all these. ... Everything was my fault. [He] accused me of having affairs with my boss or anyone else who called, that was kind of his angle but he did not worry about me having a job because I paid all the bills.' (Veronica)

Stark (2007) similarly describes the harassment of women through calls and texting to check up on their whereabouts. As in Stark's (2007) research, women in our study also described violent men checking their computers and mobile phones to monitor their contacts. Some male partners even went so far as to secretly install listening devices and surveillance cameras in the women's houses after they had left the violent relationship. In-person stalking was also mentioned, both while the women were still in the violent relationship and after they had left. A number of women in Australia and in other countries, too, have been murdered by violent ex-partners after leaving, with stalking not uncommonly leading up to this (Walby and Allen, 2004). While some men prevented women from working in order to reduce their contact with other men, others were happy for their female partners to work so that they could materially benefit from it, although they remained jealous and threatened by the arrangement nonetheless.

> 'He quit jobs and was unemployed for chunks of time – do you know what I mean? He enjoyed the fruits of my labour. So that was not an issue for him although I'm sure the power imbalance that it caused ... contributed to his actions or his attitudes so while on one hand he was quite happy for me to work and to spend my money, let's put it frankly, but he was certainly jealous. He didn't like me to talk about my work at all.' (Veronica)

As noted in the above account, some men controlled the spending of the women's earnings, which is a form of financial abuse. While the women depicted mixed attitudes on the part of their partners as to whether they should hold jobs outside the home, there seemed to be a particular dislike of, and efforts to derail, women's attempts at further education.

> 'He threw all my books out the window and every time I had an assignment due ... every time there was an assignment due he would have some, there would be some gigantic argument, the violence was huge when ... I was at university the violence was enormous.'
>
> Q: 'Okay, so this was perceived as a great threat?'
>
> A: 'It definitely was, yeah.' (Sascha)

Another woman characterised her violent partner as jealous of her opportunity to undertake university studies and as dedicated to disrupting her efforts.

> 'Once we moved in there was, quite early on, signs that things weren't quite right ... like, he ... was very jealous that I'd had the opportunity to go to Uni ... in the beginning it was just, I would have my notes out on the coffee table in the lounge room just, because I'd been at Uni just trying to consolidate all my notes and get everything together. He'd come home from work, I'd offer to make him a coffee or a tea or dinner or whatever, and in the meantime, while I'm

in the kitchen trying to get something for him, he'd throw my notes on the floor and say "Why are you making such a fucking mess?"' (Freya)

These examples speak to another important element of coercive control that has also been noted by Stark (2007), which is that the controlling tactics escalate when women try to better themselves or become more independent. One woman described how violence coincided with her becoming more independent once the children had grown.

'The domestic violence didn't really start until about the last three or four years and it sort of coincided with me becoming more independent. ... I was elected to a [local] council and he really resented that because I loved it. Part of it was very stressful later on but I found it really stimulating. He was OK with me going to the young wives clubs and mothers- and babies-type functions when the kids were little. That was no threat to him. But with this other one I was going to meetings with fellow members, mainly men, at night, and he started thinking I was having it off with them, very jealous and it just escalated from there.' (Gertrude)

Another area of coercive control described by the women focused on their domestic and child-caring practices. Stark (2007) argues that coercive control focused on the domestic realm represents a direct attack on feminine agency because the home is a highly feminised area of responsibility and activity.

'He started to get angry at me for the house being messy, and I said well hold on ... you constantly want my attention when you're home. So if I get up to do the dishes you say "Leave it" and yeah, it was just, he would constantly try to interrupt me cleaning the house, and then have a reason to yell at me ... it'd be snide remarks, sort of, more like "What have you been doing all day?" "You've been home all day, what have you been doing, why isn't the house clean if you've been doing nothing all day?"' (Freya)

Some women described retaining all or most of the responsibility for domestic chores and child-care, even when they were in paid employment and their partners were not. Many women also described the manipulation of children by violent partners, a tactic not identified by Stark (2007) in his typology of coercive control, but one which has been identified as part of the Duluth Power and Control Wheel of domestic violence (DAIP, 2008). Women described being blamed for children's behaviour while others referred to maternal alienation, where men brainwashed children into the belief that it was their mothers who were to blame for all of the family's woes (Morris, 1999).

'From the time I left there was this ongoing campaign of maternal alienation to tell the kids how stupid I was and it just went on and on and on and on. And it definitely affected my relationship with the kids and it upset them a lot.' (Sascha)

Sascha also described her partner kidnapping the children while another was prevented from taking her son with her when she tried to leave. Other men threatened to kill the children.

'He said that I would do as I was told or else he would kill the kids. And so I was very protective of the kids and [my son] never understood why I would drop him off to school while everyone else walks.' (May)

As is now well known, some violent men in Australia and elsewhere have gone on to murder the children as acts of revenge on women for leaving them (Johnson, 2006). Other women described child custody battles that were based on the men's desire for revenge for leaving rather than a genuine desire to be with and care for their children. Feminist research has shown that women will go to great lengths to protect their children from violent partners, often taking on blame and complying with unreasonable demands to keep the peace (Moulding et al., 2015). Using children as proxies for attacks on women not only strikes at a key domain of feminine agency – mothering – but also exploits a key site of vulnerability for women who have children.

Rape and other types of sexual violence were also commonly reported by almost two thirds of the women in our study (65%). Some women specifically linked rape, sexual assault and sexual coercion to male partners' fears that the women were becoming too independent: "[the rape] happened in the last year when he felt as if he was losing complete control of me." Another woman described how her partner became physically and sexually violent when he realised she was planning to leave: "That's when he first started getting physically violent. He was a bit rough in bed, is how it started. Just wanting to bring bondage into the relationship and just getting, just rough that way." Another woman described her shock when her partner raped her after she had danced with another man.

> 'That was the funny thing. I thought I had found Mr Perfect. And this one night we were out dancing and someone asked me to dance and I was dancing with him and I noticed a change in mood, but when I got home he started both raping me and slapping me across the face.'

> Q: 'Because you were dancing with someone else?'

> A: 'Because I was dancing with someone else and he said that I hadn't asked permission, and I remember lying there and thinking "Is this happening?" I was in shock.' (May)

Most women also described ongoing psychological abuse (also referred to as emotional or verbal abuse) as a central element of coercive control. For example, accusations of supposed promiscuity and unfaithfulness were tied up with violent men's efforts to restrict women's contact with other men. Verbal abuse that focused on women's weight and appearance were related to men's fears they might attract other men as well as to a proprietary sense of ownership over the women's bodies and how they should look. As noted above, criticisms of child-rearing and other domestic practices sought to control the women in traditionally feminine spheres, thereby depriving them of autonomy and agency even in these feminised domains. Calling women 'stupid' or 'mad' positioned them as incompetent and inferior to the male partner, and could also undermine women's credibility with their own children, friends and family.

The controlling tactics described by the women in our study were therefore common and multifarious, including: enforced social isolation; control of women's appearance, clothing and sexuality; stalking and monitoring of movements, particularly contact with other men; monitoring and criticism of domestic and child-rearing practices; threatening children; preventing women from working or studying; forcing women to work and controlling their earnings; and rape, sexual abuse and sexual coercion. Psychological abuse that focused on women's sexualities, bodies, intellects and mental competence served to undermine them further and bolster the men's power and control in the relationship. As noted earlier, the threat of physical violence hung over these control tactics, even if it was not always enacted (Stark, 2007). In line with Stark's observations, the coercive control experienced by the women was arguably concerned with the enforcement of a compliant and servile femininity. Coercive control in IPV can be therefore understood as a brutal and unsubtle form of sexual politics that uses the threat of physical violence to reduce women to object-like instruments for the satisfaction of the violent man's needs and entitlements (to sex, emotional support, children, domestic servicing, money, power and so on).

The practices of coercive control outlined above are based on a series of long-standing gender discourses situated within historical and continuing material gender inequalities and power imbalances that, while challenged by sexual politics, work to preserve male privilege and dominance. These gender power relations order daily lives in terms of the sexual division of labour, unequal earnings, care-giving responsibilities, institutional arrangements and the distribution of resources, but they also frame to varying extents the everyday interpersonal relationship dynamics between men and women (Anderson, 2009). Interpersonal dynamics in IPV have sometimes been understood through the relatively simplistic idea that men who most strongly identify with traditional masculinities tend to be more violent towards their partners (Anderson, 2009). In contrast, both Stark (2007) and Anderson (2009) argue that it is the inherent vulnerability and instability of masculine identities in the patriarchal gender order that leads some men to use violence and control with female partners to restore their sense of themselves as 'real men'. More specifically, it is the vulnerability and instability of these masculine identities which explains why so much coercive control is specifically concerned with the denigration of women, femininity and the feminine (Stark, 2007; Anderson, 2009). In line with this, some of the women in our study indicated that verbal abuse often involved being told that they were stupid and mad; such accusations mobilise long-standing gender discourses about inferior female intelligence and women's supposedly inherent emotionality and irrationality (Showalter, 1987).

Stark (2007) offers evidence that violent men define their own attitudes and views as reasonable, rational and correct while their female partners are seen to be emotional, irrational and immoral. This binary is hinged on long-standing socio-cultural discourses that associate the masculine with rationality, independence and control, and the feminine with irrationality, dependence and emotionality (Wirth-Cauchon, 2001). However, as Anderson (2009) points out, violent men experience the very emotions and vulnerabilities they deny and project on to women. By definition, the subjectivities of violent and controlling men are therefore highly fragile and unstable (Stark, 2007; Anderson, 2009), but also highly dangerous to their female partners as the men seek to establish difference through coercive control and violence. The establishment of difference from women through coercive control is therefore of central importance to understanding the gendered dynamics of IPV and the implications for women's sense of self and subjectivities.

Other attacks on femininity in the coercive control described earlier involve a focus on women's appearance, child-care and domestic responsibilities. As noted, these are stereotypically feminine domains and positive performances within them are commonly taken to be markers of successful femininity (Moulding, 2016). Other research undertaken by some of our team demonstrates that mothering in particular is critically important to positive identities for many women, and that refusing to leave violent relationships is not uncommonly bound up with efforts to meet mothering and homemaking expec-tations in the socially idealised and preferred structure of the heterosexual two-parent family (Moulding et al., 2015). Attacking women in these realms deprives them of agency in some of the few feminised domains of day-to-day life, and is therefore likely to be particularly damaging and distressing.

IPV and coercive control also reflect other long-standing gender discourses and practices that position women as the property of their male partners (Stark, 2007). Practices of criticising and controlling women's appearance reflect this, as do demands for emotional and domestic servicing and the monopolisation of women's earnings. These practices are borne of social and legal traditions where women were little more than the chattels of their husbands, with few or no independent rights of their own, including rights to property (Rowbotham, 1977). However, extreme jealousy, accusations of unfaithfulness, restricting women's contact with other men, and rape and sexual coercion involve a specific positioning of women as *sexual* property. Lichtenstein (2005) argues that sexual ownership of women in IPV and coercive control is enacted through jealousy and the establishment of a sexual claim on women's bodies through control, forced sex and sexual coercion.

Practices of sexual ownership reflect historical discourses about women as men's property whether they be their fathers, brothers, sons or male partners. However, these practices are also framed by more specific discourses centring the female body as the site of 'sex' and as effectively 'saturated in sex' (Foucault, 1978), and the related construction of female sexuality as dangerous and of women as sexually untrustworthy and in need of control (MacSween, 1993; Gavey,

2003). Practices of sexual ownership also enact essentialist masculinity discourses which construct men as biologically in need of and entitled to sex (Gavey, 2003). Stark (2007) has specifically identified extreme sexual jealousy and practices of sexual ownership as important elements of coercive control. He argues that violent men's jealousy involves a 'turning of the woman into a possession or thing', and while women can also be jealous, he maintains that 'the property interest men have in women gives their jealousy [a] uniquely morbid or sadistic quality' (Stark, 2007: 249). Stark describes how some controlling, jealous men 'mark' their partners through tattoos, bites and burns. In our study, rape and sexual coercion were ways for violent men to re-establish their sexual claims over women in the context of jealousy and fear about other men moving in on their turf. Stark asserts that the degrading experience of being reduced to a possession through practices of sexual control and ownership is linked to self-loathing and suicide attempts in women, and other research also bears this out (Humphreys and Thiara, 2003). Lichtenstein (2005) argues that acts of sexual control and ownership in IPV specifically diminish a woman's sense of selfhood because her identity as a non-person is confirmed.

Essentialist discourses about women, men, femininity and masculinity are therefore common to all practices of coercive control and are used to construct women as 'other', and invariably inferior, to men (de Beauvoir, 1949). Traditional gender discourses such as these rely on constructing an extreme binary between masculinity and femininity; as noted, men are positioned as rational and superior and women as irrational and inferior (Stark, 2007). Patterns of emotional abuse in IPV are therefore inherently social and gendered in character – the everyday manifestations of a wider gender order based on male privilege and dominance – rather than unique to individual couples and their supposed personality types. Essentialist discourses about women as inferior are also familiar to most women, which is likely to increase their resonance when they are repeated by intimate partners. A reduction to sexualised object status alongside a denigration of 'feminine' qualities and responsibilities is powerful because it positions women as both 'non-persons' *and* as 'failed women', drawing attention to the peculiarly gendered dimensions of the impact of IPV and coercive control on women's sense of self and subjectivities.

Looking beyond physical violence to the specific gender practices of psychological, social, financial, spiritual and sexual abuse in coercive control enables a richer, more detailed understanding of the gender dynamics of IPV and the implications for women's emotional wellbeing, capabilities and citizenship. As noted, the capacity to objectify women, including as sexual objects, is central to the enactment of coercive control. Objectification involves treating another individual as an instrument for the objectifier's purpose; the denial of autonomy and subjectivity, and the treatment of a person as something owned by another (Nussbaum, 1995). Coercive control meets each of these conditions for objectification, enabled by historic and continuing social, economic and other symbolic inequalities between men and women. It may seem almost anachronistic to suggest that expectations of female obedience, servility, deference to men and male entitlements to ownership and possession of their female partners persist at all in western societies where women have also made so many important gains in gender equality. However, coercive control is an everyday gender practice that, while common, is also hidden in plain sight (Stark, 2007). Later, we will explore this idea further when we examine how a politics of ignorance surrounds IPV and its emotional impact on women. Next, we consider in greater depth how IPV and coercive control can be conceived of as an assault on women's very sense of themselves as persons and citizens with equal rights and entitlements.

IPV as an assault on selfhood

Just over half (52%) of the women in our study reported having received a diagnosis of a mental health problem, with 86% diagnosed during or after IPV. Nearly half of the women (44%) reported depression and 41% reported anxiety, including PTSD and panic disorder. Only very small numbers of women reported bipolar disorder, personality or psychotic disorders. Just over a third of the women reporting a mental illness (34%) identified multiple mental health problems, mainly anxiety and depression. Before we examine how the sexual politics of IPV and coercive control play out in women's emotional distress, it is important to reiterate that only 13% of the women in our study had mental health problems prior to IPV. Most women indicated fair or good mental health before the violence started. As noted earlier, this challenges the idea that women who experience mental health problems in response to abuse might have had pre-existing vulnerabilities to mental illness (for example, Classen et al., 2005). Our findings clearly show that many women who were psychologically well and had no such histories struggled with mental health problems during and after IPV.

Analysis of women's text-based survey and interview responses provide more in-depth, evocative and meaningful insights into the phenomenology of IPV-related psychological and emotional distress. As indicated earlier, one of the most common themes in the women's accounts was the experience of IPV and coercive control as an assault on selfhood. Many women said that they felt they had been robbed of their sense of self through IPV and coercive control, a sense that many felt was strong prior to the violent relationship. For example, women said that they no longer felt like themselves, that they felt like different persons as a result of IPV, or that they had a reduced sense of themselves.

'It reduced my self-confidence, left me fearful, sad, undermined my belief in my ability to take care of myself. I was very self-assured and super-confident, ambitious, popular and professionally and personally successful.' (Margot)

'It has crushed me inside ... every day is a struggle to get up and face the world. Then to try and look normal to my kids so they don't feed off my feelings. Every day is a challenge to just get kids ready and then go to work and then come home do household things help with homework and prepare for next day. I was once a vibrant, well-liked, sporty and social young woman. I lost 20 years of my life and now I don't know how to be me!' (Eleanor)

Another woman said, "I am not the same person, the trauma of the relationship has left me a different person, it has absolutely shattered me," while another said, "It destroyed me mentally, physically and emotionally. I became an empty shell, completely dead inside." Psychological trauma theories similarly centre the idea of lost sense of self and identity as a result of violence and abuse (for example, Rorty and Yager, 1996). These models also recognise emotional 'numbing' as a symptom of trauma (Hund and Espelage, 2006). But trauma approaches nonetheless construct these experiences as psychological deficits and as signs of psychological dysfunction, with emotional numbing specifically categorised and pathologised as 'alexithymia'. In contrast, the psychologically healthy individual has a strong, continuous identity, sense of self and self-esteem, and appropriately controlled emotional expression.

The construct of self-esteem is central within psychological discourses and is generally understood as an individual characteristic that, when low, places the individual at risk of psychological disorder (Orth et al., 2008). However, self-esteem is also understood more broadly in theorisations of citizenship as a capability that is central to being able to act in the world and exercise agency, a vital prerequisite to the exercise of citizenship (Nussbaum, 1995; Lister, 2007). Almost one third (31%) of the women in our study specifically mentioned lost self-confidence, self-esteem and self-worth as the main effects of violence and coercive control. Our analysis shows how women's feelings of lost self-esteem and self-confidence grew directly from the specific tactics of coercive control. For some women, having every movement monitored meant that they 'walked on eggshells' in order to avoid physical and verbal assault. Women described feeling that their actions were dictated by their assessment of the violent man's wishes rather than by their own desires, reducing their confidence and capacity to choose.

> 'I lost my identity as an individual. My every movement and action was dictated by the fear of a negative reaction from [my former partner]. I adopted the "peace at any price" mentality. I lost my self-confidence, [developed] high levels of anxiety and depression, which he threatened to leave me over if it would be an ongoing issue.' (Kiara)

> 'I used to be strong-willed and positive, sure of myself and my choices. During the domestic violence I could make no choices. Now I doubt the clothes I buy and wear, the way I wear my hair and the things I say to other people. I was always told that I said the wrong thing and that I shouldn't have said whatever it was I said.' (Haley)

Feeling able to make choices is the hallmark of human agency (Davies, 1991), and knowing what one thinks, believes and feels is pivotal to this. Many women also specifically described losing self-esteem and self-confidence through repetitive psychological abuse about their capacities and characters, which was described earlier as part of coercive control. Some women went on to develop inner voices that repeated the mantras of verbal abuse.

> 'I get caught in my brain and replay and hear all the things I was called and accused of, all the threats and how I was to be murdered. I just seem to have lost my mojo over the past 13 years of hell and as much as I try I cannot regain it. I feel alone and sometimes think the shit [he] said must be true and that's why it happened. Domestic violence has made my brain weak, exposed to things I would never imagine. I believe I will never mentally be the same.' (Kylie)

Another woman said, "Inside I always have self-doubt and a very critical inner voice. I continually doubt myself." As noted, the main effect that the women identified was lost self-confidence and self-esteem, and the development of severe doubt about themselves and their place in the world. Giddens (1997: 36) defines ontological security as

> confidence or trust that the natural or social worlds are as they appear to be, including the basic existential parameters of the self and social identity having trust that the world is as it appears to be, including self and social identity.

Many women described significant ontological *in*security where their beliefs, including beliefs about themselves and the world, had been fundamentally called into question. The idea of ontological insecurity brings a sociological lens to understanding the phenomenology of women's feelings of lost sense of self in IPV by placing this experience squarely in the social world and the gendered social relationships that created it, rather than only within individual women's bodies and minds as symptoms of illness.

As part of experiencing a lost sense of self in response to IPV and coercive control, many women also described developing panic and agoraphobia. More than 40% of women reported that they had received a diagnosis of anxiety as a result of IPV, including PTSD. In their qualitative responses to the survey and in interviews some women elaborated that they had specifically experienced panic and agoraphobia, both of which can be highly debilitating for women. Agoraphobia literally means 'a fear of open spaces'; however, individual experiences are more complex than this, and other spaces and situations can also be feared and avoided such that it is usually more about other people in the spaces in question than the spaces themselves (Kirby, 1996). The experience of panic and agoraphobia are far more common in women than men in general; over two thirds of those diagnosed with agoraphobia are women (Davidson, 2000). However, there has been little attention to their associations with IPV or other gendered violence. The concept of ontological insecurity is useful to understanding how IPV and coercive control can lead to the experience of panic and agoraphobia. The next extract provides an example of one woman's experience:

> '[IPV] has impacted on my emotional wellbeing as I am afraid to leave my home. He also used family court to take my children from me even though he abused not only me

but also the children. … Court is used as a weapon by him and it is a PTSD trigger … last time no one believed or helped me and I now have a mistrust of police and judges. I have panic attacks when I leave the house. I have nightmares and I am very jumpy at every sound.' (Daphne)

Here, panic and being afraid to leave the house are directly linked to both fear of violence but also to distress about not being believed by powerful authority figures. The next extract provides a particularly graphic account of how a woman's sense of the world and her place in it changed as a result of IPV and coercive control. Vivien described violence and control as having opened a window onto a whole new world of fear that is completely outside the 'normal' world that other people inhabit:

'I think the worst things about domestic violence is not, it's almost not what you think that it would be. It's that it's disorienting, that the world that you think you know, the normal everyday world, is suddenly completely different … you'd be sitting in this unit thinking "I'm a prisoner here," and you think the doors are unlocked, there's this normal street that I know there's the shops that I know so well down there, but I can't actually get out to them … you end up not quite living in the normal world, you just see this more frightening world … When I'd walk down the street, all I would see were like predators and victims and every time I got in the taxi I thought I was being driven to be murdered. And so even when I got out unscathed, I wouldn't think "Oh, well that was silly," or "He wasn't a murderer," I'd think "He's going to kill somebody different today, lucky it wasn't me today."'

Q: 'Those thoughts are quite intrusive, still now?'

A:' It wasn't thoughts … when I talked to the psychologist, I said it's like there's two worlds and that I'm like today, I'm in the normal world … so the one that you're in, [but] when a bit much happens, it's like flicking a switch [and when I am threatened or witness violence] I'm instantly in this other world and there's no concept of the normal world existing, all I see is this sort of horror.' (Vivien)

In this account, IPV and coercive control leads to living between two worlds: the violent world peopled by predators (men) and prey (women), and the 'normal world'. Psychological trauma theory would define this phenomenon as the trauma-induced cognitive distortion of 'derealisation' or 'depersonalisation' (Michal et al., 2007), rather than as reflective of a specifically gendered perception of reality that is equally valid as the supposedly objective, gender-neutral world assumed by mainstream psychology. Other women also talked about learning that the world is an unsafe place because of IPV and coming to feel frightened outside their homes as a result.

> 'I endure flashbacks, I am often teary. I believe I will never get free of the perpetrator. ... I don't like being outside in my garden as I feel unsafe. I often feel angry ... I feel fearful a lot of the time. I see the world as an unsafe place and I am always waiting for when my ability to control my life will be impacted on again.' (Patty)

Within psycho-medical discourse, agoraphobia has been historically understood as a form of separation anxiety stemming from insecure attachment problems from childhood, with scant attention to its gender asymmetry (Parkes et al., 2006). In contrast, Bordo (1989) brings a feminist lens to understandings of agoraphobia as an exaggeration of femininity – as reflective of gender oppression, but also as protest, with the voice of sufferers saying 'You want me in the home? You shall have me in the home – with a vengeance!' (Bordo, 1989: 17). IPV and coercive control involve an attempt to entrap women in the home and a traditional femininity in one of the most extreme ways possible. Women's refusal to leave the house could be understood to signify in a broad and metaphorical way both a capitulation to the dictates of gendered violence and a protest against it. However, this plays down the severe nature of panic and fear in agoraphobia, whereby women commonly feel as if they simply *cannot* leave the house or enter certain spaces, becoming virtual prisoners in their own homes. In her research with agoraphobic women, Davidson (2000) shows how panic in agoraphobia can strip away the individual's sense of identity so that the outside world feels as if it is 'tearing in' and 'the felt boundary of the body has broken down' (Davidson, 2000: 33-4). She argues that panic involves a deep sense of ontological insecurity and that retreating into the feminised space of the home can recreate the lost boundaries of the self through the four walls of the house (Davidson, 2000). Remaining in the home can therefore provide 'the foundation of an ontologically secure existence' (Bordo, 1990: 90).

Clearly, there is an awful irony in women who have experienced gendered violence feeling safest in the very place where they have usually been most attacked and oppressed. As one woman said, "I feel safe in spaces where I probably shouldn't because the most unsafe place for me was in my home." For some women, though, fear and panic in certain spaces was more specifically related to their awareness of being at increased risk of violent attack by ex-partners in some places more than others, reflecting Kirby's point that agoraphobia is often more about the people in certain spaces rather than the spaces themselves (Kirby, 1996). Still other women felt specifically unsafe in their homes as part of violence-related agoraphobia while others emphasised the fear of being alone rather than fear of specific places. The function and meaning of home and public space consequently differed depending on the nature of the violence women had faced, as did the experience of panic, fear and agoraphobia. In all cases, though, these experiences were connected by fear and the women's sense of ontological insecurity, lost sense of self and vulnerability in a world they experienced as inherently unsafe.

Psychological and medical concepts of trauma, anxiety and depression simply cannot do justice to the phenomenology of the distress outlined above and the gendered social discourses, practices and power relations that constitute it. This is in part because the medical model 'severs the link between abuse and emotional distress' so that 'the focus shifts from the man and his responsibility for what are often criminal acts of violence and abuse to the woman and her mental health problems' (Humphreys and Thiara, 2003: 219). As noted earlier, while the diagnosis of PTSD at least acknowledges the connection between IPV and mental health problems, it prioritises fear over all other emotions while completely overlooking the sexual politics of coercive control. It was not fear that most women emphasised as much as the lost sense of themselves related to the other forms of abuse that constitute coercive control. Women described having to learn to predict violent men's emotions and desires until they felt that they had lost the capacity to feel or choose for themselves. Others felt their confidence and self-esteem evaporating as a result of repetitive verbal abuse about their supposed flaws based on negative discourses about women. Some violent men even succeeded in making their partners too anxious to walk out in the world by themselves or be alone, ironically rendering them more dependent on the very person who was actively undermining them.

At a minute-to-minute, everyday level, violent men attempted to dismantle their female partners' capacities to think, feel and act independently through processes of objectification and control based on negative femininity discourses and expectations of obedience and deference. Importantly, these control tactics were enacted against a backdrop of actual or threatened physical violence. IPV and coercive control were therefore dedicated to the erasure of women's sense of self and the creation of ontological insecurity; it is hardly surprising that many women indeed came to feel like non-persons in a hostile world. In objectifying and dehumanising women in these ways, we argue that IPV undermines women's citizenship in and of itself, before we even begin to look at its longer term personal and material effects, because it involves one group of citizen-subjects (violent men) denying another group of citizen-subjects (women) opportunities to exercise everyday micro-forms of autonomy, agency and choice. In deliberately denying women autonomy, agency and social connectedness, IPV and coercive control therefore deny women the intellectual and emotional resources required for personhood and citizenship (see also Stark, 2007). This is not to imply, of course, that violent men are necessarily entirely successful in stripping women of agency, autonomy and personhood because women actively resist and continue to exercise agency within violent relationships, including by leaving.

Haunting the women's accounts of the impact of IPV on their sense of themselves is the spectre of shame. In the next chapter, we explore shame in IPV in more detail in terms of its role in social withdrawal. Here, it is considered more specifically in relation to shame about lost sense of self and self-esteem. Individuals will avoid directly naming shame because it is shaming to do so (Budden, 2010), but women's accounts of the impact of IPV on their mental health allude to feelings of shame for losing their sense of self, self-esteem, self-confidence and independence, as well as the more general shame associated with IPV. These qualities are the hallmarks of healthy individuality, identity and selfhood in western cultures (Nettleton and Bunton, 1995), and there is shame in feeling that one does not possess them. Within individualistic western cultures, it is also shameful to be positioned as affected by other people's actions and factors external to the self (Moulding, 2003). These are the assumptions about healthy selfhood that women are likely to encounter when they seek help from mainstream health practitioners, although they will be implicit and obscured by supposedly objective gender-neutral psychological and medical knowledge and practices.

Women's health care and the politics of ignorance

In addition to the failure to properly grasp the nature of women's distress in relation to IPV, traditional psychological and medical approaches can also work, albeit inadvertently and subtly, to undermine women's capabilities further. This occurs in numerous ways, including by missing, overlooking or ignoring gendered violence; by objectifying and depersonalising women through a medical gaze focused on symptoms, diagnosis and pharmacological treatments; and by holding women to male-defined standards of mental healthiness while ignoring the gendered basis of their distress.

As noted earlier, most of the women in our study who had been diagnosed with mental illnesses had received this diagnosis during or after IPV (86%). Of these women, most (88%) indicated that they had sought help for their psychological and emotional distress, including from counsellors, doctors or hospitals. In Australia, most people will initially consult with a general practitioner about mental health problems and they can then be referred to private psychologists, social workers and psychiatrists for a series of counselling sessions. These consultations are funded through the public health system, with full coverage of costs for those on low incomes and part-coverage for others. However, only a limited number of visits can be accessed per person per year. Private counselling and therapy are also available for those with private health insurance who can afford to pay for it, which excludes many women who have left violent relationships and are on low incomes. Government-funded specialist domestic violence services provide a range of supports to women fleeing domestic violence, including psychosocial support and counselling; however these services are generally crisis-oriented and are under continued threat of de-funding and reductions in funding.

Some women reported finding the support they had accessed helpful, and they usually linked this to feeling understood by a particular counsellor. Some women specifically reported finding medicalised responses to their distress unhelpful, and were vocal and angry about having been diagnosed with mental illnesses and offered medicalised treatments in the context of IPV. In the following account, being labelled with multiple diagnoses that ignore IPV is experienced as unhelpful as compared with the more beneficial approach of a psychiatrist who understands the traumatising effects of IPV.

> '[The doctor] told me that I had ADHD [attention deficit hyperactivity disorder] and I should see a psychiatrist. So I

went and saw a psychiatrist who diagnosed me with PTSD as well. And then after we split up I saw a psychologist because I wasn't coping with it, and he told me he thought I had bipolar, so I saw another psychiatrist because mine retired. And he said that, yeah, it looked like I was bipolar. But the one I'm seeing now said that I'm not actually bipolar, I'm just a kid with a lot of issues ...'

Q: 'So how do you feel about being given all those diagnoses, do˙ they make sense to you?'

A: 'The problem is they've all got overlapping symptoms and a lot of things can be environmental, because I haven't displayed any symptoms of bipolar for about a year now. So I think in times of stress I kind of go a little bit crazy and it looks like bipolar, but yeah.'

Q: 'Maybe it's normal response to trauma?'

A: 'Yeah. ... That's what the current psychiatrist is thinking, yeah.' (Mary)

Another woman challenged a medicalised focus on brain chemicals in depression rather than the wider context of her life.

'All GPs will do is just put you on anti-depressants which don't work. The issue isn't the chemicals in my brain. The issue is my life sucks ... circumstantial depression isn't best treated by anti-depressants, anti-depressants are for ... stabilisation for chemical imbalances, it's not the right treatment, but it's all a GP can offer.' (Jane)

Other women were similarly critical of the use of medication when they were experiencing gendered violence and coercive control. One woman said that her doctor offered her a tranquiliser during a period when her partner was raping her and threatening to kill her, although she did not state whether the doctor was aware of, or attempted to clarify, her situation. Another described being offered anti-depressants during severe IPV.

'A couple of years before I left my husband I remember going to the GP and – my ex was being an absolute bugger

> ... it was one of those really bad patches and she offered me anti-depressants, in fact gave them to me there and then ... I was very nervous of taking them so I took them back a couple of months later and I said "Look it was a really bad patch, I just think I was struggling at the time with [my partner] not being there for me and him attacking me all the time." And I actually gave them back to her and I said "I want this on my record that I've given them back to you and I didn't take them," because I just didn't want it on my record.' (Lizzie)

The above account demonstrates how psychiatric diagnosis and taking medication for mental illness still carries a powerful stigma. Having depression and medication recorded on her medical record is understood by Lizzie as a judgement on her competence as a person. This is a potent reminder that receiving a psychiatric diagnosis, even in the name of providing help, involves accepting a socially devalued and pathologised identity. Moreover, women are often aware that health records can be subpoenaed by ex-partners in custody battles to portray them as unfit mothers (Humphreys and Thiara, 2003), so psychiatric diagnoses can have particularly devastating consequences for women in contexts of IPV. While a number of women were critical of medicalised approaches to their difficulties, some of these same women, and others too, embraced the diagnosis of PTSD.

> 'The courts [are] trying to say I have a borderline personality disorder. "Sorry lovie, I don't tick enough boxes for that one, I don't tick enough boxes for borderline." And I've had four other psychs tell me the same shit, who knew nothing each time. I'm suffering post-traumatic stress disorder, and my ADHD aggravates it a lot, but I don't have borderline personality disorder and I don't have bipolar.' (Amelia)

Here, a diagnosis of borderline personality disorder and of bipolar disorder are understood to be part of a campaign by the ex-partner to discredit Amelia as 'mad' and therefore an unfit mother. In contrast, a diagnosis of PTSD is considered acceptable and appropriate because it acknowledges the role of gendered violence. As in the first extract above, some women talked about seeing numerous helping professionals before finally being given a diagnosis of PTSD, which they then accepted as correct because it acknowledges the impact of IPV. Other women were not formally diagnosed with PTSD but saw themselves as traumatised nonetheless and as warranting the diagnosis. Humphreys and Thiara (2003) also found that the diagnostic category of PTSD was often preferable to women than other diagnoses because it at least acknowledges the link between IPV and psychological distress. It is also likely that some women's preference for this diagnosis is testimony to the fact that there is little else is on offer that acknowledges the IPV they have experienced and that their distress is therefore justified. Moreover, for women who experience domestic violence but do not develop trauma, there is the risk that their experiences could be overlooked or downplayed, with medical practitioners positioned as the only group qualified to identify 'proper' victimisation.

While there may be some similarities in the experience of fear (and perhaps certain other symptoms) between individuals who have been through traumas such as accidents and women who have experienced IPV, the latter is long term and is situated in the women's own homes, workplaces and other everyday spaces. The diagnosis of PTSD also defines women's trauma as 'post' despite the fact that they remain in real danger for many years after they leave, unlike other individuals whose diagnosis is related to discrete events. As such, IPV is ever-present, ongoing, gendered, patterned and unavoidable, and therefore qualitatively different to other sources of trauma that are bounded by time and/or place. While IPV is chronic in nature (Briere and Lanktree, 2012), the abusers are also women's intimate partners or former partners. Women not uncommonly reported that the relationships were very often experienced as highly romantic in the early days before violence and control took hold, and this has been reported in other studies too (Anderson, 2009). This means that profound feelings of betrayal are central to IPV (Freyd, 1996; Freyd and Birrell, 2013), while they are not necessarily relevant to other forms of trauma. Psychological and medical approaches to trauma can also be deterministic about the effects of abuse and violence on women's bodies and minds (Tseris, 2013). Gavey (2003) argues that some psychological explanations of trauma, such as John Briere's (2002) 'self-trauma model', are embraced by many feminist practitioners because they are not far off feminist social constructionist approaches to understanding women's strategies for coping with sexual abuse as 'survival strategies'. However, there is a risk that trauma models, especially those emphasising neurobiology, may bolster biological knowledge and devalue women's narratives of their experiences by centring 'the brain' rather than 'the self'; indeed, neurobiological research is already being used to deeply pathologise supposed 'deficits' in abused children (Tseris, 2013).

Perhaps most critically, a psycho-medical approach to trauma and PTSD, like all psycho-medical knowledge and practice, seeks to present itself as fundamentally 'gender-neutral' and universal. By its very nature, then, a psycho-medical approach obscures the gendered dimensions and sexual politics of IPV and its impact. A psycho-medical approach also obscures the gendered basis of the psychological and medical knowledge on which it relies. Western psychological models of mental health and illness rest on male-defined notions of mental healthiness, with agentic selfhood, autonomy, independence and confidence historically coded as masculine. The 'person' of western thought is therefore male and the 'mentally healthy individual' is synonymous with healthy masculinity (Moulding, 2003, 2006; Pease, 2010). In contrast, as noted earlier, women and the feminine are historically aligned with mental illness, dependence, emotionality, the body, lack of self-control and passivity (Wirth-Cauchon, 2001; Moulding, 2003). While IPV and coercive control rest on and exaggerate this gender binary, mainstream psychological and medical interventions also operate from these self-same (hidden) assumptions about gender and gender difference.

Feelings that are common in IPV – fear, sadness, lack of confidence, lost sense of self and self-esteem, confusion and feeling dependent on others – are all coded as feminine in western cultures (and most other cultures, too). When seeking help from mainstream practitioners, this means that women can be pathologised for displaying these behaviours and emotions because they are seen to be synonymous with both mental illness but also with femininity; they are both pathological and *expected* of women, and this can render them not particularly concerning or remarkable. On the other hand, were women to display self-assertion, anger and aggression in response to IPV, they may also be pathologised because these emotions are acceptable in men but still largely unacceptable in women (see the famous Broverman experiment, 1972).[1] Women seeking help in mainstream settings therefore run the risk of encountering what has been termed the 'double-bind' of femininity, where they could be pathologised whatever they say and do because they are judged through masculinist forms of knowledge that are predisposed to pathologise (and dismiss) women (Wirth-Cauchon,

---

[1] Broverman et al. (1972) conducted a landmark study with mental health clinicians in the US in the late 1960s. They found a 'double standard' or 'Catch 22' of mental health whereby women risked censure if they failed to be sufficiently 'feminine' but adopting 'feminine' behaviours meant they risked being defined as deficient in terms of accepted standards of adult behaviour.

2001). This is a form of epistemic disadvantage that helps to further a politics of ignorance around IPV and coercive control (Tuana, 2006).

In spite of critiques to trauma approaches, a number of feminists have argued that trauma models can be adapted so that they are appropriate for working with women who have experienced gendered violence (Herman, 1981, 1997; Tseris, 2013). Well-known feminist psychiatrist Judith Herman undertook seminal work in the US in the 1980s and 1990s to develop a feminist trauma approach to understanding and working with women who have experienced gendered violence and abuse (Herman, 1981, 1997). Herman provides a refined and nuanced understanding of the specific nature of psychological trauma caused by violence and abuse against women and children, drawing a compelling analogy between the trauma caused by war, torture and imprisonment and that caused by gendered violence and abuse (1997). Herman shows how many of the symptoms experienced by women and children following rape, sexual abuse and male-perpetrated physical violence mirror those described by combat veterans. She argues that the traumas of the public realm of war and those of the private domestic world are the same, that is, that 'the hysteria of women and the combat neurosis of men are one' (2007: 32). Herman makes a case for a new category of post-traumatic stress disorder – complex post-traumatic stress disorder (c-PTSD) – that acknowledges the specific psychological trauma wrought by gendered violence and abuse. Complex-PTSD is understood to involve more complex, diffuse and tenacious symptoms, 'personality changes' and self-harm than 'simple' PTSD (Herman, 1997). Herman's work draws on a radical feminist understanding of gendered violence and abuse as reflecting men's desire to terrorise and oppress women into submission, including sexual submission, with an understanding of patriarchy as the frame for violence against women. However, alongside this, there is a reliance on mainstream psychological theories of abnormal development and psychopathology to explain how abuse interrupts assumed 'normal developmental pathways' for women. While Herman brings a feminist eye to the impact of gendered violence on women's mental health, as in mainstream trauma theory, women are nonetheless pathologised as psychologically damaged, although not inevitably or irrevocably so.

The proposed condition of c-PTSD has not been accepted by the American Psychiatric Association and it therefore remains outside the current *Diagnostic and statistical manual of mental disorders*. Nonetheless, many feminist clinicians draw on and apply the concept in their work with abused women, although the concept of complex trauma has been mainly reserved for women who have experienced childhood abuse, particularly childhood sexual abuse (Kezelman and Stavropoulos, 2012). The diagnosis of c-PTSD has not usually been applied to women who have experienced IPV because it constructs abuse as an interruption to 'normal' development pathways while IPV affects adult women. The usual conceptualisation of complex trauma has therefore been understood as not necessarily relevant to women who experience IPV, unless they also have histories of childhood abuse, which of course a number do (Classen et al., 2005). Nonetheless, there are signs that the concept of c-PTSD is being extended to understandings of the psychological impact of gendered violence on adult women, including IPV and sexual assault (Tseris, 2013). Tseris argues that feminist workers in the area of rape and sexual assault use trauma theory in ways that stay true to feminist principles by incorporating a postmodern uncertainty about psychological 'truths' about 'trauma', a strengths-based approach, and supporting women to work through negative emotions and find new ways of living after abuse. There may be scope, then, for adapting trauma models so that they are non-pathologising and more sensitive to the sexual politics of gendered violence. Tseris's (2013) research shows that feminist practitioners in the gendered violence field in Australia draw on mainstream trauma models in novel ways that make them sensitive to gender discourses and power relations. This does not necessarily mean adopting the diagnostic category of PTSD as it is explained in the *Diagnostic and statistical manual of mental disorders*, or even Herman's concept of c-PTSD, but working with the concept of trauma from IPV in more critical feminist ways.

When the psychological impact of IPV is understood through a psycho-medical lens, responses to women's distress are limited to one-to-one intervention, diagnosis of 'symptoms' and a limited range of therapeutic interventions such as pharmacotherapy. Such responses do not usually involve looking to the context of women's lives and may overlook IPV and coercive control entirely (Laing and Toivonen, 2010). A psycho-medical perspective therefore contributes to the wider politics of ignorance about the impact of IPV on women and their lives and limited forms of state-supported psychological help for women leaving IPV. Adopting a feminist lens that seeks to understand women's subjectivities in the context of the sexual politics of gender discourses, practices and unequal power relations that they have been subjected to through IPV and coercive control offers a potentially more empowering, empathic and holistic approach to women's psychological distress. Helping professionals can therefore work in ways that recognise the gaps and deficiencies in psychological trauma theory; allow women to tell their own stories; address issues of power, betrayal, self-blame and stigma and their gendered dimensions; and focus on women's strengths and recovery, not deficits and pathology (Tseris, 2013).

Helping professionals can also work to connect women with other women who have experienced IPV and coercive control through advocacy and support groups; include psychosocial education about the patterned nature of IPV and coercive control and their impact on women's sense of self; and situate women's narratives of IPV and coercive control in wider gender discourses, practices and power relations. However, while these principles are important for guiding direct psycho-emotional support work with women, it is also imperative that state-funded responses to IPV actively engage with the complex and interconnected impact of IPV across multiple domains of women's lives.

Capabilities, mental health and the state: the ripple effect

While we have argued that the impact of IPV and coercive control on women's mental health is more usefully conceptualised as a profoundly gendered assault on women's selfhood and citizenship and a form of sexual politics, we are not suggesting that women really *are* lacking in selfhood and identity, or are powerless to resist violence and control. Most women in our study had acted decisively, leaving violent relationships and rebuilding their lives in many respects. There were also examples of women who recovered more quickly and completely after violence because they had good support from family and friends. However, many women had no such support, sometimes because violent men had turned the people in their lives against them, and feelings of low self-worth, lost confidence and self-esteem, lost sense of self and betrayal often continued into the long term, well beyond the period of the violence itself. As shown in Chapter Four, the assault on women's selfhood and citizenship therefore extends well beyond the IPV itself, reverberating across all dimensions of women's lives as well as through time, playing out much like the ripples in a pond when a stone is thrown in, multiplying as each concentric circle enlarges in response to the initial impact but also to the proliferation of other circles. We present two cases below that illustrate how the ripple effect of IPV can play out across the key domains of women's lives in diverse ways, and the role of the state in this, bringing about quite contrasting trajectories for women depending on the nature and availability of support.

Vivien is in her late forties, is single and has no children. She lived in domestic violence for four years and left three years ago. She lived in private rental with her partner in a country town. She experienced most types of violence. She is on a disability pension because of a neck injury that predated domestic violence, and which has prevented her from working. Vivien's mental health is reported as having been good before violence and very poor since, and she described feeling extreme fear and lost sense of self. Vivien was eventually offered public housing in the city. The flats she now resides in are described as "a living hell", with high levels of violence and abuse between the residents. Vivien has been physically attacked and is regularly verbally abused. Being unable to work was described as reducing her sense of self-worth and increasing isolation. She has now developed panic, agoraphobia and has attempted suicide. Vivien accesses counselling from a psychologist who describes her symptoms as PTSD. She has not found this counselling particularly helpful and says she feels hopeless about her life.

Sascha is in her late fifties, lived in domestic violence for 10-15 years and left 20 years ago. She was a co-owner-occupier of her house with her partner. She experienced all types of violence. She described herself as having "a sense of myself" before violence and as losing her self-esteem over the course of the violent relationship, resulting in anxiety and depression. When Sascha left domestic violence, she went into private rental and started doing some casual work. Her mental health initially worsened with high rent, few good job prospects and total responsibility for children. She applied for public housing and was offered a house in the "good area" she had already been living in, near schools and family. Sascha said that the house "made all the difference". The low rent meant she could engage with work slowly because she needed a lot of time and space to "recover from domestic violence". She gained back some confidence through part-time work. Sascha was also able to access free feminist-oriented counselling and a domestic violence support group. Eventually she went to university and is now a qualified professional, earns a reasonable income and has bought her house. While Sascha said she feels hopeful about her life, her mental health never bounced back to pre-violence levels.

It is important to point out that both Vivien and Sascha experienced high levels of coercive control in addition to severe physical violence. Each of these cases reveals intricate interconnections between the impact of IPV across the domains of mental health, housing, employment and social participation. Both women were living on low incomes on leaving domestic violence. While both women's mental health worsened on leaving the violent relationship, in Sascha's case, appropriate, well-located, low-cost public housing and specialist, feminist-informed counselling and support provided her with the time and space to recover from IPV and move into employment. Vivien's emotional distress was exacerbated by inappropriate housing and lack of work opportunities, while mainstream psychological counselling was experienced as not particularly helpful. In both case studies, experiences of lost sense of self and emotional distress are also central, just as they were for many of the women in this study. However, these case studies show how poor housing and limited work options on leaving IPV exacerbated this distress further. At this point, though, the women's experiences diverge because Sascha's housing was appropriate and emotional support was specialist and feminist-informed, enabling her to rebuild her self-esteem. Undertaking study and going on to gain employment was an important aspect of this. It is noteworthy that Sascha left IPV many years ago before the state housing system was dismantled and when free counselling services were more diverse and widespread than they now are. In contrast, Vivien's experience was more recent with housing that was re-traumatising and isolating, and counselling that was psychological and more diagnostic. Vivien's case was further complicated by a pre-existing physical disability. This prevented her from working both during and after domestic violence, heightening her physical and emotional vulnerability and exacerbating her economic disadvantage and lack of housing choices. The lack of appropriate services and supports therefore had particularly negative consequences for Vivien in the context of a disability, reducing her options for living and spaces for action. While most women's experiences may not fall so neatly into contrasting camps as these two cases do, these examples exemplify the pivotal role of appropriate support services in approaching women's needs in a holistic way that takes account of gender inequality, the intersections of gender, socioeconomic disadvantage and disability, and the interconnected impact of IPV across the different domains of women's lives.

As this analysis has shown, Nussbaum's (2011) citizenship capabilities – those of health, the senses, imagination and thought, and the emotions – are all directly and negatively affected by IPV. Internal abilities and the external environment are interdependent, where combined capabilities refer to the necessary connections between the conditions that produce the substantial freedoms and the characteristics of the person, including personality, intellectual and emotional capacities, states of bodily fitness and health, internalised learning and skills of perception and movement (Nussbaum, 2011). These characteristics are not innate to the person but are trained or developed through interaction with social, political and material conditions. The analysis presented in this chapter demonstrates how women's internal abilities can be severely curtailed by the sexual politics of IPV and coercive control. IPV and coercive control seek to impose a traditional femininity and gender order on women through a systematic and gendered assault on selfhood that leaves many feeling like non-selves or 'lesser', inferior selves with a reduced sense of agency and self-esteem. To borrow and expand on Nussbaum's explanation of the impact of rape, IPV similarly 'invades [a woman's] internal life of thought and emotion, changing her relationship to herself' (2011: 31); our research shows that women's changed relationships with themselves also often persists into the long term. The politics of ignorance surrounding IPV exacerbates this altered sense of self further because it also changes women's relationships with others in their lives. Most significantly, the negative impact of IPV on women's mental health carries over into other dimensions of women's lives, with poor mental health having a negative impact on work performance and inappropriate housing worsening mental health for many women, sometimes for many years. We now move on to examine the impact of IPV on the fourth dimension of citizenship: social participation.

SIX

Re-engaging lives

Introduction

In previous chapters, we have shown how the impact of intimate partner violence (IPV) on employment, housing and mental health limits women's capabilities to exercise citizenship in complex and interconnecting ways. It became increasingly clear as we analysed the data from the survey and interviews that the impact of IPV on women's social participation is particularly significant to citizenship. There has been no previous research into the impact of IPV on women's social participation. The analysis presented here therefore makes a new contribution to knowledge about how IPV interrupts and changes women's social relationships and affiliations in ways that have lasting effects on the capacity to exercise citizenship. In common with the findings in relation to employment, housing and mental health, our analysis shows that women do not regain the levels of social engagement they had prior to IPV, and that the nature of social participation is also changed by IPV in ways that are not wholly negative. In this chapter, we explore how IPV affects women's participatory citizenship and the interconnections with its impact on the three other key life domains. We also examine how women rebuild the social relationships and connections in their lives.

Social participation and citizenship

Social participation is often a focus in the health science literature as a key aspect of health and wellbeing. It is commonly understood to include undertaking an activity in preparation for connecting with others; being, interacting and doing an activity with others; helping others; and contributing to the neighbourhood and society (Levasseur et al., 2010). Research into social participation includes measures of both formal and informal activities in society. These can be activities such as church involvement, sports, hobbies such as book or arts groups, political activities such as union meetings, and socialising with friends and family (Lindström et al., 2001). We were therefore interested in the impact of IPV on women's involvement in common everyday social activities that build affiliation, enjoyment, confidence and a contribution to wider communities and societies. Our conceptualisation of social participation as an aspect of citizenship refers to women's involvement in civil society, which includes both formal and informal affiliations because 'informal social networks and social contacts in local communities and friendship circles are just as important [as formal aspects of civil society] for the cohesion of the society and the integration of individuals' (Boje, 2009: 244).

As discussed in Chapter Two, T.H. Marshall divides citizenship into three aspects: civil, political and social. Civil rights include 'the right to defend and assert all one's rights on terms of equality with others and by due process of law'; political rights include the right to participate in 'the exercise of political power'; and social rights include economic security and to 'live the life of a civilised being' (Marshall, 1950: 10-11). Social participation potentially involves the exercise of each of these categories of citizenship rights. Social participation also supports women's combined capabilities for citizenship, including being able to emotionally develop without anxiety and fear; being free to affiliate, live with and toward others and socially interact; 'being able to laugh, to play, to enjoy recreational activities'; and having control over one's political and material environment (Nussbaum, 2011: 34). Examining how IPV affects social participation is central to understanding its long-term impact on women's involvement in civil society as a key dimension of citizenship. However, as argued in Chapter Two, Marshall's and others' conceptualisations of citizenship underestimate the extent to which citizenship rights have to be won and re-won, which is certainly the case for women's rights, including efforts to address gendered violence (Walby, 1994). We therefore include a focus on how IPV affects women's participation in political activism as a further measure of the impact of IPV on the capacity to exercise citizenship.

Gender inequality not only enables IPV and shapes its impact on women's lives, it also shapes women's wider participation in society. Women have long struggled against their confinement to the so-called private sphere and their exclusion from equal participation as citizens and members of society. Feminist scholarship has highlighted how the public/private divide structures the relationship between women and the state and reproduces gender inequalities (Garcia-Del Moral and Dersnah, 2014). IPV is frequently constructed as a 'private issue' in public discourse, which helps to limit community and state responses. This separation between public/private arrangements also operates as a gendered social exclusion which prevents women from gaining access to freedom of movement and full citizenship (Franzway, 2016). One of the more significant effects of gendered violence, then, is the curtailment of women's ability to move freely in public and private spaces and the limitations that this places on their capacities to form affiliations outside the home. As outlined in the International Covenant on Civil and Political Rights (16 December 1966), Article 12, everyone has the right to freedom of movement within a country, which includes the right to choose where to live. Women's independence, citizenship and participation is dependent on being free of coercive constraints (James, 1992). Hence, while women citizens have political, civil and social rights in principle, these count for little if they are deprived of the capacity to exercise them freely through freedom of movement and the capacity to build affiliations that are borne of this.

IPV and social participation

In our national survey, we specifically asked women about their participation in friendship networks, social groups, sports, church groups, volunteering, support groups, and political groups. Hence, we asked women about their participation in formal and informal social activities because, as argued earlier, both are important to social connectedness and each contributes to women's civil, social and political engagement as citizens. Our study goes further than previous research into social isolation in IPV, which has mainly focused on IPV as a risk factor within coercive control (for example Lanier and Maume, 2009). Our concern lies with revealing how IPV and coercive control affect the social participation of women as citizens into the long term. As with the other three dimensions of employment, housing and mental health, we also asked women about their levels of involvement in these activities before, during and after domestic violence.

Friendship networks are an important reflection of an individual's levels of social connectedness and affiliation, providing opportunities for enjoyment and play. More specifically, as with family relationships, supportive friendships are pivotal to mental health and wellbeing and to recovery from psychological distress. Because IPV has such a negative impact on women's emotional wellbeing, it was essential that we consider the interconnections between mental health and social relationships. However, friendship is not just about receiving support; it also involves a two-way exchange that plays an important role in identity and self-development (Laursen and Hartup, 2002). Where these relationships are undermined, there are significant consequences for individuals in terms of sense of self but also for wider social cohesion.

Social groups were included as a further example of everyday social relations. They were understood as offering a particular opportunity to extend friendship networks, but also the companionship and recreation of undertaking shared activities with others, such as crafts, art, dancing classes, book groups, yoga classes or exercise groups.

Participation in sports was included because in Australia, as in many other countries, sport is one of the most common forms of social participation outside of work and family (ABS, 2015a). Participation in physical activities such as sport has also been found to be protective against IPV (Milner and Baker, 2017). It has been suggested that this is because sport increases women's self-esteem. Just how sports might protect against IPV is likely to be far more complex than this, though, offering women gender identities that are less traditional and influencing the performance of gender and gender relations in local sports groups and communities. Nonetheless, sports participation is an important element of many people's social lives and was included for this reason and, for the women in our study, involvement in sports groups was often through their children.

We were also keen to explore women's experiences of participating in church activities because religion remains an important social institution in most countries, even if active membership and religious affiliation is in decline in Australia as it is elsewhere in western societies (ABS, 2016b). In using the term 'church', we purposely chose the most common way of referring to participation in religious institutions in Australia, including those that are not Christian. It is important to acknowledge, though, that churches and other religious communities are often explicitly or implicitly patriarchal, with 'the concept of male headship ... often misused to promote the abuse of women and children' (Tracy, 2007: 592). Recent research yet to be published in academic journals has been profiled in the Australian media and has shown how Christian churches often silence women who seek to bring domestic violence to the attention of church leaders and communities (ABC, 2017). In Australia, as in many other countries, priests and people in other roles in religious institutions have also been directly involved in the sexual, physical and emotional abuse of children, and of adult women (Middleton, et al., 2014). Nevertheless, religious groups also sometimes provide support to women who experience domestic violence, and spirituality and religion are identified by some women as important to recovery from IPV (Wendt, 2008).

Women were asked about volunteering as a form of civic participation that expands social and human capital through the further development of social networks (Boje, 2009). Participation in the community through volunteering can also contribute to feeling a sense of control over the political and material environment (Nussbaum, 2011). Volunteering represents a form of active citizenship involving social and political participation which can affect all spheres of an individual's life and contributes to the realisation of 'democratic rights in contemporary societies' (Boje, 2009: 246).

We asked women about their involvement in support groups because we are aware from previous research, including our own, that women often rely on these groups during and after leaving violent relationships (Larance and Porter, 2004). Research has shown that support groups can be vital to women's recovery because they offer peer support, which is quite different to the type of help women might receive from professionals.

Women's involvement in political groups was included as a form of participation in public interest groups and social movements; such activities represent a key element of civil society and citizenship (Boje, 2009: 244). As noted earlier, we also included participation in political groups in recognition of the fact that citizenship rights have to be won, and are not simply bestowed, and feminist activism continues to be central in forcing the state to address gendered violence. Women's participation in such movements is therefore one of the most cogent examples of participatory citizenship; gaining insight into how IPV affects this type of social participation is of critical importance to an examination of the impact of IPV on citizenship.

As indicated in the graph below, our findings show that all forms of social participation decreased significantly during IPV, and while there was some recovery of pre-violence levels, these were not fully regained in most categories.

Figure 4 presents women's social participation prior to experiencing IPV, during the relationship and after separation. Women's levels of social participation before IPV are difficult to compare to those in the wider Australian population because data is available only for some categories of participation and the types of questions asked in other studies, usually by the Australian Bureau of Statistics (ABS), were different in emphasis to our own. We purposely asked a quite broad question about what other activities outside work and family women had been involved in before, during and after IPV because we were primarily interested in change over time. Nonetheless, there is some comparative data in relation to three categories of social participation: sport, church groups, and volunteering. It is important to remember, though, that unlike census data and other population surveys undertaken by the ABS, our survey was not a prevalence study; our sample is not necessarily fully representative of the wider population of women who have left IPV and not all women answered all questions. Participation in sports and physical recreation sits at around 60% for both women and men in the wider Australian population (ABS, 2015a). The women in our sample reported higher participation rates than this before IPV, at just under 75%. This might reflect the fact that participation in sports decreases with age; most women in our sample will have been in younger age groups before violence started. It may also reflect women's involvement in their children's sporting activities.

Figure 4: Social participation

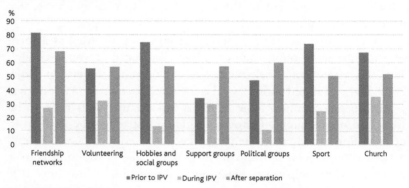

Source: Authors' calculations

Women in the general population report church involvement at higher rates than men (22% and 15% respectively) (ABS, 2017a). More than two thirds (67%) of the women in our research reported participating in church activities; this higher rate is likely to reflect the emphasis on 'active' involvement in the ABS survey. Women are also more likely to participate in voluntary work than men (34% and 29% respectively) (ABS, 2015b). More than half of the women in our sample (55%) reported participating in volunteering before IPV. As noted in Chapter Four, volunteering is highest for people in the 35–44 age group, and this is also likely to be related to parents providing assistance to groups in which their children are involved. Large numbers of the women in our study had dependent children, so the high rates of volunteering before IPV most likely reflects this.

Women's participation in all categories of social activity fell dramatically during IPV. The most severe falls from levels before IPV occurred in participation in friendship networks (more than 50%); sporting groups (almost 50%); hobbies and social groups (over 60%), and political groups (37%). Volunteering and involvement in churches fell, too, but not quite so dramatically (23% and 22% respectively). Perhaps these activities are less threatening to violent and controlling men than the other social activities we asked about. Participation in support groups showed the smallest decline (4%) during IPV of all the categories of social participation, most likely reflecting women's needs during this difficult period, particularly if there had been loss of friendship networks and reduced access to other forms of social participation because of coercive control. It is interesting that over a third of women (34%) reported participation in support groups before experiencing IPV, perhaps indicating their awareness of relationship problems prior to the descent into violence and coercive control.

While participation in most social activities did not return to pre-violence levels once women were no longer experiencing IPV, participation in volunteering did rebound to pre-violence levels of just over half of women (56%). In addition, participation in support groups almost doubled from 34% before IPV to 62% after IPV and participation in political groups rose to 60%, which is 13% higher than before IPV. Women described their continuing involvement in volunteering post-violence as at least in part concerned with gaining confidence in engaging with others and the potential pathways to paid employment it offers. Many women had experienced periods away from paid work during IPV and felt insufficiently qualified, skilled or confident to seek paid work. Volunteering offered them meaningful opportunities to regain skills, confidence and a sense of being valued, as well as social interaction with others. For some women, poor mental and physical health meant that part-time volunteering also best matched their felt capabilities at that point in time. Some women also expressed a degree of altruism in their motivation for volunteering. As one women who had retired from the workforce explained, "I need to 'give back' for as long as I can," and she mentioned valuing the support she had received after escaping from a violent partner. For some women, then, volunteering is a way of exercising responsibilities towards other citizens, particularly other women experiencing IPV.

The increased level of participation in support groups after IPV is not surprising given the fact that many women need significant social and emotional support to re-establish their lives and recover from the trauma of IPV. Participation in support groups showed the largest increase from before IPV to after, rising by 28%. As noted, the peer support available in these groups is vital, and many women pointed to only feeling properly understood and accepted by other women who had also experienced IPV. Women described the groups as offering a sanctuary from a wider community where they felt judged and stigmatised. As one woman said, "People don't understand, there is a lack of education around it. I felt judged." Such groups therefore function as socially safe spaces in social contexts involving denial and a politics of ignorance about IPV; in these groups, women do not need to explain 'why it happened to them' or 'why they did not leave earlier'. Some women were also motivated to help other women through support groups. We explore women's experiences of support groups and their important role in more detail later when we discuss the qualitative data.

Of all the categories of social participation the increase in women's participation in political groups involved the most dramatic rebound after IPV from the levels during violence (from 11% to 60%). We know from some women's comments in the survey and in interviews that this increased involvement was sometimes specifically focused on political activism in relation to gendered violence and related issues. One woman, Sascha, described in her interview how her involvement in a domestic violence support group grew into political activism that has continued to this day in spite of the fact that IPV ended for her some two decades ago. This increase in political activism is an extremely important finding because it demonstrates that while IPV has dramatic negative effects on women's capabilities to exercise citizenship, for some women, IPV also gives rise to new or enhanced forms of political activism. Such activism represents the exercise of citizenship in one of the most striking ways possible. As with support group involvement, we explore women's involvement in political activism in greater detail later.

As can be seen, then, the impact of IPV on social participation is not clear cut. Nonetheless, IPV and coercive control do have lasting effects on the nature of women's social affiliations into the long term. Moreover, the increased participation of women in political activism after IPV may also reflect inadequate responses from the state, as well as by family, friends and the wider community. Increased political activism could be to some extent a symptom of the politics of ignorance surrounding IPV and its impact on every other dimension of women's lives and citizenship.

Coercive control and social participation

In the previous chapter, we examined women's narratives of coercive control to reveal its impact on sense of self and emotional wellbeing. We now revisit these narratives to interrogate the specific impact coercive control has on social participation. As noted in Chapter Five, one of the central purposes of coercive control is to increase the violent man's sense of power and control over his partner by restricting or even completely preventing her from forming or maintaining relationships with other people. In the following accounts, the women explain how the social and emotional abuse of coercive control combined to affect their relationships with family, friends and the wider community. Our analysis includes: consideration of verbal abuse in coercive control and its role in severing women's social relationships; the role of shame and shaming in social withdrawal; the links between self-confidence, mental health and social participation; and the multiple demands women experience after leaving IPV and how they result in retreat from social participation.

Verbal abuse and 'making a scene'

Many women described verbal abuse and 'making a scene' in public as a form of coercive control that was central to their violent partner's attempts to prevent their engagement with the outside world. Women particularly described men's use of verbal abuse to isolate them from others.

> 'I had no involvement in any activities outside of work and home. I was completely isolated from friends. He made up stories about my friends and told me I had to choose between him and them. He confiscated my mobile phone so that I could have no contact with friends. It was difficult to restore those friendships after the relationships ended.' (Tabitha)

Coercive control that sought to isolate women commonly included verbally denigrating friends and family, verbal threats, and more direct face-to-face abuse of family and friends. As Tabitha mentioned, she found it difficult to restore friendships after she left the relationship. The practice of 'making a scene' was also a common way of preventing women from connecting and relating to other people.

> 'I was not allowed to join in anything as he needed complete control over me. If I did manage to go anywhere, he would sabotage it by causing a scene or constantly calling me while I was out making more and more threats towards me and others.' (Kristin)

Like Cat below, many women choose not to disclose IPV and coercive control when they are still in violent relationships as a way of protecting themselves and their families. However, this can mean that when they eventually do disclose, often on the point of leaving, they are not heard or believed and are deprived of critically needed informal support networks.

> 'I found it really hard to be around my family as he always put them down so it was easier to avoid. All my friends were his friends and when I left they all took his side, as they had no idea what was going on. I lost everyone and even some of my extended family. The ongoing stress and pressure put on me caused me to drop out of many [university] courses …' (Cat)

Here, as in other cases, friends and family are presented as siding with the violent man, in part because they were unaware of the violence until the woman left. Some of the women stated that the people in their lives had difficulty grasping and understanding IPV, particularly the more hidden forms of coercive control that take place out of public sight. One woman said, "normal people don't understand". Another said, "My ex-husband looked like a nice guy to everyone [but] behind the closed doors he would be a Jekyll and Hyde." Yet another said that neighbours could not believe her husband was violent because "he was such a nice man outside the house. He was a devoted father and a devoted husband – but only if you did what he wanted to do." It is well known that violent, controlling men carefully present a different face to the wider world, purposefully 'stage managing' their private and public behaviour so that other people never see the abuse (Stark, 2007). This can make it difficult for women to gain support because people do not equate women's stories with the man they think they know. Hence, because IPV and coercive control occur largely out of sight behind closed doors, and men usually ensure that no one sees it, women's pre-existing epistemic disadvantage is exacerbated, restricting access to much needed support.

Other women pointed to lack of understanding on the part of others in their lives about the impact of IPV on their capacity to participate in social activities. Shauna talked about feeling criticised and excluded at her children's sporting activities by others who seemed not to understand the limitations on her capacity to volunteer:

'I took the kids to Little Athletics this season and got berated for not helping out – they didn't understand just how much effort it took to even go there, and that I cannot parent the way others can. Suffice to say, I will not be going back next season.'

As we have argued, denial and disbelief on the part of the broader community as well as family and friends reflect the politics of ignorance surrounding IPV (Tuana, 2006; Franzway, 2016) and has significant material repercussions for women. As we show later, our qualitative survey and interview data indicate that women who are supported by family and/or friends are able to rebuild their lives much more effectively and quickly than women who are not.

Shame, shaming and social withdrawal

In her account, Shauna implies a level of anger at not being understood by other parents. A more common response among the women to lack of understanding and criticism was shame. Shame and shaming in response to IPV plays an important role in reducing women's social worlds and their social participation more generally. Shame is a fundamentally social emotion that speaks to our relationships with others, and it is also a highly gendered phenomenon because it is associated with women's subjugation in gender power relations (Probyn, 2005). Previous research by some members of our team has shown that IPV in and of itself is viewed as a shameful experience reflective of a 'failed' family, for which women are often held (by themselves as well as others) particularly responsible (Buchanan et al., 2015). One woman said, "I feel ashamed, I feel ostracised from my family, as I am the only one that has separated, not once, but twice. I brought shame on the family." As another explained, "I feel embarrassed that others may know my situation, and therefore avoid as many social situations as possible." Another said, "... when you are in a mentally and physically abusive relationship you keep it quiet because you are embarrassed". Others said, "You lose confidence and become isolated and it feels like you are being judged by the people around you," and "I don't talk about it with anyone, I feel embarrassed." One woman specifically mentioned feeling ashamed about her reduced material circumstances, which she connected to her feeling associated with her perceived class status: "I feel I have no self-worth. I feel empty. I feel that I have lost my old self. I feel dirty and lower class to my peers." Another mentioned hiding physical injuries from IPV because of shame and a sense that she would be seen as responsible for the abuse: "... it was shameful to be beaten because it was always assumed that you must have done something to trigger the behaviour, especially when your partner was as charming as mine could be". Scheffer Lindgren and Renck (2008) also found that women feel high levels of shame and guilt in relation to IPV, which can lead them to withdraw from others.

Stigma is closely related to shame and shaming, and can be thought of as a marker of social disgrace that involves placing judgemental labels on people associated with negative stereotypes, thereby creating a sense of separation from the norm with negative outcomes for the stigmatised groups (Murray et al, 2016). Like the woman who said she felt ashamed for being 'lower class' after IPV, other women also specifically mentioned feeling ashamed about their reduced material circumstances because of IPV, compounding their desire to avoid socialising with others. For example, one woman told how she felt ashamed about not progressing in her career: "I lack the self-esteem to start another career, as I am ashamed to be at this career level in my forties." Another woman mentioned moving geographical locations because she felt ashamed in front of the neighbours: " ... we as a family moved from the house due to me being embarrassed by the neighbours' knowledge of the abuse". Other women mentioned feeling ashamed and anxious about applying for rental accommodation, with one saying "I felt shame, fear and anxiety in applying for rentals." Mina, who left her violent husband in the 1990s and identified as being of Southern/Eastern European background reflects on how she felt the compounded stigma of living in public housing while being a 'single parent':

> '... we had to go into Housing Commission rental. That was very demoralising for me ... my children suffered as some parents wouldn't let their children come and play with them because I was a "single parent living in a housing commission house" and they didn't want their children associating with the likes of us ... that was over 22 years ago.'

Women's comments show that they felt demoralised because of family and societal attitudes, their reduced class status and their visibly declining material status symbolised by having to go into rental or public housing.

One of the most common practices of shaming is victim-blaming, which can be perpetrated by the violent man himself, but also by family and friends who are influenced by, and participate in, a politics of ignorance surrounding IPV. Victim-blaming can be internalised by women into self-blame, further reducing their sense of confidence in themselves and their loss of trust in others. Victim-blaming was alluded to when women talked about their violent partners turning friends and family against them. Women experienced significant feelings of betrayal and distrust of others, which in turn fed into a general social withdrawal and isolation from the community. Jodie said that "friends who supported me when I left the relationship don't talk to me". Some women saw that rejection by others was the direct result of manipulation by partners as part of coercive control.

> 'I find it difficult to trust people such as family and friends as during the DV [domestic violence] my ex turned my parents against me and my sister also. I won't allow myself to get close to friends ... I can't enjoy my life like I should because I am always safe-guarding myself from hurt.' (Tiffany)

Withdrawing from social engagement became a way for women to protect themselves from the likelihood of additional pain. Many women reported similar experiences of people turning away from them because of IPV and the subsequent loss of these relationships. Miranda also described rejection by family members as well as by friends, leading to distrust, loss of confidence and self-esteem. These feelings contributed to a particular discomfort about intimate heterosexual relationships:

> 'I am distrusting of people – men – lost faith in people, I do not feel comfortable entering into another relationship. My confidence and self-esteem were eroded. Some family members and friends turned away, adding insult to an excruciatingly painful experience.' (Miranda)

Another woman said "I can't trust anyone anymore. I feel people want to use me and hurt me like I'm just a joke," alluding to feelings of shame and humiliation. Annabel talked about fear of being hurt again, and not wanting to share information about herself and her life because of IPV:

> 'I tend not to get involved with many people outside my family because I'm afraid I will get hurt. As well as, people ask questions about my life and I don't want to lie but I also don't want to share either.'

Many women also blame themselves for the violence, in part because their partners claim that the women's behaviour incites their violence (Scheffer Lindgren and Renck, 2008). Self-blame was common among the women in this study and extended beyond feeling they were the cause of the violence. One woman said, "I always blamed myself for being too tired to work, for being flaky, for not being confident enough to get jobs I deserved." Another said, "... the domestic violent relationship sunk me into a place I have never been in my life – scared, hated myself, felt like I was to blame for everything". Social isolation is therefore strongly intertwined with feelings of shame, self-blame and the stigma of being considered a 'victim'. The fear of judgement from others and related self-blame negatively influences women's social engagement, with specific shaming, stigmatising and self-stigmatising social practices that contribute to social marginalisation and withdrawal. Stigma and shame also erodes women's confidence and trust in others, contributing further to social isolation.

We draw particular attention to our data that shows how different the trajectory for women after IPV can be when they are believed and supported by family or friends. It underlines our argument that the impact of IPV is not only a matter of individual violence and conflict; rather, the effects (as well as the causes) are shaped by the sexual politics of gendered discourses and social institutions. Veronica offers a quite different account from those of other women who described not having their situations believed or understood. She described her mother's realisation of her partner's violent and controlling behaviour when she came to stay with the family:

> 'She was really gobsmacked and so I could tell her "Look," I could ring her and just, I could tell her that I had a plan and then the plan would take eight months but I told her because I think it's very hard for people who are not in there to understand how you can still be with that person. "Why don't you just kick him out or isn't that just usual arguing?" People don't really understand until they see it.' (Veronica)

Veronica went on to describe how her mother provided material and emotional support that helped her leave IPV safely and rebuild her life because she understood. Other women also talked about family and friends who supported them emotionally and materially, including families who gave financial assistance or accommodation, so they could rebuild their lives.

Self-confidence, mental health and social participation

Denial and disbelief on the part of family and friends have emotional consequences for women, whose sense of self and self-belief are usually already damaged by IPV and coercive control. Here, we specifically examine the interconnections between reduced self-confidence and women's withdrawal from social activities and relationships. In the previous chapter, some women described themselves as strong and confident before IPV. Many also portrayed themselves as socially outgoing and engaged before violence: "... prior to my experience of domestic violence I was the most outgoing and physically active of all my friends and now I feel I am the least active". Another described the impact of IPV on her personality, saying "... it was huge ... I went from a social butterfly to not coming out my shell". Yet another said, "I am more of an introvert now ... I have no zest for life, go to work and go home, no social life." Many women described themselves now as 'introverted' and less trusting, with implications for maintaining friendships.

'I am less confident, less optimistic, often pessimistic. I find it hard to establish and maintain friendships and have difficulties opening up to people, trust is something I find challenging. I've become introverted.' (Trina)

IPV was therefore seen by the women to have long-term effects on shaping their personalities, sociability and social relationships. These negative effects of IPV are not peripheral to partner abuse; as Evan Stark (2007) among others has argued, they are caused by deliberate actions of coercive control. Deborah provides a clear example of the process:

'Domestic violence starts with mental abuse and undermining your self-worth, that's how they isolate you from family and friends and social activities, when you feel worthless you stay home and do not participate in life or activities outside the home. Breaking free of that torment is very difficult when you feel worthless and can't do anything right.' (Deborah)

Creating feelings of worthlessness is an effective way to isolate women from others, which in turn can make leaving more difficult. As women's social worlds become increasingly smaller through coercive control, their mental wellbeing, sense of self-worth and identity are further undermined in a self-perpetuating cycle. While many women do attempt to regain earlier levels of social engagement after leaving violent men, they often find it difficult because, as pointed out in the previous chapter, the abusive words that were hurled at them continue to affect their sense of self and self-belief.

> 'I was completely isolated during my marriage, which was the opposite of my life before being married. I'm trying to become more involved but it's extremely hard because my ex-husband's voice is still in my head and it's taking a lot of time and work to move on from his words.' (Mikeala)

Women's social isolation after leaving violent relationships is therefore in part a function of the sexual politics of discourses deployed in coercive control and, as noted in the previous chapter on mental health, these clearly live on well beyond the verbal and emotional abuse itself. Other women linked social withdrawal more directly and simply to their struggles with anxiety and depression. For example, one woman described how IPV "reduced my levels of involvement due to depression and anxiety. I did not want to associate with people as I felt I had nothing to contribute," while another said, "I suffer from depression and anxiety and do not want to do any social activities now after 19 years away from the abuse." As can be seen here, women's experiences of social isolation can persist for many years. Some women specifically described the impact of IPV-related poor mental health on specific social activities such as attending church:

> 'I don't go out unless I have to. I become extremely anxious when I have to go out. Sometimes I become so depressed I hibernate for days. I no longer feel able to go to church. My faith has always been very important to me and still is, but I practise it alone. I have to force myself to do things outside my home.' (Pearl)

Withdrawal from church groups not only means reduced social contact, but also being prevented from practising one's faith with others in a faith community, which could specifically reduce women's spiritual wellbeing (Wendt, 2008). Women affected by mental illness because of IPV can also be doubly shamed and stigmatised for being 'crazy' as well as victims of IPV through gendered discourses about women being prone to madness. This further reduces self-confidence and trust in others, in turn exacerbating social isolation. Women who experience IPV are therefore often managing multiple forms of shaming and stigma, which have negative implications for their readiness to engage in social relationships.

Fear also played a specific role in shrinking some women's social worlds, exacerbating the impact of IPV on confidence and trust. As discussed in the previous chapter in relation to agoraphobia, some women spoke of not being able to leave the home because of panic and fear, while others were not able to leave because of the fear of being stalked and actually being physically attacked by their ex-partners. Feeling fearful and unsafe pertained mostly to the women's continuing fear of their violent partners but also, in some instances, to the fear of other men's potential use of violence. Some women therefore struggled with participating in activities outside of work and family because they feared for their safety.

The severity of the effects of IPV are mediated and complicated by numerous factors, including the length and extent of the violence and how this intersects with personal issues such as mental health, as well as external conditions such as family and community responses. We argue in addition that women's recovery is strongly mediated by how the state responds to IPV, which includes facilitating access to income security, education, employment, housing, practical and mental health supports.

Multiple demands, exhaustion and retreat from the public realm

Many women described feeling too exhausted to participate in social activities due to IPV-related mental health problems, increased caring roles, financial pressures and heightened vigilance about safety. The caring demands were also very often compounded by IPV-related trauma in their children. Many women reported simply not having the energy for a social life outside the private sphere of home and the simultaneous demands of their paid and unpaid work, and managing their own and their children's trauma. In the following account, Melissa linked loss of trust in others, "bad social skills" and feelings of exhaustion as being related to "keeping my guard up every day":

> 'I am extremely troubled, and I have extreme trust issues, almost a fear of people. I feel everyone wants to hurt me, I have bad social skills, and I am depressed constantly.... I am extremely exhausted from keeping my guard up every day.'

This account alludes to how unenjoyable and difficult social interaction can be when one is distrusting and fearful of other people. However, in spite of a desire to avoid social interaction, all women have to interact with others to some extent in the course of their day-to-day lives.

Many women also linked exhaustion to undertaking increased child-care after leaving IPV, with some also working longer hours in their jobs, while at the same time experiencing IPV-related anxiety and depression. As Blanche explained (quoted in Chapter Four) the combined effects of exhaustion and stress, and the associated financial costs of this, can result in women finding it simply 'too hard to put themselves out there', exacerbating social exclusion and isolation. Not dissimilarly, Yasmin drew attention to how her capacity for social relationships outside the realms of home and work was reduced, when the economic costs of IPV combined with the loss of trust, self-esteem and self-confidence:

'I have lost friendships. The economic cost has stopped me from doing many things. My damaged sense of trust, self-esteem and confidence have made it very hard for me to try to make new friendships. I now bury myself in work or stay at home. My children are in 50:50 shared care. My life is extremely lonely when they are away.'

Both Nussbaum (2003, 2011) and Kelly et al (2014) emphasise that women must have control over the material conditions of their lives in order to fully participate in society. The above accounts demonstrate how financial problems not only contribute to exhaustion that in turn limits social participation, but also present a concrete barrier because participation in many social activities requires money.

As discussed in Chapter Four, escaping violent partners through frequent geographical moves also had a significant impact on women's capacities to maintain social relationships and connections. As one woman said, "... having had to move so many times has meant it's really hard to make any true friends". Women (and their children) had to make frequent and significant geographical moves to escape violence (42% of total survey respondents). Another woman said, "We have moved six times in less than six years ... it is expensive and disruptive." Such moves contribute further to exhaustion and limit women's abilities to affiliate with others and have meaningful relationships.

Women who are migrants or who are living in rural and remote locations already confront social isolation and are at particular risk of having their social worlds reduced even further as a result of IPV (Lanier and Maume, 2009). Research does indicate that in general, migrant women are vulnerable to social isolation when living in

IPV because of fewer family supports, fear of disclosure, community sanctions about domestic violence, cultural and language barriers, and limited knowledge about their legal rights, including domestic and family violence clauses in immigration policies (Ghafournia, 2011). Some migrant woman who we interviewed, such as Mariana, who was an Australian citizen, spoke of her church-based supports, financial independence and professional employment as providing her some security and hope for the future.

In Australia, some residents live on a diverse range of so-called temporary visas, which leave them with fewer rights and claims on the state than full citizens. Of the five women who completed the survey and reported being temporary residents, two were still living with their violent partners. Their different stories give some hint of the wide variations in the experiences of migrant women (Pease and Rees, 2008; Reina et al., 2014). For example, Alina was born in Russia, identified as Christian of North African/Middle East background, and had a Bachelor's degree, but was currently employed as a clerical worker. She said she lived "in housing at the mercy of a friend" on a semi-rural property:

'My experience of IPV made my worst nightmares seem very real. Because of visa dependence, it's now made me extremely fragile and anxious.' (Alina)

Alina's ex-partner had isolated her from her overseas family and from their social networks in Australia. As a temporary resident and new migrant , Alina had relatively few of her own established social and family networks or institutional supports. Alina's fear and anxiety were closely connected to her precarious position as an individual woman with liminal status in relation to her citizenship rights, associated with temporary visa eligibility and requirements. Migrant women without citizenship status cannot access state-funded support services, public housing, sustainable employment and affordable further education, which invariably limits their social participation.

In addition to the impact of coercive control as an aspect of IPV, it is important not to underestimate the damaging consequences of physical abuse and its implications for social participation. Meredith described how severe physical violence reduced her ability to participate in activities such as sport:

'I can't play sport or exercise like I'd like to, as I encounter pain in neck and head location where I was last beaten

by my violent ex. I also get dizzy spells and blackouts
that penetrate from a spot on my forehead that I received
punches bumps from my violent ex … . Most of the time
I think it's better and easier for me to be alone and just
be a mum because I know how to be a mum. I no longer
know how to be a friend.'

Here, physical damage directly attributable to IPV prevents Meredith
from participating in sport, with all its health-promoting and social
benefits. These health problems, combined with the familiarity of
isolation because of IPV and coercive control, led Meredith to conclude
that it is simply easier to focus on her child and mothering and to give
up on friendship altogether. Other women also talked about focusing
their energies on their relationships with their children as part of
retreating from the wider social world. As can be seen, this reproduces
and reinforces women's location in the private realm of the home
rather than in the wider public realm. Unfortunately, then, while IPV
and coercive control result in many women leaving violent partners
obsessed with the imposition of a traditional domestic femininity,
many nonetheless find that they remain to some extent trapped in the
domestic realm because of a lack of support and understanding from
family, friends and the wider community. As we note in Chapter Four,
the numbers of women involved in full-time caring roles (usually of
children) increased after IPV. There is an awful irony in women seeking
their freedom from entrapment by leaving violent and controlling men,
only to find that they are trapped in the home by community denial,
ignorance and shaming.

A lack of support from the state is a critical aspect of the difficulties
women find in seeking to regain their capabilities to engage in a full
range of social participation after IPV, a lack that is underpinned by
institutionalised denial of, and ignorance about, IPV and its impact.
Many of the women were confronted by rejection or outright refusal
when they attempted to obtain state assistance and support. In one
example of many, Camilla explained how impossible she found it to
locate adequate support for herself and her child:

'Although I actively reach out and seek understanding and
have sought support continuously from all avenues I can find
for six years, I have not found the awareness or resources
required to assist or help me and my child to free ourselves
from the situation we endure.'

It is the lack of understanding and appropriate support from the state that ultimately locks women into a struggle on the margins of society that includes a long-term reduction in their social participation. Women particularly commented on the lack of support and understanding from the legal system, the education system and police departments, in addition to the low levels of income and housing support we identified earlier. We argue that these are part of the hidden effects of sexual politics. For example, as one woman observed, there are negative consequences of the family court system's failure to acknowledge women's overall disadvantage relative to men in judicial proceedings, in spite of rhetoric that this is taken into account: "We are disadvantaged in so many ways and the family law does not honour this, even though they say they do."

Over the past two decades, there has been a tendency within the Australian family court system to prioritise fathers' rights to contact with children over child safety, with many women reporting that their fears for their children fall on deaf ears (Buchanan et al., 2015). In relation to the education system, women found it difficult to access support for traumatised children, with one woman saying "I must be a child advocate for my children within the school system." It is well documented that children exposed to domestic violence can experience emotional, behavioural, social and academic difficulties, and that schools should provide supportive interventions if children cannot access supportive services outside of the school environment (Thompson and Trice-Black, 2012). In relation to police and the wider criminal justice system, Luciana explained that she had no faith that she would be protected or supported, thereby choosing not to report IPV:

'As there was inadequate support available from police I chose not to report it. ... I would not put my life at risk by reporting my partner's actions to the police ... I have absolutely no confidence in the legal system's ability to protect people from domestic violence after it has been reported. In fact, it appears to only antagonise the offender and create increased danger for the victim.'

As can be seen, denial, rejection and victim-blaming on the part of friends and family is often matched by institutional denial in the form of lack of understanding and support from agencies. Below, we present the case of Felicity to demonstrate in greater detail how shame and loss of social networks conspire with lack of institutional support and understanding to lock women into the private sphere after IPV. This also shows how Felicity is rebuilding social connections in different ways after experiencing IPV, to support other women and advocate for improving community and state responses to IPV.

> Felicity is aged between 35-44 years and has two sons, who are five and two years old. Her income comes from government benefits and is under $30,000 per annum. She receives minimal child support from her ex-partner and has significant debts created by him that she has to pay off. Felicity has a university degree. The violence lasted for six years. Felicity was able to stay in her private rental house, but because of her financial problems she is very stressed about managing. This in part pertains to paying her ex-partner's creditors and lack of child support, but also to her perception that her children could not cope with more than one day of child-care. She also left work in part because of shame about the domestic violence and her husband's affair. She says that because of caring responsibilities, she has no social life and only sees family. Friends tell her she has changed, which she says is due to hypervigilance caused by the violence. Consequently, she does not have strong friendship networks. Her ex-partner also criticised her and put her down to many of her friends and family, including accusations of 'craziness'. Counselling was described as very unhelpful and victim-blaming. Felicity has had very little in the way of formal help that has been effective. She is struggling on in a very small world where the children's needs are at the centre and her own needs do not really feature. Felicity is angry about her experiences and is very involved in the White Ribbon Foundation and advocacy. She describes herself as 'on the soap box about domestic violence'. She also supports other women in domestic violence on Facebook through a single mothers' forum.

The politics of ignorance surrounding IPV therefore operates at multiple levels that serve to increase shame, stress and exhaustion for women by rendering them entirely responsible for protecting themselves and their children and for rebuilding their lives after IPV. Ultimately, these processes increase women's social marginalisation and exclusion, and reduce their participation in the wider social world. IPV therefore has a significant impact on women's social participation in complex and intersecting ways. Most importantly, though, our analysis shows that the negative impact of IPV on social participation interconnects with, and is compounded by, its negative impact on other domains of women's lives. Interconnections between the impact on mental health and social participation are perhaps the most obvious, with women describing reduced confidence, and feeling anxious, depressed, exhausted and distrustful, as leading them to withdraw from social contact with others. Women also pointed to shame about IPV as a factor in their withdrawal, as well as the added burden of shame about IPV-related poor mental health and reduced socioeconomic circumstances, which exacerbates social withdrawal and isolation. However, the capacity and desire for social participation was also negatively affected by the deterioration of women's actual material circumstances in terms of income, work and housing, not just shame about their changed social status, such that they no longer had the means or the energy to engage. Social withdrawal is compounded by the lack of adequate material support to women leaving IPV, including from the state, which is further exacerbated by the shame associated with stigmatisation and community denial of IPV.

Rebuilding connections: spaces for action after IPV

As is evident in the case study of Felicity above, women in this study did find some 'spaces' for taking action after they had escaped from the IPV. These spaces include mothering in a safe environment; being able to grow personally, emotionally and spiritually; engaging with new situations; rebuilding a sense of self as well as a sense of home and community; reconnecting with friends and family; seeking help; feeling a sense of competence; safety and emotional and physical wellbeing, and obtaining financial independence (Kelly et al., 2014: 15). We are particularly concerned here with women's capacities to rebuild a sense of community, reconnect with friends and family, seek help, and feel safe as aspects of social participation. Strong social connections and affiliations can be understood as vital spaces for action that contribute to other aspects of the individual's life, such as increasing confidence, building a strong sense of self, building a home, and good relations with children.

Expanding social worlds

Many women in our study described reconnecting with friends and activities outside the home after leaving violent relationships. Vicki captures the idea of a lack of volitional space caused by a violent partner's coercive control when she says, "I was never allowed to be involved with activities outside of home." She contrasted this with more her recent experiences of joining groups and developing a friendship network:

'Since then over the past few years I am now joining in with groups, going out with small groups of friends. I have

a good network of friends now, which I was not allowed
to have previously.' (Vicki)

Leaving IPV therefore allowed Vicki to re-establish spaces for action
that had been lost because of coercive control. Other women talked
about their increasing social involvement with both formal and informal
supports and social activities. They were rebuilding their involvement in
what appear to be apparently innocuous activities such as participating
in a church choir, which could be treated as a cause for partner violence.

'Since leaving a violent relationship I am heavily involved
in church, friendship groups and my choir and have strong
connections with family. During the violence, the only
connection I could maintain was choir, and this was a cause
of regular and increasing violence.' (Eliza)

Many other women mentioned church groups as important sources
of support after IPV. Another woman said, "Since I am no longer
experiencing domestic violence I am able to pursue external activities
safely, and not fear any repercussions from doing so ... I have built a
strong network after separation." Another used a celebratory tone to
describe her new freedom to participate in whatever activities she wants
to: "Since leaving the domestic violent relationship I have been free
to be involved and do many social activities that I wasn't able to do
before. It's wonderful." Overall, women described their increasing social
participation in collective groups and activities after IPV in positive
terms, although some reported that their social participation increased
slowly: "... so that I can meet new people, as I lost a lot of friends. I
also do more activities to learn new skills and build my confidence."
This is consistent with Kelly et al's (2014) finding that when women
no longer experience coercive control, they can find safe spaces for
action because they have increased freedom of movement.

Material conditions, power and social participation

Kelly et al (2014) point to the importance of social support networks
to wellbeing and social participation, but the authors warn that these
networks can only really develop when women are financially able,
settled and not in temporary accommodation. Thus, as we have already
argued, expanding women's space for action depends on women having
a measure of control over their material environments. Our findings
demonstrate the links between increased financial independence, self-

confidence and a widening of women's social worlds. Emilia described feeling "a prohibitive and controlling sense of insecurity and instability" and the related anxiety, poverty, stigmatisation, discrimination and exclusion from rental properties so that she never "knew a home". She then went on to describe the experience of new-found power and social relationships once she gained paid employment and a new social network.

> 'My ex-partner continued to survey and control the local environment, being "in the area", and intruding upon new relationships, forcing a sense of isolation, even amongst new friends and environments. Nowhere was ever safe, until I recently gained employment and have been financially independent. My financial independence seems to have intimidated my ex-partner, and he less frequently makes an effort to engage me, and may be aware that most of the people and environments I encounter now are well above his education level. He would not feel superior amongst my new environments or friends.' (Emilia)

Emilia suggested that her ex-partner detected a shift in power relations once she was employed and financially independent, and moving in more educated circles, subsequently backing off in his attempts to control her. This account articulates particularly well how classed power relations associated with employment and education can have an impact on how IPV is enacted. It also shows how interconnections between mental illness, poverty, financial dependence and housing problems can together lead to shame, a sense of powerlessness and social isolation. It demonstrates how work, increased finances and positive social relationships can mitigate against these effects and bring a sense of power and control for women over their material environments. Veronica's account earlier also demonstrates how family and social supports are central to women leaving, successfully rebuilding their lives and intimately connected to women's material circumstances. Below, we present Veronica's case in more detail to demonstrate how social support connects to the other dimensions of women's lives.

Veronica is 45 years of age and has a five-year-old son. Veronica's annual income is over $90,000 and she has a university degree. She experienced violence for five years. Veronica was the primary income earner on a good salary during the violent relationship, and lived in a privately owned home during this period. She remained in the home when the violent relationship ended. Her mother provided emotional support and was aware of her partner's violent and controlling behaviour. Her mother was also a mortgagee on the house. Veronica had the advice of a good lawyer in relation to the separation. Veronica worked in an organisation where domestic violence was understood and she was supported through workplace counselling services, flexible hours and a good carers' policy. While the violence caused anxiety attacks, Veronica was not diagnosed, does not depict herself as having had mental health problems and has largely bounced back in this regard with non-pathologising, pro-active support from her doctor. Veronica has been able to bounce back across all dimensions of citizenship.

Veronica's class privilege is evident in this case study. She was the primary income earner on a good salary and because she contributed most to the mortgage payments for the family house, she was able to make her ex-partner leave. Her mother's support, as well as her role as one of the mortgagees, also meant that Veronica was not taking this action alone. Veronica had the advice of a good lawyer; she had the education and the foresight to document her partner's violence; and her mother was able to acknowledge the violence, provide emotional support and act as a witness. Her economic, social and cultural capital were therefore important to managing well in the aftermath of violence. The state plays little part in this narrative because Veronica had sufficient economic and social resources to manage leaving violence. As such, Veronica has been able to bounce back across all dimensions of citizenship in a way that many other women have not. She was therefore protected from the more extreme fall-out experienced by many other women in our study.

Online worlds: new spaces for action

An emerging issue in the literature on IPV is the misuse of the internet by violent men who continue stalking and harassing women to exert power and control (Lee and Anderson, 2016). Yet, the online environment can also offer a platform to women for collective support and feminist activism (Schuster, 2013). Our survey and recruiting for interviews took place largely in an online environment, and women reported that even taking part in the survey felt like a form of advocacy against gendered violence. We did not specifically seek information about online social participation in the survey or interviews, so we cannot say how common this experience is, but a small number of women volunteered that belonging to online groups was important to rebuilding their lives and themselves after IPV. One woman particularly noted that she maintained this form of social participation over face-to-face participation in support groups, "I don't go out as much, I removed myself from a lot of support groups, apart from those I have which are online." Daphne complements online support with attending church, which she identified as the only place she feels safe "in the real world":

> 'All the friendship networks I am involved with are online,
> as are the support groups. I was meeting people in the real
> world before domestic violence. Church is the only thing
> I have found to meet people in the real world as I feel safe
> there.'

In contrast, Amelia had to change her church as well as her network of friends, although she did manage to start her own online domestic violence support.

> 'I had to change my network of friends because they all
> knew him. I had to change the church that I had been
> involved in for 20 years. I started my own support group
> for domestic violence victims after joining one online and
> one in real life but couldn't attend after he bad-mouthed it
> to my kids so that they refused to attend the crèche.'

After experiencing IPV, Celia also garnered support from "a few trusted friends, online social justice groups and a domestic violence service". Both during and after violence, participation in internet technology can be important for women. There is arguably a need for further research, so we can better understand how technology can help and support women in this emerging new space for action that is not bounded by geography or time. However, women are also well aware that internet and online technology offers ample opportunities for men to abuse them, thus knowing how to use it 'safely and privately' is important (Lee and Anderson, 2017: 32).

Retreating from social spaces

A final space for action previously overlooked in research into how women rebuild their lives after IPV is the opportunity to retreat from others and spend time alone. While this might be considered the converse of social participation, all individuals arguably need quiet and a measure of solitude to rebuild their sense of self, particularly if they are recovering from the trauma of abuse. Once women had physically removed themselves from the constant intrusion of coercive control, they often expressed sheer relief at having found safe spaces in their new homes which offered them the option of being in their own company. This finding draws attention to the fact that being alone is not necessarily problematic or isolating when it is chosen, particularly for women who have been denied even the most basic control over their private lives and spaces. Valeria talked about preferring her solitude now that she was living in a safe space:

> 'I'm currently living in a small town where I prefer not to leave my house too often. I've even named my home *Il Mio Posto Sicuro* which is Italian for *My Safe Place*.' (Valeria)

Others said, "I like my couch, quiet, and cooking," or "I prefer to avoid outside and people and activities, I like being alone." When describing themselves, some women used the terms 'recluse' or 'hermit' because they said that most of their time was spent in the home alone. For some, this had a negative connotation, suggesting a shift from who they were before violence. Other women presented themselves as more contented this way, for example, "I'm a bit of a hermit now. And loving it – a counterbalance to a super-busy rewarding work life." For these women, a self-imposed retreat from social relationships offered a peaceful haven after long periods of intense vigilance and fear. Moreover, retreat into these safe havens was often presented as central to rebuilding a stronger sense of themselves after years of IPV. Thus, some women used the language of retreat and aloneness as reflective of agency rather than of pathology or social isolation willed by the violent man rather than themselves. One woman captured in a very evocative and celebratory way her hopes to be able to revel in her own company after IPV when she said, "I want to laugh more, dance in my own lounge room, eat chocolate and have a cup of tea while reading a book and other small achievements before I die." These accounts of women enjoying their own company, or hoping to in the future, resist the dominant discourse of social isolation as a negative consequence of male violence over which they have had little control. The practice of seeking and enjoying one's own company also resists the assumption that being alone and not connected to others is invariably a problem or symptomatic of mental illness; for these women, being alone was instead associated with healing and recovery.

Peer support and political activism

As noted earlier in discussion of the quantitative survey data, women's participation in collective social support and political groups increased to higher levels than before IPV. Analysis of the qualitative data demonstrates how participation in support groups is an important space for action, playing an important role in rebuilding women's confidence, trust, social networks and social lives after IPV. As Larance and Porter (2004: 676) note, support groups involve 'female victims of domestic violence challenging the social isolation imposed by their dominant partners as they search for meaning in their lives' through connecting with and 'building trustful relationships and establishing supportive networks during the group process'. Sascha mentioned how important a domestic violence support group was for her in ending a violent relationship:

> 'I was regularly going to the women's group and without that support I would not have gotten through this with no doubt about it at all, I had a whole network of people helping me to get rid of him ... I needed to go to that women's group because that was the only way I could make sense of it all. Once I started hearing all these stories about how all these other people had been in the same situation and same pattern of behaviour and because of the huge amount of harassment and parental alienation that continued, I needed all this ongoing support. It was completely exhausting ... they had a "sister system" so it would be six years later and I was still going to the family court, I was still doing this, I was still doing that. People from that group would come with me and that made all the difference.'

Hearing other women's stories and coming to see the patterns in abusive men's behaviour was critically important for Sascha in the decision to leave, as was support from the 'sister system' in attending court. Not dissimilarly, Emilia explained how she restricts her social life to spending time only with women who have had similar experiences:

> 'I only invest in people who understand domestic violence and single motherhood and poverty. ... my network is reliable, and empathic. I have no friends who have not experienced domestic violence ... they [who have not

experienced domestic violence] often betray confidence and do not realise how dangerous the perpetrator is ... I am untrusting of other people.'

Feeling safe and understood by women who had been through IPV was therefore central to Emilia as it was to other women in the context of lack of understanding from others. Mindy also said that a domestic violence support group is her main source of support and her only activity outside work and family.

'I used to do volunteer work however my violent partner was extremely angry and jealous about this so I stopped during the relationship and I have not had the confidence to return. I now attend a support group for domestic violence victims which is the only activity I do outside work and family now.'

In addition to participating in a domestic violence support group, Sascha also described her work as a volunteer in the group, emphasising the importance of helping other women, but also the positive effects on her own recovery:

'[Domestic violence] had a big detrimental effect. I left the relationship with health issues. However, I now work as a volunteer with a domestic violence group, helping other women and their children leaving domestic violence. Being involved with this work has helped in my own recovery.'

As noted earlier, involvement in political groups after IPV increased by 60% compared to during IPV, with a small number of women expanding on this in their qualitative responses in the survey or interviews. Some women specifically talked about becoming involved in political activism on gendered violence or related issues. Activism involves speaking out or raising awareness about gendered violence, informing and improving policy, legislation and services, joining action groups, protest and public media campaigns, and establishing and being involved in ventures to promote sexual equality in the community (Noble and Verity, 2006: 3). While activism includes formal involvement in groups and movements, it also describes more informal and individual acts of awareness-raising and advocacy. Earlier, we noted three women's accounts of undertaking advocacy in the legal and education systems in relation to IPV and children's rights.

When women reflected on their experience of domestic violence, some also noted that they had become more aware of persistent gender inequalities and were more outspoken about injustices and conscious of helping others in need.

> 'Domestic violence made me a more sheltered and anxious person. On the flipside, it has made me more understanding of others in similar situations, and more outspoken on their behalf. I still avoid confrontation, but I try to be an advocate for fairness as much as I can within those constraints... . I've become fiercely independent financially and can be quite defensive about it. I feel like I owe my friends for their help during the abusive relationship and try to go above and beyond if they need help for any reason.' (Daisy)

IPV is presented here as leading to a more general awareness about the difficulties people face and a greater willingness to advocate for justice. Ursula described her efforts to speak out and raise awareness in spite of her anxiety and fear of people resulting from IPV.

> 'I suffer anxiety in large crowds I do not go out alone. But I have also found my voice and for the past year I continue to put myself in harm's way knowing we must speak out even if it puts my life in danger. I will never be free. My power and my voice is about reclaiming who I am. I demand accountability of the individual and systemic failure that failed me then and continues today.'

Ursula specifically emphasises her awareness of the individual and systemic failures she encountered which other women continue to face and the need to speak out as part of addressing them. A number of women also mentioned going on to study in particular areas because of their experiences of IPV and their awareness that other women continue to be unsupported or understood, including studies in law or mental health. One woman talked about taking up a role as a mental health advocate after her experiences of IPV-related poor mental health. Other women described their increased involvement in political activism specifically related to IPV.

> 'I'm much more, I feel like I'm kind of more of a spokesperson. I'm really, I'm really, really into the White Ribbon Foundation. I've changed my profile and put my

little, you know, "never be silent" and blah, blah, blah. I do take a real interest in anything that's about domestic violence, like I'll talk about it, you know? I've often said to people, you know, "Oh yeah, look, you're talking about the sharks but one women is killed every week in Australia, every week by a partner or an ex – generally, ex." I'm going "That is news, not a shark," do you know what I mean. I get the shark cull, yeah, everyone's big on it, and excited, but no one's standing up and making protests about the fact that one women is killed every week. And you think about all of those children, do you know what I mean?'

Q: 'It's kind of politicised you.'

'I am, I'm … and I'm like a soap box. But that for me feels empowering, you know that's a part of, a part of being a survivor of that situation and knowing that I don't want to ever have that kind of situation again. And that so many women experience it, just makes me really angry.' (Felicity)

Felicity went on to describe meeting women through Facebook who have also experienced IPV and supporting them. Sascha described how her participation and volunteer work in a domestic violence support group resulted in the establishment of a domestic violence action group.

'Through that [support] group they started another group because women are treated so badly by the police, the legal system, the family court and the child support agency, a group of women the year before I joined, so it would've been … they started a group that lobbies and does stuff to change domestic violence and support women and I still work with that group. I joined it and I'm still in it … I have been involved [for over 20 years] in the domestic violence action group.'

Sascha's involvement in activism on domestic violence continues to this day, some 20 years after she left the violent relationship. As argued earlier, these examples of political activism are among the most cogent examples of the exercise of political rights and active citizenship, which are in part borne of the failure of the state to guarantee women's freedom from violence and support to rebuild their lives. As Buchanan and Wendt (2017: 9) argue, the very act of participating in domestic violence research involves women taking opportunities to speak out and raise awareness; to help other women; to affirm their emotional experiences; to make sense of memories leading to new insights; and 'to feel part of a wider movement to address domestic violence'. A number of women mentioned similar motivations for participating in our research. Women's participation in all types of activism on gendered violence and related issues, from individual acts to group actions, can be understood as contributing to a feminist sexual politics that seeks transformation and change, particularly around state responses to IPV.

One of the unique contributions of our study is that we asked women whether specific forms of social participation changed over time, including before, during and after IPV. This has enabled development of a more detailed understanding of how women's social participation is altered by the experience of IPV and the interconnections with its impact in other life domains. Our findings confirm that women's social participation shrinks dramatically during IPV and that, in almost all categories, it never regains its former levels after women leave. We have shown how a sexual politics of ignorance surrounding IPV and coercive control is central to this and includes gendered social practices of shaming, denial, victim-blaming and rejection as well as institutionalised denial on the part of the state. We show how deterioration in women's material conditions intersects with shaming, community and institutional denial to reduce women's capabilities and desire to engage socially. However, our analysis also demonstrates that many women do open up new spaces for action by re-engaging with relationships, the community and society across all categories of participation. This includes taking the opportunity to retreat from the social world to recover and heal from IPV.

In particular, we have shown how women's combined capabilities can be enhanced through engagement in collective support and political activist groups. These groups can be important spaces for action in assisting women to develop new personal relationships and social networks, and they also bolster civic, political and social engagement. Involvement in political groups working towards the prevention of gendered violence and the provision of support to women contributes to feminist activism more broadly. Such activism calls the state to account by demanding that it address violence in the 'private' sphere, complicating traditional notions of state responsibility, citizenship and human rights and entering, directly and purposefully, into feminist sexual politics to bring about change. In the next chapter, we consider in more detail the history of feminist activism on gendered violence and directions for the future.

SEVEN

Campaigns for women's freedom from violence

Introduction

The women who participated in this research project have provided compelling evidence of the long-term negative effects that gendered violence is likely to have on individual women and their children across interconnected aspects of everyday life. Both the quantitative data and the women's accounts uncover the damage caused by such violence to their mental health and identity, employment and income, and their housing and social engagement. However, their experiences are not uncommon for women whenever and wherever they have lived. As both Max Weber in the 20th century and Sylvia Walby in the 21st have argued, violence is woven into the fabric of (almost all) societies. The form of violence on which we are focused here, namely intimate partner violence (IPV) against women, lies at the extreme end of the spectrum of gendered power that is always being contested. We encapsulate this struggle in the term 'sexual politics'. Women's rights to exercise all the capabilities necessary to live decent flourishing lives have not been easily won, and clearly need to be constantly defended against the gender inequalities produced by male-dominated sexual politics. Our argument that violence against women erodes, even prevents, their achievement of full citizenship is rooted in the work of feminist activists and the reflexivity of women's experiences of unequal power and force in many communities and over many decades.

Violence against women continues; however, there have been shifts in moral and political attitudes towards gendered violence. Naming violence against women as a problem has not been a straightforward matter, even for the alert and aware feminists of the early years of the women's liberation movement, the so-called second wave of feminism. The shift in attitudes and contemporary condemnation of violence against women has taken considerable and persistent effort, mainly on the part of feminist activists. As we have shown, campaigning continues to be necessary if we are to reach gender equality and stop gendered violence. Such campaigning is taking different forms in the contemporary environment through global access to digital technologies which are changing both the knowledge available to the community and campaigning strategies.

Feminists' efforts have included active engagement with the state. Feminist calls for the state to counteract and prevent men's violence against women have largely focused on three areas: housing, including emergency accommodation such as shelters, as well as affordable long-term housing; law reform and legislation to criminalise and prevent further violence; and policies and programs designed to enable government and non-government agencies to respond effectively to the needs of victims and to promote the principles of freedom from public and private violence (Chung, 2015). Gains have been made in each of these three areas across different forms of welfare, policy and legislative structures in several nation states such as Australia, the United Kingdom, New Zealand, Canada and the US. Such changes have enabled some women and children to escape violence and have increased public awareness about violence as a serious and damaging problem. These initial state funded responses were heavily concentrated at the point of crisis with physical violence causing a threat to life. While a wider range of responses has evolved the major focus remains with crises associated with physical violence. State and societal responses are not necessarily framed by feminist principles with women's equality and human dignity at their centre. These gains were hard fought both in relation to debate and disagreement among feminist activists but also the persistence required to attain the changes and retain legal and civil rights for women subjected to male violence. For example, criminalising domestic violence required police to attend, act in ways that promoted safety for the woman victimised and charge the perpetrator with criminal offences. This occurred infrequently in the early days and decisions about a perpetrator's removal were often based on whether he was physically violent or abusive to the police and not what had transpired with the female victim.

As we show in this chapter, feminists themselves have struggled with the obstacles created by the fitful and damaging politics of ignorance that help to sustain gender inequality. Whether unequal gender relations are merely natural, or whether men's identity depends on maintaining their dominant position as patriarch of the family by necessary force, or whether somehow women's psychology or childhood socialisation leads them to attract abusive men into their lives, or whether women need to learn how to manage their violent partner for the sake of the marriage, the children or their relationship with god are all questions that feminists have needed to work through (Gordon, 1988;

Schneider, 2000; Lister, 2003). And, we are saddened to report, this work must continue. The discursive effects of a politics of ignorance about violence against women have an impact on women as much as on men, and on our social and political understanding of violence as much as on social institutions and the state. Women must work to overcome discourses and practices that construct them as causing or deserving of ill-treatment, abuse and discrimination, a task that has engaged feminists for over a century.

How violence becomes a problem

'I may have been his excuse, but I have never been the reason.' (Martin, 1981: 3)

Del Martin opens her early US study of 'battered wives' with a graphic four-page letter written by a woman who had attended a public meeting on the issue of wife-beating. Locating the reason for the violent abuse of women and working out what to do about it has been the motivation of many feminist activists from diverse backgrounds and cultures. As a result, there have been different views about the reasons for and the solutions to violence against women. Likewise, histories about violence against women are framed in varied terms and stress different campaigns. Our account in this chapter pays particular attention to the debates around the sexual politics of gendered violence, as well as the attempts that have been made to counter violence across the world.

The ways in which violence against women is understood has changed a great deal in the modern period during which the civil, political and social rights of citizenship have been achieved within the nation state. The links between women's rights as citizens and their rights to freedom from violence and abuse cannot be established until women achieve other capabilities. Early campaigners recognised the ways that gender inequalities limited women's access to those rights. Black feminists have also led the way in their campaigning and writing to highlight how multiple interlocking and intersecting forms of oppression operate, which undermine women's rights as citizens and entrap women in violence and poverty, preventing them living a safe and secure existence (Collins, 1990; Crenshaw, 1994). Their work has been influential in understanding the importance of how racism, ableism, classism and heterosexism combine with sexism to limit women's capacities to live without male violence (Anthias, 2013). As we argue in Chapter Two, a key aspect of citizenship is the assumption that all citizens are equal. The political right to vote was fought for on the grounds of equality and required complex and persistent campaigns to tackle both the material and discursive conditions that would make this possible. So too do the challenges of winning women's citizenship rights to freedom from violence and abuse demand substantial activist effort. The right to vote was hard won, but eventually it was extended to all citizens regardless of class, race or gender (in almost all contemporary nation states). Rights equality is foundational to citizenship but is rarely achieved or retained without being contested. Perhaps one of the most significant features of recent times is the complete acceptance of discourses of citizen equality, even though race, class and gender inequalities persist or even intensify (for example, through the erosion of welfare state support or voter de-registration).

Although violence against women has been a focus of feminist concern since the 1800s (Murray, S., 1999), it was not their central issue. Rather, it was a lack of economic and political rights which led to poverty and homelessness that were the focal points. In Australia, Caroline Chisholm who famously campaigned for the establishment of settler families in the colonies opened the Female Immigrants Home in 1841 to relieve women's homelessness and poverty from unemployment (Summers, 1975: 300). Chisholm's approach was very much in accord with other women in the early 19th century in western countries who

> ... began to organize in the name of social reform, reclamation, and moral purity. Essential to this mobilization was the rise of domestic ideologies that stressed women's differences from men, humanitarian concerns for the conditions of child life and labor, and the emergence of activist interpretations of the gospel ... (Koven and Michel, 1990: 1085)

Other historians argue that campaigns against violence beginning in the late 19th century were mounted from different perspectives. For example, temperance campaigners sought to protect women and children from violence by prohibiting alcohol, while feminists as well as social purist reformers maintained that violence against women stemmed from a husband's property rights over his wife's body and campaigned for emancipation to remove that privilege (Schneider, 2000: 15).

The protection of children against cruelty 'that occurred only in the lower classes' (Gordon, 1988: 20) was the first stage of the historical and political attention to family violence identified by Linda Gordon in her study of documented cases in Boston from 1880-1960. She reviewed the documents across four periods to demonstrate that 'family violence has been historically and politically constructed' (1988: 3). Gordon proposes that definitions of domestic violence depend on what she termed 'political moods' and the force of political movements, and second, that family violence usually arises out of power struggles, which in turn depend on changing norms and conditions. Her first point is now widely accepted, but the notion of contested power within the family has lost ground.

In Gordon's schema, the problem of family violence meaning cruelty to children shifted to one of child neglect caused by poverty and unemployment; hence it was still seen as an issue of class until the Depression era when family violence overall was obscured by sympathy for the unemployed husband. During the 1940s and 1950s the problem of violence was understood in terms of psychiatric views of frigid wives and frustrated husbands. Wife-beating finally began to become visible during the 1960s. In Gordon's argument, each shift in understanding was consequent on the strengths or weaknesses of feminist movements for women's rights. Notably, Gordon shows how the so-called 'clients' of the newly created child protection agencies use 'the powers of the weak'. They sought to protect themselves and their children by enlisting middle-class agency visitors and social workers as their allies over the course of the shifting interpretations of their experiences of violence. Gordon's periodisation of the changing understandings of violence against women in the US is similar to patterns in most western states (Koven and Michel, 1990).

Suffrage movements became long-lived women's organisations and continued to campaign against violence after vote rights for women had been achieved (Breitenbach, 2010). Many new women's organisations were formed in the UK after women gained the right to vote, including organisations campaigning against violence against women and children, and service provision organisations addressing health and childcare. These continued through the interwar period (Breitenbach and Thane, 2010a). During the post-war period of the 1950s and 1960s, what we now label intimate partner violence or IPV was known as wife-beating or wife battery and was largely understood in psychoanalytic terms. Nevertheless, women's unequal access to housing, education and employment, often exacerbated by poverty, was of considerable concern to women-oriented organisations such as United Australian Women. Such organisations aimed to provide support for women in the face of hardships that were not corrected or relieved by the state or the community. For example, the first shelter for battered women in the US was set up by Al-Anon in 1964 (Schechter, 1982: 55). Intended for the victims of alcohol related violence, it became a support for battered women, although Al-Anon was not a self-described feminist organisation.

What are the solutions?

During this period, the emerging 'second wave' of feminists saw themselves as breaking the silence on gender inequality in their personal lives and in political and civil society. Prevailing norms of everyday life of the family and gender relations were called into question, producing tensions within the women's movement around the new and competing attempts to explain gender inequality (was it caused primarily by capitalism or by patriarchy?), as well as disagreement about the best solutions (self-help, collective action, reformation of the state or independence from the state?).

Feminists in the Women's Liberation Movement shared their experiences as women in conscious-raising groups, conferences, shared-house meetings, collectives, and in an outpouring of articles, magazines, images and books. Among the most influential publications in the early 1970s were books by Germaine Greer (1970), Shulamith Firestone (1970), Juliet Mitchell (1966) and Kate Millett (1969). Their arguments were sophisticated, intellectual and tough. Greer gave a clear warning: 'Women have very little idea of how much men hate them' (1970: 249). Discussing masculine aggression, Millett says '...to confuse this neurotic hostility, this frank abuse, with sanity, is pitiable' (2000: 313). The authors addressed the issue of violence against women in relation to rape and sexual assault. Whatever violence or abuse women suffered was seen as integral to women's sexual repression (Firestone), oppression (Mitchell), and overall, caused by their abject position as men's property within the family. This period was associated with the understanding that feminists could speak about 'women' as a social category or group with some level of shared identity through common experiences of oppression.

How to overcome the complex causes and conditions of this male-dominated sexual politics was the most urgent question for second wave feminists. The diversity and the extent of violence within the family became more visible; 'rape, like charity, begins at home' (Hall cited in Rowbotham, 1989: 9). The growing focus on male violence was fraught with much controversy, which saw splits between those who argued that it was a keystone of women's oppression (radical feminists) and those who insisted on the role of capitalism in the oppression of women, as well as men (socialist feminists) (Mackay, 2015: 51). Liz Kelly (2013: 134) observed of the UK environment: 'Violence against women was a fault line in the many acrimonious debates between socialist and radical feminists in the 1970s'. The UK historian Sheila Rowbotham characterises the most significant conflict as whether violence could occur in the family, or was actually 'the determining aspect of the family' (1989: 9; see also Horsfall, 1991). If the family is the site of violence, it followed that viable heterosexual relationships were not possible, which seemed an untenable proposition for a successful egalitarian society. Despite these very sharp debates among feminists, those in the UK were able to agree on adding a demand for freedom from men's violence to the original four demands produced by the Women's Liberation Movement:

> Freedom from intimidation by threat or use of violence or sexual coercion, regardless of marital status; and an end to all laws, assumptions and practices which perpetuate male dominance and men's aggression towards women. (cited in Mackay, 2015: 50)

Feminists grappled with these debates at the same time as they made practical efforts to support women, particularly those suffering from male violence. '[A]t the local level, the reality was always more complex. Feminists of all shades established refuges and rape crisis centres in small towns and cities' (Kelly, 2013: 134). In the UK, Erin Pizzey lays claim to having set up the first refuge for battered women – Chiswick Women's Aid – in 1971. The first Australian women's shelter, Elsie Women's Refuge, was set up by feminists who occupied two small houses in Sydney in 1974 with the aim of providing free, temporary accommodation without the constraints of bureaucratisation or institutionalisation (Summers, 1975). Elsie Women's Refuge was the alternative to what feminists saw as the lack of state financial support and viable accommodation for women and their children. The violence perpetrated by husband violence was seen as only one of the multitude of problems women faced due to gender inequality.

Other shelters were set up, mainly in large cities. In Australia, there were an estimated one hundred in operation by 1979, about half of which were run by women's groups and the remainder by church groups (McGregor and Hopkins, 1991: 11). However, the debates and disputes meant that they were also sites of conflict among all those involved. Not only were the feminist activists confronted by hostile communities and a serious lack of resources, there were also disruptive conflicts between adversarial feminist groupings (Otto and Haley, 1975; McFerran, 1993; Mackay, 2015). Otto and Haley documented one of the early conflicts, concluding that feminists should concentrate on the bigger picture rather than provide substitute refuge support. Until the 1980s, Australian feminist refuge workers who campaigned for state funding as well as legal protection and education 'were a very lonely voice' (McFerran, 1993: 153). In the UK, Erin Pizzey herself became a point of contention when she became a very public advocate for men's rights groups. Documenting the shelter movement in the US, Susan Schechter observes:

> Power struggles, difficult in any organization, took trusting feminists by surprise and left them paralyzed … Some dedicated women were driven out of the movement by 'trashing'… [some] shelters or groups came precariously close to dissolving … (Schechter, 1982: 77)

Nevertheless, the creation of refuges was central to the feminist movement against domestic violence. Importantly, 'these were not institutions, but houses formed through collective action to provide a safe haven from male violence' (Bumiller, 2013: 194; see also Murray, S., 1999; Weeks, 2003; Kim, 2015). Refuges are a key example of feminist activism aimed at overcoming the lack of support provided to women by the state, their communities and families. Feminists who focused on violence against women were not alone in their activism as Heather Gautney (2010: 112) points out: 'Feminists of all stripes founded their own abortion clinics, shelters for rape and victims of domestic violence, and formed consciousness raising groups to deal with issues specifically related to patriarchy and its manifestations in the lives of women' in parallel with other movements who aimed to develop alternative structures outside/alongside the state.

Feminists continue to debate the values and principles of pursuing the creation of feminist-based services in contrast to pushing for larger changes to achieve equality of state support for their civil, political and social rights. Part of the dilemma is that even state-based services are rarely adequately funded with the result that service workers are often overloaded as they deliver services beyond what they are funded for (Weeks, 2003). Some argued that such state-based services were at risk of becoming institutionalised, professionalised, hierarchical and bureaucratised, and limited by state funding priorities (Charles, 2010; Nichols, 2011; Bumiller, 2013; Munshi, 2013; Abraham and Tastsoglou, 2016b).

Calling on the state

Despite the debates about whether feminists should establish shelters and other services for women, and despite the denial in many societies of the problem of violence against women, feminists have made consistent demands on the state to ensure civil, political and social rights for all women. In relation to IPV, efforts have largely been directed towards emergency accommodation, law reform, specialist policies and services. Many western nation states now have a range of responses to violence against women. For those seeking support, demand for services always outstrips supply. However, it is important to observe the complexities inherent in these responses that are rooted in the sexual politics of the state, violence and gender inequality. One of the issues associated with states accepting responsibility for addressing domestic violence is the notion that it is an issue of the private sphere. By calling for states to address actions in the 'private' sphere feminists have complicated traditional notions of state responsibility, citizenship and human rights (Flax, 1990; Walby, 1990). The 'challenge to the public/private divide inherent in the feminist understanding of due diligence has opened avenues for changing the terms on which women engage with these institutions, potentially reconfiguring women's citizenship in its national and transnational dimensions' (García-Del Moral and Dersnah, 2014: 663). The feminist challenge to the state to support gender equality and to prevent violence against women demands substantial change to prevailing white male–dominated sexual politics.

There are many and diverse options available to those who resist or deny the need for change, enabling the deflection of policies and practices that could produce effective change (DeKeseredy, 2011). For example, a national statement against gendered violence may be accepted by the national government, but insufficient funds are attached to ensure its implementation. This is not to argue that there is a Machiavellian cabal actively opposing gender equality in state headquarters, but only to restate that sexual politics involves constant struggle and conflict that is often likely to produce piecemeal outcomes. And, as we argue, these are contingent on contemporary political and social conditions.

Hence, the state in many countries does respond in material and policy terms to violence against women, including IPV. However, the long shadow cast by IPV over women's lives continues to raise feminist concerns about the role of the state (Lister, 2011; Franzway, 2016). The state's main focus has become high-risk (and highly visible) incidents of men's use of physical violence and the subsequent crisis this creates by endangering women and their children. High-risk incidents certainly deserve close attention; however, as our research shows, this focus can obscure the effects of other forms of violence. As more than one participant said – 'Do I have to die first?' Feminist activists and researchers have pushed successfully for the recognition of the multiple forms of violence, including coercive control as well as financial, spiritual and emotional abuse (Stark, 2007; Wendt and Zannettino, 2015). The invisibility of those aspects of IPV that receive the least attention in policy, practice and research is maintained by a politics of ignorance that denies the complexity of violence and IPV. This includes the state's continuing dominant focus on incidents of crisis and risk management, which are no doubt difficult and demanding to resolve, but which obscures the sexual politics of violence that requires consistent efforts to prevent or punish.

The political conditions in some western states have been strongly influenced by neoliberal agendas which seek small government, reduced welfare services and free markets. In response, some domestic violence policies and services have reframed the problem of violence from being caused by gender power relations to being 'an infringement of women's rights and an economic drain on society' (Ball and Charles, 2006: 174). The 'framing of domestic violence in terms of legislation, policies, and state intervention tends to fit disturbingly well within the neoliberal framework' (Abraham and Tastsoglou, 2016a: 569). Weissman (2007: 403) argues that engagement with the state 'continues to sap energy from the grassroots shelter organizations, narrow their political agenda, and alienate the advocates from potential allies in other facets of the justice struggle'. Bumiller (2013) goes so far as to argue that the feminist movement against domestic violence has been shaped by its interaction with the neoliberal state.

Although the influence of neoliberalism may be declining (Prügl, 2016), its focus on individual initiative is in direct contrast with feminist principles which are now under threat (Ishkanian, 2014; Rios, 2014). The degree to which feminist organisations are co-opted by the neoliberal state is ambiguous; state funding is beneficial, but at what cost?

A recent study conducted during a period of growing austerity measures in the UK provides strong evidence of the extent to which the state and its policies affect women's well-being (Kelly et al., 2014). Women's combined capabilities and citizenship rights may be either supported or undermined by the state. Kelly, Sharp and Klein's research, which followed UK women over a three- year period, found that:

... barriers to accessing the resources women needed to rebuild their lives – protection from further abuse, housing, financial resources, employment, divorce and safe child contact – were exacerbated by legal and social policy changes that were not anticipated at the start of the study. Over the three years the rights which had been won for women and children fleeing domestic violence over the past four decades were eroded, undermining their opportunities to achieve safety and freedom. The rationing of Legal Aid resulted in some women giving up rights that previously might have been enforced by the courts, raising the costs of safety and freedom considerably. (Kelly et al., 2014: 5)

Neoliberalism's anti-welfare ideology has led to reduced and punitive welfare assistance, and market-based responses to domestic violence (Weissman, 2016). Enforcement of child support mechanisms, which displace welfare obligations from the state to individuals, has been a focus of the neoliberal state, even where this endangers women and children.

The critical role of the state to women's lives and freedoms in the aftermath of IPV has received little attention in practice or research. The crisis orientation of state responses has reinforced the idea that the only safe solution for women and children is to flee. And yet, it is well known that leaving the violent situation is also the most dangerous time for women and children (Kelly, 2013). Post-separation violence occurs in numerous ways and can include physical violence (such as stalking and harassment); economic violence (such as men not paying the required amounts of child support regularly, interference in women's employment and training, coercing women to settle for less than the financial and material resources to which they are entitled, and drawing out Family Law processes which are costly and time consuming); as well as social violence (such as being humiliated in front of colleagues and family, threatening and intimidating friends, further isolating women).

Women who do flee IPV are not only at risk of further violence, but their identities are also publicly reconstituted. They are no longer victims entitled to state support, but rather are wage earners or beneficiaries of state income support where they must demonstrate their entitlement to the rights of citizenship. Discourses endorsed by neoliberal states stigmatise welfare recipients, and, in the case of women escaping violence, give little regard to the immediate risks as well as the long-term damaging effects of IPV. This highlights the ambivalent relationship between women and the state, which may aggravate their experience of gender inequality or may provide support and opportunities for women to develop complex capabilities, including adequate shelter and decent work. Importantly, our research shows that women do not just 'bounce back' to fully re-engage in public and private life, not only because post-separation violence may continue but also because the experience of violence has long-term effects on women's wellbeing as starkly demonstrated in the earlier chapter on mental health.

Feminist activism diversifies

Although this debate about service delivery has been lengthy and heated, it has not been a significant question for feminist movements in all countries. In Croatia the primary goal is to win human rights for women (Rošul-Gajić, 2016). In China, the goal has been to create awareness about gender inequality among policy makers and the general public. 'The urban intellectuals who are active in popular organizing in Beijing did not think domestic violence was a problem in Chinese society and certainly not in urban society' (Milwertz, 2003: 649). No attempts to provide services such as shelters were made until the 1990s, and then only with little success. In Beijing, plans for a shelter for women experiencing domestic violence were abandoned when the party/state agencies pulled out, and in Shanghai, a shelter was short-lived as it was closed by authorities. A decade later the Shanghai Anti-Domestic Violence Rescue Center offered accommodation services for homeless people affected by domestic violence. However, only 18 people were received in the first five years and equally small numbers used a rescue centre in Guangzhou City. Women in China who experience IPV are more likely to turn to their family than to state agencies (Qui and Zufferey, 2017). Nevertheless, awareness and concern about violence against women has increased as Chinese women's organisations were exposed to overseas non-governmental organisations' (NGO) tactics and practices (Keech-Marx, 2014).

The growth in activism by global women's rights activists, global conferences and global conventions helped to place domestic violence on the political agenda as a global epidemic that threatens both women and children (de Silva de Alwis, 2012: 184). At international levels, the issue of violence against women was given additional impetus by campaigns against gendered violence in war (Cockburn, 2012). Significant events, such as the Beijing Women's Conference in 1995, brought new attention to domestic violence and opened spaces of action, giving local campaigners access to new analyses and vocabulary

(Milwertz, 2003; de Silva de Alwis, 2012; Keech-Marx, 2014). In Asian Muslim societies, international feminist movements as well as local activists worked to raise awareness of domestic violence (Fulu and Miedema, 2015).

One of the key issues for feminist activism internationally has been to find ways to integrate the intersectionality of women's varied experiences of oppression and identity while opening up spaces for alliances and coalitions that would strengthen movements against gender injustice (Moghadam, 2005; Wendt and Zannettino, 2015). In London, groups working with South Asian women challenge 'the context and experience of abuse' and address intersections of poverty, race and gender to increase women's influence over their own lives and the specific experience of women of colour in the west (Sen, 1999). Self-described nomadic activist Lina Abirafeh (2009) points out that violence against women may also be compounded by problematic understandings of issues such as HIV/AIDS.

As we noted in Chapter One, international discourses on human rights and the elimination of violence against women have been important in feminist activism. Women's movements generally have made use of international human rights conventions as lawmaking tools in their efforts to change gender inequality. Such conventions have enabled successful challenges to the sexual politics of violence by defining domestic violence as a human rights violation, for example by many countries in Asia (de Silva de Alwis, 2012: 230). International women's rights activism has contributed to local movements around the world. The emergence of the international women's rights regime has had a tremendous impact on social movements locally. The inclusion of domestic violence directly into the United Nations agenda legitimised women's felt needs on the ground by informing local and grassroots movements (de Silva de Alwis, 2012: 183). This approach is not without its critics as we observed in Chapter Two. Some feminists (see for example, Ishkanian, 2014) argue that framing domestic violence as a human rights issue marginalises less radical agendas, a familiar dilemma for political activists around balancing strategies between compromise and effectiveness.

Varied tactics

Activism involves speaking out or raising awareness about gendered violence; informing and improving policy, legislation and services; joining action groups, protest and public media campaigns; and establishing and being involved in ventures to promote sexual equality in the community (Noble and Verity, 2006: 3). Individual acts of resistance to violence can be understood as valuable forms of activism. Although small acts may operate at different scales they 'cumulatively constitute a transformative politics of encounter' (Pain, 2014: 145). In our research, women described their own individual acts of resistance which served to build their confidence and courage. As Buchanan and Wendt (2017: 9) argue, the very act of participating in domestic violence research involves women wanting to speak out and raise awareness, to help other women, to be heard, to affirm their emotions and 'to feel part of a wider movement to address domestic violence'.

The tactics used by activists around the world have varied according to local conditions, cultures and political opportunity structures (Breitenbach and Thane, 2010a). In our study, women who had left a violent relationship became engaged in personal and public forms of activism, although it took some time. As one of the participants in our study said, "I'd say I'm a more active citizen than I used to be." The feminist repertoire of contention (Della Porta, 2013) or forms of activism against injustice has developed across the decades in the face of damaging changes to state policies and new mediums for action (Evans, 2011; Ryan et al., 2012). In the west, efforts in the 1970s and 1980s focused on service provision, welfare, housing and law reform (Weeks, 1994; Fraser, 2014). As we have noted, early political action in Australia focused on housing and income support (Jamieson, 2012) and the provision of counselling, information services and legal advice (Milwertz, 2003).

Criminalising violence

Efforts have shifted to gaining recognition of violence against women as crime and to criminal justice frames and methods for addressing violence against women, including IPV (Radford and Tsutsumi, 2004). Historically, criminalisation was advocated as a means of making private violence against women a crime, demanding equal response by the law to a stranger being assaulted in public. Domestic violence was made into a matter for the criminal justice system, whereupon the state, through law enforcement agencies, legislatures, the courts, and prisons, acted to punish men for violence against women and thus restored women to their full humanity (Weissman, 2007: 396). More recently, law reform and criminalisation strategies have been described as congruent with the neoliberal climate in which domestic violence was constructed as a crime 'perpetrated by deviant individuals that could only be controlled by prosecution and penalties' (Abraham and Tastsoglou, 2016a: 570) rather than a form of gender inequality produced by sexual politics.

The goal was that criminal prosecution would be triggered if domestic violence was recognised as a crime against women, and thus 'women could begin to dismantle male hierarchy and social subordination based on gender' (Weissman, 2007). However, criminalisation has proved to be a 'double edged sword' (Abraham and Tastsoglou, 2016a: 575). The sexual politics of legal reform has seen the criminal framing of domestic violence rely on 'racist, classist, and homophobic understandings of criminality and sexuality; and co-opt feminist rhetoric to advance antifeminist goals' (Corrigan, 2013: 490). It may also be submerged within the broad rhetoric of tough on crime campaigns promoted by many socially conservative advocates (Charles, 2010: 222).

Where laws have been introduced, implementation and enforcement have tended to be weak and inconsistently applied (Schneider, 2008; de Silva de Alwis, 2012; WHO, 2013). Some states actively resist and oppose claims for women's rights and domestic violence laws. For example, in Ghana, domestic violence continues to be trivialised and not seen as a serious crime in spite of new legislation (Manuh and Dwamena-Aboagye, 2013). Services are not adequately funded by the state while NGOs do not have the capacity to provide alternatives. In India, when implementation has been under-funded and resourced, NGOs have stepped in. Women's NGOs are recognised in legislation as official service providers of legal aid and casework (Roychowdhury, 2015). In addition, in other jurisdictions, law enforcement may discriminate among women according to their race and class (Cheers et al., 2006; Reina et al., 2014; Roychowdhury, 2015). In our study, women reported that the legal and court systems failed to acknowledge the effects of gender inequality. One woman for example, described how she felt "let down ... by the family court system, which seems more interested in its core philosophy and system needs than my son's wellbeing ... I am taking desperate action to protect children from family court idiocy!"

Domestic violence may be recognised as a crime, but legislation often constrains the work of NGOs within criminal justice framing, takes attention and funding from other aspects of the problem and undermines women's autonomy by framing them as 'victims' (Bailey, 2010). Where 'mandatory arrest' policies have been introduced, control is taken from victims, and women are at risk of prosecution and unwanted state interventions (Bumiller, 2013). However, legal protections do not necessarily produce victimhood, as women also engage tactically within available discourses (Roychowdhury, 2015).

In contrast, Weissman (2007: 402) believes that criminalisation 'has produced troubling results for individual victims, the communities in which they live, and the domestic violence movement generally'.

Our research with Australian women found that becoming involved in the criminal justice system can be frustrating and even traumatic:

> 'I would not put my life at risk by reporting my partner's actions to the police ... I have absolutely no confidence in the legal system's ability to protect people from domestic violence after it has been reported. In fact, it appears to only antagonise the offender and create increased danger for the victim.' (Daisy)

In the US, the sexual politics of criminal justice responses are complicated by the often dangerous politics of race where whole communities of colour are criminalised (Weissman, 2007). Indigenous communities such as those in Australia likewise are disadvantaged by politics of race. Incarceration rates of Indigenous men and women are far greater than non-Aboriginal Australians. Twenty-seven percent of Australia's prison population identifies as Aboriginal or Torres Strait Islander, yet they represent only 2% of the population (ABS, 2017a). Indigenous women are more likely to be killed by a partner or family member and are 21 times more likely to be imprisoned than non-Indigenous Australian women (Human Rights Law Centre 2017). The vast majority of all of the women incarcerated have experienced family and domestic violence and are unable to care for children and other family members while in prison. The shadow of the colonial past has considerable consequences for Aboriginal women whose lives are marred by violence and trauma. Some Aboriginal women can be highly reluctant to bring law enforcement into their lives as they may be incarcerated themselves for matters such as outstanding fines. If the perpetrator is taken into custody, the economic consequences may lead to retributive violence from their extended family (Cheers et al., 2006). The experiences of Australian Aboriginal and Torres Strait Islander women starkly demonstrate how intersecting forms of sexism, racism, colonialism and poverty align to compound their oppression and maintain the risk of being subjected to further violence.

Framing domestic violence through criminalisation 'has complex consequences for women's lives and, also, deflects attention from the social, economic, and political realities that contribute to abuse' (Abraham and Tastsoglou, 2016a: 569). Weissman (2007: 404) argues that the apparent 'convergence of interests between the domestic violence movement and the criminal justice system is illusory'. When legal reform is achieved, even with these limitations, feminist activism is necessary for the maintenance, implementation, resourcing and continuation of reforms (Htun and Weldon, 2012; Manuh and Dwamena-Aboagye, 2013). For example, in India, the average case takes 10 to 20 years to reach court (Roychowdhury, 2015: 799). Domestic violence survivors depend on women's organisations to navigate the legal system and achieve their claims.

Movement activism

In addition to pushing for legal reforms and establishing support services, feminist activists have undertaken and created campaigns designed to challenge the politics of ignorance that allow violence against women, and IPV in particular, to be denied as a significant and damaging issue to women as well as their children and their communities. For example, feminist groups make themselves visible by organising marches, such as the Chicago-based group Furie's march against rape culture, and the annual Reclaim the Night and Take Back the Night marches that occur all over the UK, Australia and the US (Evans, 2016). New groups and campaigns are:

> undertaking creative forms of protest to highlight the ways in which women's lives are put at risk by the cuts to domestic violence services (see for instance the occupation of a council flat in Hackney, London, to protest against cuts to women's refuges by Sisters Uncut. (Evans, 2016: 94)

NGOs have used 'edutainment' in India, Vietnam and South Africa, utilising theatre, documentaries and visual art (Pham, 2015). Among some of the most evocative media are songs that have become popular in their own right, as well as for their message, for example, iconic Australian Archie Roach's 'Walking into doors', still performed since its release in 1993, in addition to being used on TV and film soundtracks.

Feminist activists in trade unions have campaigned for unions to recognise women's specific issues and to advocate for gender equality (Colgan and Ledwith, 2002; Franzway and Fonow, 2011). The dilemma for this strategy involves persuading unions that domestic violence, particularly IPV, falls within their ambit of concern. As our research shows, women may be subject to IPV in the workplace itself, but perpetrators of violence may also be union members. 'Union officers are required to fulfil their responsibility and "duty of fair representation", whilst still considering safety issues, by referring both parties to appropriate services, advocating for the woman and letting the abuser know his violence is not acceptable' (Franzway et al., 2009: 31). Trade unions have developed policies around domestic violence aimed at protecting women members, educating delegates and officials, and working in partnership with feminist and anti-violence organisations such as White Ribbon (Urban and Wagner, 2000; Elger and Parker, 2007; True, 2012). Key ways to assist female employees include ensuring security, safety and protection at work; allowing flexible time and work arrangements; providing information about services and resources; and providing awareness training about domestic violence.

In Australia, trade unions have supported issues raised for 'women at work', but only a few have included domestic violence initiatives. For example, the Australian Service Union (ASU) supports the 'Say No to Violence against Women' initiatives, including White Ribbon Day, 16 days of Activism Against Gendered Violence, and Reclaim the Night marches, as well as offering information about 'Violence against women in Australia' on their website. A recent initiative has seen Australian unions include a clause allowing for family and domestic violence leave to be included in workplace agreements. By 2016, more than 1.6 million Australian workers had access to domestic violence leave through union-negotiated workplace agreements (Baird et al., 2014; Kaine, 2016).

Recent campaigns have used social media, including Twitter (Evans, M., 2011; Clark, 2016), Facebook and video creation and sharing (Mudavanhu and Radloff, 2013). Bräuer (2015) describes the use of performance art and social media to raise awareness of domestic violence in China. The Million Women Rise campaign in the UK has focused on cuts to domestic violence funding and shelters facing closure (Evans, M., 2011). The groups Everyday Sexism and Hollaback! record sexist harassment and assault across the US and UK, and The Counting Dead Women campaign in the UK raises awareness of women killed by male violence (Evans, E., 2016). The Facebook page 'Destroy the Joint' publishes its count of every known death due to violence against women in Australia. It was founded in 2012 in response to the conservative claim that 'women are destroying the joint' during the term of the first woman Prime Minister of Australia, Julia Gillard.

A public health issue?

We have discussed the main strategies employed to campaign against domestic violence, but the focus of the struggle to eliminate violence against women never stands still. We now move to reflect on the recent links between domestic violence as a human rights issue and a public health concern. We have noted that the criminalisation strategy has helped to reframe violence against women as a serious problem for the whole of society, but it has largely failed to make everyday life safer for those women who find themselves with a violent partner (Abraham and Tastsoglou, 2016a, 2016b). The argument that freedom from violence is an international human right and one that should be upheld by states has no doubt made some inroads into state policies and programmes. Without that endorsement, women are unable to exercise their full rights as citizens.

In the struggles around the sexual politics of violence against women, what are the consequences of identifying IPV as a matter of public health? In 2013, the World Health Organization (WHO) reported on the first global systematic review of scientific data on the prevalence of two forms of violence against women: violence by an intimate partner (IPV), and sexual violence by someone other than a partner (non-partner sexual violence) (WHO, 2013). The definition of IPV endorsed by the WHO is behaviour within an intimate relationship that causes physical, sexual or psychological harm, including acts of physical aggression, sexual coercion, psychological abuse and controlling behaviour. Public health is not about individuals, but emphasises interdisciplinary and collective action (Dahlberg and Krug, 2002). In this it serves as a counterweight to the explicit medicalisation of problems, as we discuss in Chapter Five.

The public health approach sees IPV as preventable, and that it has an important, even unique, role in addressing it. Niolon et al (2017: 43) argue that 'public health agencies, which typically place prevention at the forefront of efforts and work to create broad population-level impact, can bring critical leadership and resources to bear on this problem'. The public health approach has contributed to the development of creative projects aimed at prevention as well as protection. For example, in Uganda, Nambusi Kyegombe and her team (2014) framed their investigation of community-based violence prevention interventions in terms of human rights and public health. They saw that IPV in low-income settings is a serious public health concern owing to its effect on women's physical, mental and emotional health and its association with increased HIV risk.

In Australia the public health approach to preventing violence against women has been largely led by VicHealth, a state-wide health promotion agency in Victoria with responsibility for health promotion and prevention (see for example, VicHealth, 2017). VicHealth led a substantive programme on preventing violence against women in Australia, including research examining the morbidity and mortality effects from violence against women and a large-scale attitude survey, with all of its work underpinned by a detailed prevention framework based on an ecological understanding of violence against women. The significance of this framework was that it located the continuation of violence against women within the sexual politics of gender inequality and paid attention on income inequalities and child-care responsibilities as well community and individual understandings and attitudes. This public health prevention model required all social institutions, including agencies of the state (such as education, health, police), as well as employers and workplaces, and sporting and social clubs to play a role in eliminating sexism and ending violence against women.

The public health approach adopted by VicHealth and other organisations has much potential to alleviate the direct and indirect damage caused by violence against women. It has won acceptance, and resources from significant international agencies, which has some impact on state policies and practices; the recognition of gender inequality as implicated in the causes and persistence of IPV can rebut the politics of ignorance in relation to violence. However, we signal caution when the problem of gender is rendered as 'harmful gender norms', meaning 'harmful beliefs and expectations about the roles and behaviour of men and women' (Niolon et al., 2017: 9). This concept relies on the equivocal notions of role and a limited binary of gender. As we have argued in earlier chapters, gender norms and roles fail to recognise the fluidity of gender and its contested nature. The definition of 'harmful' in this case appears to be taken for granted, which also warrants challenge when the intention of this approach is to offer remedies and solutions across the diversity of cultures and communities. What is regarded as harmful in one social setting may not be in another.

Why feminist activism continues

Persistent, creative feminist activism has doubtless challenged the sexual politics of violence against women with some success both materially and discursively. Women's citizenship rights have been strengthened allowing the development of the necessary combined capabilities to achieve decent lives. However, the rate of violence perpetrated against women continues to be substantial. As we noted earlier, the WHO (2013: 2) records that 'overall, 35% of women worldwide have experienced either physical and/or sexual IPV or non-partner sexual violence'. In some states, increased awareness of the problem of violence has not reduced the stigma against it or increased support for the victims of IPV. According to Nichols (2011), current workers in the field can be unaware of feminist histories of activism, and continue to regard domestic violence as a problem for the individual. In spite of the expansion of policies and services, much remains to be done to enhance their effectiveness. Australian women reported to us that they could not be confident about their safety if they attempted to utilise services:

> 'Some states have extremely temporary measures to protect people from violence. But then what? There will never be honest reporting of domestic violence until victims can be reasonably assured of their safety once they have reported it to authorities.' (Luciana)

Other state and community institutions and agencies, such as schools and churches, were also felt to be unreliable as sources of support or protection.

Feminists have worked to raise the expectation that freedom from violence is a right of all genders, adult or child, whether citizen or not. However, the dynamics of sexual politics continues to see attempts to reclaim and retain men's dominance. For example, the changes arising from the unpredictable processes of globalisation have created new opportunities or conditions that are oppressive to women. Sex tourism has expanded to become a large global business, which produces safer profits than drugs (Radford and Tsutsumi, 2004). Women and children are abused with little risk to the perpetrators. The global sex trade continues to grow, increasing the scope for violent men to evade risks associated with crime control policies on violence against women at home by enabling them to entice, entrap or force women on the 'periphery' into abuse and exploitation (Radford and Tsutsumi, 2004: 5; see also Suchland, 2015). Sex trafficking has become equally unbounded, particularly over the last two decades of destructive wars and terrorism.

Globalisation also opens up new opportunities to campaign as women achieve combined capabilities that enhance their social political and civil rights. As women gain better conditions in education, employment and legal status, they are able to participate in political activism (True, 2012; Fulu and Miedema, 2015). However, the current policies, resources and practices dedicated to reducing if not eliminating violence against women continue to demand that persistent effort on the part of activists be maintained.

On the face of it, violence in the form of familial, domestic and IPV should obviously be thoroughly rejected in any community that values human rights. However, violence against women remains a deeply controversial issue that incites strong and contradictory responses. Dahlberg and Krug argue that 'violence is an extremely emotional issue and many countries tend to be reluctant to take initiatives challenging long-established attitudes or practices. It can take considerable political courage to try new approaches in areas such as policing and public security' (2002: 19). But is it the violence which is at issue? Or is it the sexual politics in which male dominance seeks to maintain its power and control?

We are not the first to observe that contemporary responses to acts of violence continue to be highly selective, with men-on-men assaults for example causing enormous outrage. In Australia, the so-called 'king hit' when one man is struck powerfully by another without any warning is now dubbed the 'coward's punch'. Yet every week, individual women are killed by their intimate partners who are often described as 'quiet, good blokes'. We ask what has changed since the woman who wrote to Del Martin more than 40 years ago said: 'Everyone I have gone to for help has somehow wanted to blame me and vindicate my husband ….' (1981: 3).

And yet, as we show in this chapter, much has been gained by feminists in mitigating the damage to women and their rights. The first United Nations special rapporteur on violence against women, Radhika Coomaraswamy, argues that the violence against women movement is 'perhaps the greatest success story of international mobilization around a specific human rights issue leading to the articulation of international norms and standards and the formulation of international programmes and policies' (de Silva de Alwis, 2012: 186). As our research together with that of many scholars has shown, the changes in attitude, public policies and discourse have been the direct result of pressure by feminist activism and women's movements (Schechter, 1982; Franzway et al., 2009; Ball and Charles, 2006; Schneider, 2008; True, 2012; Kelly, 2013; Roychowdhury, 2015; Wendt and Zannettino, 2015).

In addition to achieving legislative change, activists have had direct impact on the outcomes for survivors through service delivery and refuges. Refuges succeeded in 'establishing themselves as "experts" on domestic violence and in attracting more substantial amounts of money' (Charles, 2010: 212). The refuge movement has engaged in cultural change and policy-focused action combining service delivery and strategising for social change. Feminist civil society mobilisation was the most important factor in establishing government action on violence against women in the 70 countries studied by Htun and Weldon (2012; Weldon and Htun, 2013). They found that autonomous feminist mobilisation – not 'intra-legislative political phenomena such as leftist parties or women in government or economic factors' (2012: 548) – accounts for the differences in policy among the range of countries.

EIGHT

Transforming sexual politics

I write for those women who do not speak, for those who do not have a voice because they/we were so terrified, because we are taught to respect fear more than ourselves. We've been taught that silence would save us, but it won't. Audre Lorde (cited in Hall, 2004: 90)

The social invisibility of women's experience is not 'a failure of human communication'. It is a socially arranged bias persisted in long after the information about women's experience is available. Joanna Russ (1983: 48)

Feminist research into gendered violence has provided many women around the world with the opportunity to share their experiences and contribute to increased understanding of its nature and impact. Drawing on the responses and narratives of the women who participated in our study, we have been able to show how intimate partner violence (IPV) casts a long shadow over women's lives in complex and interconnected ways that have not been widely appreciated until now. What is particularly distinctive about the approach we have taken is the adoption of sexual politics as our lens and citizenship as our primary concern. This has enabled us to show that gender inequalities not only produce and sustain IPV itself, but that they also shape the very nature, direction and intensity of its impact on women and their capabilities to exercise full citizenship into the long term. We have shown that women do not recover former levels of mental health, housing, work or social participation after IPV, reducing their capacities to exercise full citizenship. A sexual politics of ignorance about gendered violence and its basis in gender inequality exacerbates this impact further because it silences women about the impact of IPV and deprives many of the formal and informal support that is so crucial to the successful rebuilding of lives.

As we have argued, there has been a tendency in research, policy and practice to focus on the immediate effects of individual incidents of men's physical violence. Expanding our perspective on IPV to include coercive control, and taking a sociological approach through the foundational concepts of sexual politics and citizenship, has enabled us to take theorisation of the impact of IPV beyond a one-dimensional, linear conceptualisation of the 'effects' of individual men's violence on individual women. Our intention has been to produce a more dynamic account of how IPV limits women's capacities for citizenship across the interconnected domains of work, housing, mental health and social participation. Drawing on analysis and argument in previous chapters, we propose that IPV can be understood as an assault on citizenship, driving at the very heart of women's full participation in society and exacerbating the gender inequalities which make violence against women possible in the first place. Bringing citizenship into the picture turns attention to questions of fundamental human rights and state responsibilities, as well as questions about citizens' responsibilities towards each other. We took as our jumping-off point a concern that despite some 40 years of feminist activism, research, policy development and on-the-ground support work marked by many important achievements, gendered violence has not reduced in any country in the world and community denial remains widespread. What our analysis has shown at the most fundamental level is that inadequate responses from the state as the guardian of citizenship is central to both the persistence of IPV itself, but also to its long-term and often devastating impact.

This cannot and should not be the end of the story. As we have noted at different points in the book, one of the main barriers to the full acknowledgement of gendered violence and the taking of effective steps to eradicate it and support women is the widespread misconception, at least in western societies, that gender equality has been won. This means that women are often taken to be the equals of men in terms of rights, power and influence *in reality*, not just in principle. As a corollary, women are then held equally responsible for so-called 'relationship problems' that so often include violence. In too many countries, women continue to battle for basic acknowledgement of their rights, but they also confront outright denial of the reality of gendered violence and its relationship to gender inequality. We have drawn on Tuana's (2006) concept of the politics of ignorance and women's epistemic disadvantage to help explain this widespread refusal to believe and accept the reality of gendered violence and its fundamental basis in continuing gender inequality. We found that IPV has social, material and economic costs to women and children, and therefore the wider community. It invades and erodes key domains of life over time such as housing, employment, mental health and social participation. IPV damages women's capabilities to be employed, to enjoy good mental health and to have access to quality safe housing; furthermore, it limits the fundamental freedom and opportunity to engage and participate in society as full and equal citizens. However, there are also more dangerous forces at work in the denial of gendered violence than overcommitment in some countries to the idea that women's equality has been achieved.

As we note throughout the book, and particularly in Chapter Six, denial of gendered violence often morphs into a sexual politics based on victim-blaming where women are held primarily responsible for violence not only by violent men themselves but also by friends, family and the wider community. Following Tuana (2006), we have argued that the sexual politics of ignorance and blame surrounding IPV is symptomatic of women's epistemic disadvantage, where men are constructed as credible knowers while women are frequently discredited. We have argued that knowledge practices imbued with prejudices about women's characters, bodies, intellectual capacities and natures result in epistemic disadvantage for all women (Mills et al., 2013; Tuana, 2006), with IPV exploiting and exacerbating this disadvantage. In particular, we show in Chapter Five how the reduction of women to sexualised objects and the domestic servicers of men is pivotal to the perpetration of coercive control in IPV, as is the deployment of discourses about women as mad, stupid, inferior and as sexually untrustworthy. We have also shown how these long-standing gender discourses enable violent, controlling men to position women as abject possessions in their efforts to galvanise vulnerable masculine identities in the patriarchal gender order.

Violent men enact these subjugating discourses about women in extreme ways, but similar notions and sensibilities continue to inhere across almost all societies and cultures even if they are no longer laid out in explicit terms. To borrow Stark's (2007) terminology, negative and oppressive gender discourses and practices effectively 'hide in plain sight' in many communities because discourses about gender equality are more socially acceptable. Nonetheless, these disparaging ideas do sometimes emerge into public view. As the accounts of women in our study testify, some of the most illustrative examples are when women come forward to disclose domestic violence, as well as rape or sexual abuse. The laying of blame at the feet of women (and girls), and a refusal to acknowledge and accept the reality of gendered violence and its basis in gender inequality remains almost as common as it ever was, even if it is sometimes more subtle than in the past (Gavey, 2005). Long-standing ideas about women as untrustworthy (especially sexually), irrational and overly emotional, as less competent than men and as primarily responsible for relationships, families and the domestic realm underpin denial and victim–blaming in IPV, just as they enable IPV itself. Such discourses and practices are borne of historical and continuing male privilege and persistent gender inequality; they also run entirely counter to the idea that women are equal to men and enjoy equal rights as citizens, either in principle or in practice. In many ways, then, IPV persists and continues to have a devastating impact on women because in most countries there remains a deep ambivalence and fear about women and female autonomy. As we have shown, this fear is embedded in historical gender discourses and practices that are hinged on hierarchical binaries of (superior) masculinity and (inferior) femininity which, in turn, are intertwined with structural gender inequalities as well as other social inequalities.

While we recognise the durability of a gender order based on unearned male privilege and gender inequality, we also recognise that this is not fixed or inviolable. As we argued in Chapter Two, sexual politics acknowledges that gender relations are continually contested and that gender relations are therefore dynamic and open to change, including transformative challenges to women's disadvantage (Franzway, 2016). And as we went on to argue in Chapter Seven, women's rights to exercise all the capabilities necessary to live good lives and fully exercise citizenship are not easily won. These rights have to be constantly defended against the gender inequalities produced by male-dominated sexual politics. The efforts from women's rights activists around the world to achieve a condemnation of gendered violence have been considerable and intense, but pushback from male-dominated sexual politics is constant, and perhaps never more so as when so-called 'strong men' take power across the world, bringing with them a disdain for women and for women's rights that emboldens others to indulge in the same.

There have been achievements in many countries in terms of housing, law reform, policy development and the provision of support services for women leaving IPV. In Australia, some of the most important developments over the past decade include establishment of a national plan to eliminate violence against women and their children (COAG, 2010), and the development under this plan of national standards for working with men who use violence in intimate partner relationships (COAG, 2015). A national organisation for research into domestic, family and sexual violence – Australia's National Research Organisation for Women's Safety – has also been created with bi-partisan and state support. At the coalface, there is now provision for intervention orders to be recognised across state borders (ABC, 2017). In some parts of the

UK, there is now recognition of coercive control as a crime (Home Office, 2015), with debate about the need for this change building in Australia, the US and Ireland.

While these developments are important and could go some way towards improving the safety of women and their children, not all state responses are sufficiently informed about the nature of the gender inequalities that enable violence, nor of the specific impact of IPV. As shown in Chapter Five, state-supported responses to poor mental health as a result of IPV are typically psycho-medical in nature, diagnosing and pathologising women rather than their male abusers with little awareness of the gender discourses and practices deployed in IPV and coercive control, and how they affect sense of self. Other state responses are more accurately described as hostile to the welfare of women seeking to leave violent relationships. For example, an anti-welfare neoliberal ideology and so-called market-based responses to domestic violence in the US have led to reduced and punitive welfare assistance for women attempting to re-establish their lives (Weissman, 2016). Reductions in funding to women's domestic violence services have also occurred in both Australia (ABC, 2016) and the UK (Buchan, 2017) at a time when political rhetoric about the need to respond to domestic violence has been high.

Our research points to many areas where state responses to IPV must improve in order to build women's capabilities to exercise full citizenship. These include but are not restricted to: the provision of well-funded and resourced crisis shelters for women and children fleeing domestic violence, staffed with appropriately trained workers; early intervention, prevention and education campaigns about domestic violence in the community; increased behaviour change programmes for men; 'whole of government' responses to IPV; culturally appropriate support programmes for women experiencing family violence in Indigenous and ethnic communities; higher levels of income support for women leaving IPV; family court and criminal justice processes that recognise the priority of safety for women and children; the provision of long-term, affordable and appropriate housing near informal and formal supports; the provision of counselling and support for women and children by practitioners who are knowledgeable about gendered violence and its impact; and peer support groups for women who have experienced IPV. However, to significantly reduce IPV and its impact on women's citizenship it is imperative to look beyond crisis-specific and IPV-specific interventions to the wider context of gender inequality that frames and enables violence against women. This will require substantial state intervention in diverse areas ranging from improved access to low-cost child-care for all women to enable opportunities for paid work, and further and higher education; increased representation of women, including women from diverse backgrounds, in all public arenas; the achievement of equal pay for all women across all sections of the labour market; the systematic challenging of gender discrimination in all its forms from cradle to grave; and the challenging of binary and essentialist discourses about gender and the inferiority of women wherever they appear.

As we have argued, male-dominated sexual politics continues to locate IPV as an issue of the private sphere while, at the same time, claiming that gender equality has been won anyway and is therefore irrelevant. Feminists in turn continue to complicate traditional notions of state responsibility and citizenship by calling on the state to take action in the 'private' realm (Flax, 1990; Walby, 1990), based on the understanding that gender inequality is fundamental to gendered violence. Importantly, women who have experienced IPV not uncommonly become involved in feminist sexual politics on gendered violence themselves, exercising their rights as citizens on the back of their lived experience of silencing, marginalisation and the denial of citizenship rights. We add to these demands by pointing out that IPV casts a very long shadow over women's lives that no governments have sought to address in any systematic way. Our and others' feminist demands clearly speak to the need for substantial change to prevailing male-dominated sexual politics. As we and other researchers have shown, questions about how gender inequalities enable and maintain IPV and coercive control continue to be largely side-stepped. As a result, IPV has not reduced and many women continue to live constrained lives focused on day-to-day survival, deprived of the necessary capabilities to flourish and participate as active citizens. Women also continue to die in large numbers every day around the world at the hands of men whose abusive controlling behavior remains invisible when the disadvantage caused by gender inequality is denied. This book and the research on which it is based is part of a wider practice of feminist sexual politics which we hope will contribute to further activism and change into the future, until such time that women and girls are able to enjoy freedom from violence and full citizenship.

References

ABC (Australian Broadcasting Commission) (2016) Funding cuts impact migrant women. www.abc.net.au/news/2016-07-08/funding-cuts-impact-migrant-women-suffering-domestic-violence/7578968

ABC (2017) *Domestic Violence Order Scheme comes in to effect providing nationwide protections.* www.abc.net.au/news/2017-11-25/national-domestic-violence-order-scheme-comes-in-to-effect/9189800

Abirafeh L. (2009) Activism to counter gender-based violence and HIV and aids: overcoming obstacles to movement building in Papua New Guinea. *Development* 52(2): 233-8

Abraham H. (2010) *Rebuilding lives after domestic violence: Understanding long-term outcomes.* London: Jessica Kingsley

Abraham M. and Tastsoglou E. (2016a) Addressing domestic violence in Canada and the United States: the uneasy co-habitation of women and the state. *Current Sociology* 64(4): 568-85

Abraham M. and Tastsoglou E. (2016b) Interrogating gender, violence, and the state in national and transnational contexts: framing the issues. *Current Sociology Monograph* 64(4): 517-34

ABS (Australian Bureau of Statistics) (2006) Trends in Women's Employment. Cat. No. 4102.0. Canberra: Commonwealth of Australia

ABS (2007) National Survey of Mental Health and Wellbeing. Cat. No. 4326.0. Canberra: Commonwealth of Australia

ABS (2013a) Wage and Salary Earner Statistics for Small Areas. Cat. No. 5673.0.55.003. Canberra: Commonwealth of Australia

ABS (2013b) Gender Indicators. Housing Circumstances. Cat. No. 4125.0. Canberra: Commonwealth of Australia

ABS (2014a) Employee Earnings and Hours. Cat. No. 6306.0. Canberra: Commonwealth of Australia

ABS (2014b) Average Weekly Earnings. Cat. No. 6302.0. Canberra: Commonwealth of Australia

ABS (2014c) Gender Indicators, Australia. Cat. No. 4125.0. Canberra: Commonwealth of Australia

ABS (2014d) General Social Survey. Cat. No. 4159.0. Canberra: Commonwealth of Australia

ABS (2015a) Participation in Sport and Physical Recreation, Australia. 2013-14. Cat. No. 4177.0. Canberra: Commonwealth of Australia

ABS (2015b) General Social Survey: Summary Results, Australia, 2014. Cat. No. 4159.0. Canberra: Commonwealth of Australia

ABS (2016a) Census of Population and Housing: Australia Revealed. Cat. No. 2024.0. Canberra: Commonwealth of Australia

ABS (2016b) Cultural Diversity in Australia – Reflecting Australia: Stories from the Census. Cat. No. 2071.0. Canberra: Commonwealth of Australia

ABS (2016c) Gender Indicators, Australia. Cat. No. 4125.0. Canberra: Commonwealth of Australia

ABS (2017a) Census of Population and Housing: Australia Revealed 2016. Cat. No. 2024.0. Canberra: Commonwealth of Australia

ABS (2017b) Prisoners in Australia, 2017. Cat. No. 4517.0. Canberra: Commonwealth of Australia

Acker J. (2006) Inequality regimes: gender, class, and race in organizations. *Gender & Society* 20(4): 441-64

AIHW (Australian Institute of Health and Welfare) (2014) *Child protection Australia 2012–13*. www.aihw.gov.au/

Ailwood S., Easteal P. and Kennedy J. (2012) Law's indifference to women's experience of violence: colonial and contemporary Australia. *Women's Studies International Forum* 35(2): 86-96

Akyüz A., Yavan T., Şahiner G., et al. (2012) Domestic violence and woman's reproductive health: a review of the literature. *Aggression and Violent Behavior* 17: 514-18

Alexander J. (2014) Social justice and Nussbaum's concept of the person. In: Comim F. and Nussbaum M. (eds) *Capabilities, gender, equality*. Cambridge: Cambridge University Press

Alhabib S., Nur U. and Jones R. (2010) Domestic violence against women: systematic review of prevalence studies. *Journal of Family Violence* 25: 369-82

Al-Sharmani M. (2013) *Feminist activism, women's rights, and legal reform*. London: Zed

Altman D. (2013) *The end of the homosexual*. St Lucia, Queensland: University of Queensland Press

Anderson K.L. (2009) Gendering coercive control. *Violence Against Women* 15(12): 1444-57

Anthias F. (2013) The intersections of class, gender, sexuality and 'race': the political economy of gendered violence. Special issue on 'Gender, Sexuality and Political Economy', *International Journal of Politics, Culture and Society* 27: 153-71

APA (American Psychiatric Association) (2013) *Diagnostic and Statistical Manual of Mental Disorders – DSM-5*. Arlington: APA

Australian Health Ministers Conference (2009) National Mental Health Policy. Canberra: Commonwealth of Australia

Bacchi C.L. and Beasley C. (2002) Citizen bodies: is embodied citizenship a contradiction in terms? *Critical Social Policy* 22(2): 324–52

Bailey K.D. (2010) Lost in translation: domestic violence, 'the personal is political', and the criminal justice system. *The Journal of Criminal Law and Criminology* 100(4): 1255–300

Baird K. and Kracen A.C. (2006) Vicarious traumatization and secondary traumatic stress: a research synthesis. *Counselling Psychology Quarterly* 19(2): 181–8

Baird M., McFerran L. and Wright I. (2014) An equality bargaining breakthrough: paid domestic violence leave. *Journal of Industrial Relations* 56(2): 190–207

Baird S. and Jenkins S.R. (2003) Vicarious traumatization, secondary traumatic stress, and burnout in sexual assault and domestic violence agency staff, *Violence and Victims* 18(1): 71–86

Baker C.K., Billhardt K., Warren J., et al. (2010) Domestic violence, housing instability, and homelessness: a review of housing policies and program practices for meeting the needs of survivors. *Aggression and Violent Behavior* 15(6): 430–9

Baker C.K., Cook S.L. and Norris F.H. (2003) Domestic violence and housing problems: a contextual analysis of women's help-seeking, received informal support, and formal system response. *Violence Against Women* 9(7): 754–83

Baker E. and Tually S. (2008) Women, health and housing assistance: implications in an emerging era of housing provision. *Australian Journal of Social Issues* 43(1): 123–38

Ball W. and Charles N. (2006) Feminist social movements and policy change: devolution, childcare and domestic violence policies in Wales. *Women's Studies International Forum* 29(2): 172–83

Barrett M. and McIntosh M. (1982) *The anti-social family*. London: Verso

Batliwala S. (2013) *Engaging with empowerment: An intellectual and experiential journey*. New Delhi: Women Unlimited

Bauman Z. (2005) Freedom from, in and through the state: T.H. Marshall's trinity of rights revisited. *Theoria: A Journal of Social & Political Theory* 52(108): 13–27

Beasley C. and Bacchi C. (2000) Citizen bodies: embodying citizens – a feminist analysis. *International Feminist Journal of Politics* 2(3): 337–58

Beaumont J. (2013) *Broken nation: Australians in the Great War*. Sydney: Allen & Unwin

Benhabib S. and Cornell D. (1987) Beyond the politics of gender. In: Benhabib S. and Cornell D. (eds) *Feminism as critique: Essays on the politics of gender in late capitalist societies*. Cambridge: Blackwell

Boje T.P. (2009) Organized civil society, volunteering and citizenship. In: Enjolras, B. and Sivesind K.H. (eds) *Civil society in comparative perspective* (*Comparative Social Research*, vol 26). Bingley: Emerald Group Publishing, 243-62

Bordo S. (1989) The body and the reproduction of femininity: a feminist appropriation of Foucault. In: Jaggar A. and Bordo S. (eds) *Gender/body/knowledge: Feminist reconstructions of being and knowing.* New Brunswick, NJ: Rutgers University Press, 13-34

Bordo S. (1990) Reading the slender body. In: Jacobus M., Keller E.F. and Shuttleworth S. (eds) *Body/politics: Women and the discourses of science.* New York: Routledge, 83-112

Bradley H. (2013) *Gender.* Cambridge: Polity

Bräuer S. (2015) Becoming public: tactical innovation in the Beijing anti-domestic violence movement. *VOLUNTAS: International Journal of Voluntary and Nonprofit Organizations* 27(5): 2106-30

Breckenridge J. (1999) Subjugation and silences: the role of the professions in silencing victims of sexual and domestic violence. *Challenging silences: Innovative responses to sexual and domestic violence* 6-30

Breitenbach E. (2010) Scottish women's organizations and the exercise of citizenship c. 1900–c.1970. In: Breitenbach E. and Thane P. (eds) *Women and citizenship in Britain and Ireland in the 20th century: What difference did the vote make?* London: Continuum, 63-78

Bride B.E., Radey M. and Figley C.R. (2007) Measuring compassion fatigue. *Clinical Social Work Journal* 35: 155-63

Briere J. (2002) Treating adult survivors of severe childhood abuse and neglect: further development of an integrative model. In: Myers J.E.B., Berliner L., Briere J., et al. (eds) *The APSAC handbook on child maltreatment.* Thousand Oaks: SAGE Publications

Briere J. and Lanktree C. (2012) *Treating complex trauma in adolescents and young adults*, London: SAGE Publications

Broverman I.K., Vogel S.R., Broverman D.M., et al. (1972) Sex-role stereotypes: a critical appraisal. *Journal of Social Issues* 28: 59-78

Browne K., Lim J. and Brown G. (2007) *Geographies of sexualities: Theory practices and politics.* Brookfield, VT: Ashgate

Brush L. (2003) Effects of work on hitting and hurting. *Violence Against Women* 9: 1213-30

Buchan L. (2017) Women's refuge budget cuts. *The Independent*, 17 October. www.independent.co.uk/news/uk/politics/women-refuge-budget-cut-quarter-domestic-violence-victims-children-support-a8003066.html

Buchanan F. and Wendt S. (2017) Opening doors: women's participation in feminist studies about domestic violence. *Qualitative Social Work* 1-16

Buchanan F., Wendt S. and Moulding N. (2015) Growing up in domestic violence: what does maternal protectiveness mean? *Qualitative Social Work* 14(3): 399-415

Budden A. (2010) Moral worlds and therapeutic quests: a study of medical pluralism and treatment-seeking in the lower Amazon. UC San Diego (Dissertation)

Bumiller K. (2010) The nexus of domestic violence reform and social science: from instrument of social change to institutionalized surveillance. *Annual Review of Law and Social Science* 6(1): 173-93

Bumiller K. (2013) Feminist collaboration with the state in response to sexual violence: lessons from the American experience. In: Tripp A.M., Feree M.M. and Ewig C. (eds) *Gender, violence, and human security.* New York: NYU Press, 191-213

Bussemaker J. and Voet R. (1998) Citizenship and gender: theoretical approaches and historical legacies. *Critical Social Policy* 18(56): 277-307

Cantón-Cörtes D. and Cantón J. (2010) Coping with child sexual abuse among college students and post-traumatic stress disorder: the role of continuity of abuse and relationship with the perpetrator, *Child Abuse & Neglect* 34(7): 496-506

Chappell D. and Di Martino V. (2006) *Violence at work.* Geneva: International Labour Office

Charles N. (2010) The refuge movement and domestic violence policies in Wales. In: Breitenbach E. and Thane P. (eds) *Women and citizenship in Britain and Ireland in the 20th century: What difference did the vote make?* London, UK: Continuum, 209-24

Charlesworth S. and Macdonald F. (2015) Women, work and industrial relations in Australia in 2014. *Journal of Industrial Relations* 57(3): 366-82

Cheers B., Binell M., Coleman H., et al. (2006) Family violence: an Australian Indigenous community tells its story. *International Social Work* 49(1): 51-63

Childe G. (1954) *What happened in history.* Harmondsworth, Middlesex: Penguin Books

Chung D. (2015) Domestic violence: UK and Australian developments. In: Evans T. and Keating F. (eds) *Policy and social work practice.* London: SAGE Publications, 137-50

Chung D.R., Kennedy R.J., O'Brien B.A., et al. (2000) *Home safe home: The link between domestic and family violence and women's homelessness.* Canberra: Commonwealth of Australia.https://wesnet.org.au/wp-content/uploads/2011/05/homesafehome.pdf

Clark C.J., Lewis-Dmello A., Anders D., et al. (2014) Trauma-sensitive yoga as an adjunct mental health treatment in group therapy for survivors of domestic violence: a feasibility study. *Complementary therapies in clinical practice* 20(3): 152-8

Clark R. (2016) 'Hope in a hashtag': the discursive activism of #WhyIStayed. *Feminist Media Studies* 16(5): 788-804

Classen C.C., Palesh O.G. and Aggarwal R. (2005) Sexual revictimization: a review of the empirical literature. *Trauma, Violence, & Abuse* 6(2): 103-29

Clough A., Draughon J.E., Njie-Carr V., et al. (2014) 'Having housing made everything else possible': affordable, safe and stable housing for women survivors of violence. *Qualitative Social Work* 13(5): 671-88

COAG (Council of Australian Governments) (2010) *National plan to reduce violence against women and their children 2010–2022.* CanberraCOAG

Cockburn C. (2012) *Antimilitarism: Political and gender dynamics of peace movements.* Basingstoke: Palgrave Macmillan

Coles J., Astbury J., Dartnall E., et al. (2014) A qualitative exploration of researcher trauma and researchers' responses to investigating sexual violence. *Violence Against Women* 20(1): 95-117

Colgan F. and Ledwith S. (2002) *Gender, diversity and trade unions: International perspectives.* London: Routledge

Collins, P.H. (1990) *Black feminist thought: Knowledge, consciousness and the politics of empowerment.* London/New York: Routledge

Connell R. (1987) *Gender and power: Society, the person and sexual politics.* Sydney: Allen & Unwin

Connell R. (1995) *Masculinities.* Sydney: Allen & Unwin

Corrigan R. (2013) Building theory and making change: the challenges of studying feminist activism. *Politics & Gender* 9(04): 489-93

Cox P. (2015) *Violence against women in Australia: Additional analysis of the Australian Bureau of Statistics' Personal Safety Survey, 2012: Key findings and future directions.* Compass Report, Australian National Research Organisation for Women Safety (ANROWS), NSW.

Crenshaw, K. (1994) Mapping the margins: intersectionality, identity politics and violence against women of color. *Stanford Law Review* 43: 1241-99

Dahlberg L. and Krug E. (2002) Violence – a global public health problem. In: Krug E., Dahlberg L., Mercy J., et al. (eds) *World report on violence and health*. Geneva: WHO

DAIP (Domestic Abuse Intervention Programs) (2008) The Duluth Model. Understanding the Power and Control Wheel. www.theduluthmodel.org/wheels/

Davidson J. (2000) '...the world was getting smaller': women, agoraphobia and bodily boundaries. *Area* 32(1): 31-40

Davies B. (1991) The concept of agency: a feminist poststructuralist analysis. *Social Analysis: The International Journal of Social and Cultural Practice* 30: 42-53

de Beauvoir S. (1949) *The second sex*, London: Jonathon Cape

de Silva de Alwis R. (2012) Domestic violence lawmaking in Asia: some innovative trends in feminist lawmaking. *Pacific Basin Law Journal* 29(2): 176-233

DeKeseredy W. (2011) Feminist contributions to understanding woman abuse: myths, controversies and realities. *Aggression and Violent Behavior* 16: 297-302

Della Porta D. (2013) Repertoires of contention. *The Wiley-Blackwell Encyclopedia of social and political movements*. Wiley-Blackwell

Department of Social Services (2016) *Third Action Plan 2016-2019 of the National Plan to Reduce Violence against Women and their Children*. Canberra: Commonwealth of Australia. www.dss.gov.au/sites/default/files/documents/10_2016/third_action_plan.pdf Canberra: Commonwealth of Australia

Devaney J. (2008) Chronic child abuse and domestic violence: children and families with long-term and complex needs. *Child & Family Social Work* 13(4): 443-53

Dobash R. and Dobash R. (1980) *Violence against wives: A case against the patriarchy*. London: Open Books

Dobash R. and Dobash R. (1992) *Women, violence and social change*. London: Routledge

Drigo M., Ehlschlaeger C.R. and Sweet E.L. (2012) *Modelling intimate partner violence and support systems*, Boston, MA: Springer US

Ehrenreich B. and English D. (1978) *For her own good*, New York: Anchor Books

Ehrenreich B. and Hochschild A.R. (2002) *Global woman: Nannies, maids, and sex workers in the new economy*. New York: Metropolitan Books/Henry Holt

Elger T. and Parker A. (2007) Widening union agendas? The case of British union policies to combat domestic violence. Paper presented at the Work, Employment and Society Conference, University of Warwick, 12-24 September

Elizabeth V., Gavey N. and Tolmie J. (2012) '. . . He's just swapped his fists for the system': the governance of gender through custody law. *Gender & Society* 26(2): 239-60

Evans E. (2016) Feminist resistance. *Renewal* 24(3): 9-95

Evans M. (2011) 'Social kettling' and the closure of domestic violence shelters are amongst the new challenges for feminists in 2011: they are responding with a new activism, using social media and collective action. *British Politics and Policy at LSE* (19 Jan) Blog entry

Eveline J. (1998) Heavy, dirty and limp stories. In: Gatens M. and Mackinnon A. (eds) *Gender and institutions: Welfare, work and citizenship.* Melbourne: Cambridge University Press, 90-106

Firestone S. (1970) *The dialectic of sex. The case for feminist revolution.* London: Jonathan Cape

First Dog on the Moon (2016) A how not to guide on men's violence against women. Thanks, Donald Trump. *The Guardian*, Australia edition, 18 October (cartoon) www.theguardian.com/commentisfree/2016/oct/18/a-how-not-to-guide-on-mens-violence-against-women-thanks-donald-trump

Fischbach R.L. and Herbert B. (1997) Domestic violence and mental health: correlates and conundrums within and across cultures. *Social Science & Medicine* 45(8): 1161-76

Flax J. (1990) Postmodernism and gender relations in feminist theory. In: Nicholson L.J. (ed) *Feminism/postmodernism.* New York: Routledge

Fonow M.M. and Cook J.A. (1991) *Beyond methodology: Feminist scholarship as lived research.* Indiana University Press

Foucault M. (1978) *The history of sexuality: Volume I.* New York: Vintage

Franzway S. (2001) *Sexual politics and greedy institutions: Union women, commitments and conflicts in public and private.* Sydney: Pluto Press Australia

Franzway S. (2016) The sexual politics of citizenship and violence. *Women's Studies International Forum* 58: 18-24

Franzway S. and Fonow M.M. (2011) *Making feminist politics: Transnational alliances between women and labor.* Urbana, IL: University of Illinois Press

Franzway S., Court D. and Connell R. (1989) *Staking a claim: Feminism, bureaucracy and the state.* Sydney: Allen & Unwin

Franzway S., Sharp R., Mills J.E., et al. (2009a) Engineering ignorance: the problem of gender equity in engineering. *Frontiers: A Journal of Women's Studies* 30(1): 89–106

Franzway S., Zufferey C. and Chung, D. (2009b) *Sustainable economic futures: Women, work and domestic violence*. Research Centre for Gender Studies, University of South Australia (for the Department of Families and Communities (DFC), and Office for Women (OFW), South Australian Government

Fraser J. (2014) Claims-making in context: forty years of Canadian feminist activism on violence against women. Department of Criminology, University of Ottowa (PhD thesis)

Freyd J.J. (1996) *Betrayal trauma: The logic of forgetting childhood abuse.* Cambridge, MA: Harvard University Press

Freyd J. and Birrell P. (2013) *Blind to betrayal: Why we fool ourselves we aren't being fooled.* Hoboken, NJ: John Wiley & Sons

Fulu E. and Miedema S. (2015) Globalization and changing family relations: family violence and women's resistance in Asian Muslim societies. *Sex Roles* 74(11–12): 480–94

García-Del Moral P. and Dersnah M.A. (2014) A feminist challenge to the gendered politics of the public/private divide: on due diligence, domestic violence, and citizenship. *Citizenship Studies* 18(6–7): 661–75

Gardiner M. (2004) Citizenship and women. In: Patmore G and Jungwirth G (eds) *The vocal citizen: Labor essays.* Melbourne: Arena Publishing

Garner H. (2014) *This house of grief.* Sydney: Text Publishing

Gatens M. (1996) *Imaginary bodies: Ethics, power and corporeality.* London: Taylor & Francis

Gautney H. (2010) *Protest and organization in the alternative globalization era: NGOs, social movements, and political parties*, New York, NY: Palgrave Macmillan

Gavey N. (2003) Writing the effects of sexual abuse. In: Reavey, P. and Warner, S. (eds) *New feminist stories of child sexual abuse: Sexual scripts and dangerous dialogues*, London: Routledge

Gavey N. (2005) *Just sex? The cultural scaffolding of rape.* Brighton: Routledge

Gerth H.H. and Mills C.W. (1948) *From Max Weber: Essays in sociology.* London: Routledge and Kegan Paul

Ghafournia N. (2011) Battered at home, played down in policy: migrant women and domestic violence in Australia. *Aggression and Violent Behavior* 16: 207–13

Giddens A. (1997) *Modernity and self-identity.* Cambridge: Polity

Goldenson J., Geffner R., Foster S.L., et al. (2007) Female domestic violence offenders: their attachment security, trauma symptoms, and personality organization. *Violence and Victims* 22(5): 532

Gordon L. (1988) *Heroes of their own lives: The politics and history of family violence*. London: Virago

Greer G. (1970) *The female eunuch*. London: Paladin

Gringeri C.E., Wahab S. and Anderson-Nathe B. (2010) What makes it feminist? Mapping the landscape of feminist social work research. *Affilia* 25(4): 390-405

Hague G. (2006) Domestic violence survivors' forums in the UK: experiments in involving abused women in domestic violence services and policy-making. *Journal of Gender Studies* 14(3): 191-203

Hall, J.W. (ed) (2004) *Conversations with Audre Lorde*. Jackson, MS: University Press of Mississippi

Hall R. (1981) Introduction to Women Against Rape (pamphlet). In: Feminist Anthology Collective (ed) *No turning back: Writings from the Women's Liberation Movement (1975-1980)*. London: Women's Press.

Hall S. and Held D. (1990) Citizens and citizenship. In: Hall S. and Jacques M. (eds) *New times*. London: Lawrence and Wishart, 173-88

Hearn J. (2002) Men, fathers and the state: national and global relations. In: Hobson B. (ed) *Making men into fathers: Men, masculinities and the social politics of fatherhood*. Cambridge: Cambridge University Press, 245-72

Hearn J., Oleksy E. and Golanska D. (2010) *The limits of gendered citizenship: Contexts and complexities*. New York: Routledge

Herman J. (1981) Father–daughter incest. *Professional Psychology* 12(1): 76-80

Herman J.L. (1997) *Trauma and recovery*. New York: Basic Books

Hobson B. and Lister R. (2001) Citizenship. In: Hobson B., Lewis J. and Siim B. (eds) *Contested concepts: Gender and social politics*. Northampton, MA: Edward Elgar

Hoffman J. (2004) *Citizenship beyond the state*. London: SAGE Publications

Home Office (2015) *Controlling or coercive behaviour in an intimate or family relationship: Statutory guidance framework*. www.gov.uk/government/uploads/system/uploads/attachment_data/file/482528/Controlling_or_coercive_behaviour_-_statutory_guidance.pdf

Horsfall J. (1991) *The presence of the past: Male violence in the family*. Sydney: Allen & Unwin

Htun M. and Weldon S.L. (2012) The civic origins of progressive policy change: combating violence against women in global perspective, 1975–2005. *American Political Science Review* 106(03): 548-69

Hughes M.M. and Brush L.D. (2015) The price of protection: a trajectory analysis of civil remedies for abuse and women's earnings. *American Sociological Review* 80(1): 140–65

Human Rights Law Centre (2017) *Over-represented and overlooked: The crisis of Aboriginal and Torres Strait Islander women's growing over-imprisonment.* Sydney: Change the Record Coalition. www.hrlc.org.au/news/2017/5/10/over-represented-overlooked-report

Humphreys C. and Thiara R. (2003) Mental health and domestic violence: 'I call it symptoms of abuse'. *British Journal of Social Work* 33(2): 209–26

Hund A.R. and Espelage D.L. (2006) Childhood emotional abuse and disordered eating among undergraduate females: mediating influence of alexithymia and distress. *Child Abuse & Neglect* 30(4): 393–407

Isaacs D. (2011) Corporal punishment of children: changing the culture. *Journal of Paediatrics and Child Health* 47(8): 491–2

Ishkanian A. (2014) Neoliberalism and violence: the Big Society and the changing politics of domestic violence in England. *Critical Social Policy* 34(3): 333–53

Isin E.F. and Turner B.S. (2002) *Handbook of citizenship studies.* London: SAGE Publications

Jackson N. (2007) *Encyclopaedia of domestic violence.* New York: Routledge

James P. (2014) Faces of globalization and the borders of states: from asylum seekers to citizens. *Citizenship Studies* 18(2): 208–23

James S. (1992) The good-enough citizen: citizenship and independence. In: Bock G. and James S. (eds) *Beyond equality and difference: Citizenship, feminist politics and female subjectivity.* London: Routledge, 48–67

Jamieson G.G. (2012) *Reaching for health: The Australian women's health movement and public policy.* Canberra, Australia: Australian National University Press

Janoski T. and Gran B. (2002) Political citizenship: foundation of rights. In: Isin E. and Turner B.S. (eds) *Handbook of citizenship studies.* London: SAGE Publications

Jasinski J.L. (2010) *Hard lives, mean streets: Violence in the lives of homeless women.* Boston: Northeastern University Press

Jessop B. (1978) Capitalism and democracy: The best possible political shell? In: Littlejohn G (ed) *Power and the State.* London: Croon Helm, 10–51.

Joachim J.M. (2007) *Agenda setting, the UN, and NGOs: Gender violence and reproductive rights.* Washington, DC: Georgetown University Press

Johnson M.P. and Ferraro K.J. (2000) Research on domestic violence in the 1990s: making distinctions. *Journal of Marriage and Family* 62(4): 948–63

Kaine S. (2016) Women, work and industrial relations in Australia in 2015. *Journal of Industrial Relations* 58(3): 324–39

Keck M.E. and Sikkink K. (1998) *Activists beyond borders: Advocacy networks in international politics*, Ithaca, NY: Cornell University Press

Keech-Marx S. (2014) Airing dirty laundry in public: anti-domestic violence activism in Beijing. In: Unger J. (ed) *Associations and the Chinese state: Contested spaces.* New York: Sharpe, 174–99

Kelly L. (1988) *Surviving sexual violence.* Cambridge: Polity

Kelly, L. (2003) The wrong debate: reflections on why force is not the key issue with respect to trafficking in women for sexual exploitation. *Feminist Review* 73: 139–44

Kelly L. (2013) Changing it up: sexual violence three decades on. In: Appignanesi L., Holmes R. and Orbach S. (eds) *Fifty shades of feminism.* London: Virago, 133–7

Kelly L., Sharp N. and Klein R. (2014) *Finding the costs of freedom. How women and children rebuild their lives after domestic violence.* London: Solace Women's Aid and Child and Woman Abuse Studies Unit, London Metropolitan University

Kezelman C. and Stavropoulos P. (2012) *'The last frontier': Practice guidelines for treatment of complex trauma and trauma informed care and service delivery.* Sydney: Adults Surviving Child Abuse

Kim S.K. (2015) *Korean American women's community activism and their response to domestic violence.* Philadelphia, PA: University of Pennsylvania

Kimmel M. (2002) Gender symmetry' in domestic violence: a substantive and methodological research review. *Violence Against Women* 8(11): 1332–63

Kirby K.M. (1996) *Indifferent boundaries: Spatial concepts of human subjectivity.* London: Guilford Press

Koven S. and Michel S. (1990) Womanly duties: maternalist politics and the origins of welfare states in France, Germany, Great Britain, and the United States, 1880–1920. *The American Historical Review* 95(4): 1076–108

Kwesiga E., Bell M.P., Pattie M., et al. (2007) Exploring the literature on relationships between gender roles, intimate partner violence, occupational status, and organizational benefits. *Journal of Interpersonal Violence* 22(3): 312–26

Kyegombe N., Starmann E., Devries K.M., et al. (2014) 'SASA! is the medicine that treats violence'. Qualitative findings on how a community mobilisation intervention to prevent violence against women created change in Kampala, Uganda. *Global Health Action* 7(1): 25082

Kymlicka W. (1995) *Multicultural citizenship: A liberal theory of minority rights.* Oxford: Clarendon Press

Laing L. and Humphreys C. (2013) *Social work and domestic violence: Developing critical and reflective practice.* London: SAGE Publications

Laing L. and Toivonen C. (2010) Bridging the gap: evaluation of the domestic violence and mental health pilot project – Joan Harrison Support Services for Women. Faculty of Education and Social Work, University of Sydney. http://hdl.handle.net/2123/6118

Lanier C. and Maume M.O. (2009) Intimate partner violence and social isolation across the rural/urban divide. *Violence Against Women* 15(11): 1311–30

Larance L.Y. and Porter M.L. (2004) Observations from practice support group membership as a process of social capital formation among female survivors of domestic violence. *Journal of Interpersonal Violence* 19(6): 676–90

Laursen B. and Hartup W.W. (2002) The origins of reciprocity and social exchange in friendships. *New Directions for Child and Adolescent Development* 95: 27–40

Lee K. and Anderson J. (2017) The internet and intimate partner violence. Technology changes, abuse doesn't. *Strategies: The Prosecutors' Newsletter on Violence against Women*, 16

Leopold T.A., Ratcheva V. and Zahidi S. (2016) *Global gender gap report 2016.* Geneva: World Economic Forum

Levasseur M., Richard L., Gauvin L., et al. (2010) Inventory and analysis of definitions of social participation found in the aging literature: proposed taxonomy of social activities. *Social Science & Medicine* 71(12): 2141–9

Lichtenstein B. (2005) Domestic violence, sexual ownership, and HIV risk in women in the American deep south. *Social Science & Medicine* 60(4): 701–14

Lindström M., Hanson B.S. and Östergren P.-O. (2001) Socioeconomic differences in leisure-time physical activity: the role of social participation and social capital in shaping health related behaviour. *Social Science & Medicine* 52(3): 441–51

Lister R. (1997) Citizenship: towards a feminist synthesis. *Feminist Review* 57: 28–48

Lister R. (2002) Sexual citizenship. In: Isin E. and Turner B.S. (eds) *Handbook of citizenship studies.* London: SAGE Publications

Lister R. (2003) *Citizenship: Feminist perspectives.* New York: New York University Press

Lister R. (2007) Inclusive citizenship: realizing the potential. *Citizenship Studies* 11(1): 49-61

Lister R. (2011) From the intimate to the global: reflections on gendered citizenship. In: Hearn J., Oleksy, E.H. and Golanska, D. (eds) *The limits of gendered citizenship: Contexts and complexities.* Abingdon: Routledge

Lister R., Williams F., Anttonen A., et al. (2007) *Gendering citizenship in Western Europe: New challenges for citizenship research in a cross-national context.* Bristol: Policy Press

Lombardo E. and Verloo M. (2009) Contentious citizenship: feminist debates and practices and European challenges. *Feminist Review* 92: 108-28

Longo P. (2001) Revisiting the equality/difference debate: redefining citizenship for the new millennium. *Citizenship Studies* 5(3): 269-84

Lumby B. and Farrelly T. (2009) Family violence, help seeking and the close knit Aboriginal community: lessons for mainstream service provision. *Australian Domestic & Family Violence Clearinghouse* 19: 1-24

Lundgren E. (1998) The hand that strikes and comforts: gender construction and the tension between body and symbol. In: Dobash.R.E. and Dobash R.P. (eds) *Rethinking violence against women.* London: SAGE Publications, 169-96

Mackay F. (2015) *Radical feminism: Feminist activism in movement.* London: Palgrave Macmillan

MacSween M. (1993) *Anorexic bodies: A feminist and sociological perspective on anorexia nervosa.* London/New York: Routledge

Manjoo R. (2014) *Violence against women, its causes and consequences.* New York: United Nations General Assembly

Mann M. (1987) Ruling class strategies and citizenship. *Sociology* 21(3): 339-54

Manuh T. and Dwamena-Aboagye A. (2013) Implementing domestic violence legislation in Ghana. In: Al-Sharmani M. (ed) *Feminist activism, women's rights, and legal reform.* London, UK: Zed, 203-33

Marshall T.H. (1950) *Citizenship and social class and other essays.* Cambridge: Cambridge University Press

Martin D. (1981) *Battered wives,* Volcano Press

McFerran L. (1993) Domestic violence - stories, scandals and serious analysis. In: Refractory Girl (ed) *Refracting voices: Feminist perspectives from Refractory Girl.* Southwood Press, 152-9

McFerran L. (2011) *Safe at home, safe at work? National Domestic Violence and the Workplace Survey (2011)*. Sydney: Australian Domestic Violence Clearinghouse and Micromex Research

McGregor H. and Hopkins A. (1991) *Working for change. The movement against domestic violence*. Sydney: Allen & Unwin

McNay L. (2004) Situated intersubjectivity. In: Marshall B. and Witz A.M. (eds) *Engendering the social: Feminist encounters with sociological theory*. Maidenhead: Open University Press, 171–86

Medlin J.A. (2012) Domestic violence and working women: The relationship between employment status and women who seek assistance. Ann Arbor, MI: Capella University (Dissertation)

Michal M., Beutel M.E., Jordan J., et al. (2007) Depersonalization, mindfulness, and childhood trauma. *The Journal of Nervous and Mental Disease* 195(8): 693–6

Middleton W., Stavropoulos P., Dorahy M.J., et al. (2014) The Australian Royal Commission into institutional responses to child sexual abuse. *Australian & New Zealand Journal of Psychiatry* 48(1): 17–21

Millett K. (1969) *Sexual politics*. New York: Avon Books

Mills J.E., Franzway S., Gill J., et al. (2013) *Challenging knowledge, sex and power: Gender, work and engineering*. London/New York: Routledge

Mills J.E., Gill J., Sharp R., et al. (2011) Getting it together: feminist interdisciplinary research on women and engineering. *Women's Studies International Forum* 34: 13–19

Milner A.N. and Baker E.H. (2017) Athletic participation and intimate partner violence victimization: investigating sport involvement, self-esteem, and abuse patterns for women and men. *Journal of Interpersonal Violence* 32(2): 268–89

Milwertz C. (2003) Activism against domestic violence in the People's Republic of China. *Violence Against Women* 9(6): 630–54

Mitchell J. (1966) *Woman's estate*. Harmondsworth, Middlesex: Penguin

Moghadam V. (2005) *Globalizing women: Transnational feminist networks*. Baltimore: Johns Hopkins University Press

Montero I., Escriba V., Ruiz-Perez I., et al. (2011) Interpersonal violence and women's psychological well-being. *Journal of Women's Health* 20: 295–301

Morris A. (1999) Adding insult to injury. *Trouble & Strife* 40: 30–5

Mouffe C. (1992) Feminism, citizenship and radical democratic politics. In: Butler J. and Scott J.W. (eds) *Feminists theorize the political*. New York: Routledge, 369–84

Moulding N. (2003) Constructing the self in mental health practice: identity, individualism and the feminization of deficiency. *Feminist Review* 75(1): 57–74

Moulding N. (2006) Disciplining the feminine: the reproduction of gender contradictions in the mental health care of women with eating disorders. *Social Science & Medicine* 62(4): 793–804

Moulding N. (2016) *Gendered violence, abuse and mental health in everyday lives: Beyond trauma.* London/New York: Routledge

Moulding N.T., Buchanan F. and Wendt S. (2015) Untangling self-blame and mother-blame in women's and children's perspectives on maternal protectiveness in domestic violence: implications for practice. *Child Abuse Review* 24(4): 249–60

Mudavanhu S. and Radloff J. (2013) Taking feminist activism online: reflections on the 'Keep Saartjie Baartman Centre Open' e-campaign. *Gender & Development* 21(2): 327–41

Munday J. (2009) Gendered citizenship. *Sociology Compass* 3(2): 249–66

Munshi S. (2013) *Negotiating violence, navigating neoliberalism: Domestic violence advocacy efforts in South Asian communities in post-9/11 New York City.* New York: City University of New York

Murray C., Crowe A. and Akers W. (2016) How can we end the stigma surrounding domestic and sexual violence? A modified Delphi study with national advocacy leaders. *Journal of Family Violence* 31(3): 271–87

Murray G. (2007) Who is afraid of T. H. Marshall? Or, what are the limits of the liberal vision of rights? *Societies Without Borders* 2(2): 222–42

Murray S. (1999) Taking action against domestic violence in the 1970s. *Studies in Western Australian History* 19: 190–203

Murray S. (2002) *More than a refuge: Changing responses to domestic violence.* Crawley, WA: University of Western Australia Press

Murray S. (2008) 'Why doesn't she just leave?' Belonging, disruption and domestic violence. *Women's Studies International Forum* 31: 65–72

Murray S. and Powell A. (2009) 'What's the problem?' Australian public policy constructions of domestic and family violence. *Violence Against Women* 15(5): 532–52

Nash K. (2001) Feminism and contemporary liberal citizenship: The undecidability of 'women'. *Citizenship Studies* 5(3): 255–68

Nettleton S. and Bunton R. (1995) Sociological critiques of health promotion. In: R. Bunton, S. Nettleton and R. Burrows (eds) *The sociology of health promotion: Critical analyses of consumption, lifestyle and risk.* London: Routledge.

Netto G., Pawson H. and Sharp C. (2009) Preventing homelessness due to domestic violence: providing a safe space or closing the door to new possibilities? *Social Policy & Administration* 43(7): 719–35

Nichols A.J. (2011) Feminist advocacy in community based responses to domestic violence: gendered identity, ideology and practices. University of Missouri (Dissertation)

Niolon P.H., Kearns M., Dills J., et al. (2017) *Preventing intimate partner violence across the lifespan: A technical package of programs, policies, and practices.* Atlanta, Georgia: National Center for Injury Prevention and Control, Centers for Disease Control and Prevention

Nixon R.D., Resick P.A. and Nishith P. (2004) An exploration of co-morbid depression among female victims of intimate partner violence with posttraumatic stress disorder. *Journal of Affective Disorders* 82(2): 315–20

Noble J. and Verity F. (2006) *Imagine if. A handbook for activists.* Kent Town: Wakefield Press

Nussbaum M.C. (1995) Objectification. *Philosophy and Public Affairs* 24(4): 249–91

Nussbaum M.C. (2000) Women's capabilities and social justice. *Journal of Human Development* 1(2): 219–47

Nussbaum M. (2003) Capabilities as fundamental entitlements: Sen and social justice. *Feminist Economics* 9(2–3): 33–59

Nussbaum M.C. (2005) Women's bodies: violence, security, capabilities. *Journal of Human Development* 6(2): 167–83

Nussbaum M.C. (2011) *Creating capabilities: The human development approach.* Cambridge, MA: Belknap of Harvard University Press

Okin S.M. (1991) Gender, the public and the private. In: Held D. (ed) *Political theory today.* Stanford: Stanford University Press

Orth U., Robins R.W. and Roberts B.W. (2008) Low self-esteem prospectively predicts depression in adolescence and young adulthood. *Journal of Personality and Social Psychology* 95(3): 695–708

Otto D. and Haley E. (1975) Helter shelter: a history of the Adelaide women's shelter. *Refractory Girl* Winter: 11–16

Paglione G. (2006) Domestic violence and housing rights: a reinterpretation of the right to housing. *Human Rights Quarterly* 28(1): 120–47

Pain R. (2014) Seismologies of emotion: fear and activism during domestic violence. *Social & Cultural Geography* 15(2): 127–50

Parkes C.M., Stevenson-Hinde J. and Marris P. (2006) *Attachment across the life cycle.* London/New York: Routledge

Pateman C. (1988) *The sexual contract.* Cambridge: Polity

Pateman C. (1989) Feminist critiques of the public/private dichotomy. In: Pateman C. (ed) *The disorder of women: Democracy, feminism and political theory.* Cambridge: Polity, 118-40

Pateman C. (1992) Equality, difference, subordination: the politics of motherhood and women's citizenship. In: Bock G. and James S. (eds) *Beyond equality and difference: Citizenship, feminist politics and female subjectivity.* London: Routledge, 17-31

Pateman C. (2011) The legacy of T.H. Marshall. In: Carver T. and Chambers S.A. (eds) *Carole Pateman: Democracy, feminism welfare.* London: Routledge

Pateman C. and Grosz E. (1986a) Introduction. In: Pateman C. and Grosz E. (eds) *Feminist challenges: Social and political theory.* Sydney: Allen & Unwin

Pateman C. and Grosz E. (1986b) *Feminist challenges: Social and political theory.* Sydney: Allen & Unwin

Pavao J., Alvarez J., Baumrind N., et al. (2007) Intimate partner violence and housing instability. *American Journal of Preventive Medicine* 32(2): 143-6

Pease B. and Rees S. (2008) Theorising men's violence towards women in refugee families: towards an intersectional feminist framework. *Just Policy: A Journal of Australian Social Policy* 47: 39-45

Peetz D. and Murray G. (2017) *Women, labor segmentation and regulation.* NY: Palgrave Macmillan

Pettman J.J. (1996) *Worlding woman: A feminist international politics.* Sydney: Allen & Unwin

Pham T.T.G. (2015) Using education–entertainment in breaking the silence about sexual violence against women in Vietnam. *Asian Journal of Women's Studies* 21(4): 460-6

Plummer K. (2001) *Documents of life 2: An invitation to a critical humanism.* London: SAGE Publications

Pocock B. (2003) *The work/life collision: What work is doing to Australians and what to do about it.* Sydney: Federation Press

Pollack K.M., Cummiskey C., Krotki K., et al. (2010) Reasons women experiencing intimate partner violence seek assistance from employee assistance programs. *Journal of Workplace Behavioral Health* 25(3): 181-94

Ponic P., Varcoe C., Davies L., et al. (2011) Leaving ≠ moving housing patterns of women who have left an abusive partner. *Violence Against Women* 17(12): 1576-600

Probyn E. (2005) *Blush: Faces of shame.* Sydney: University of New South Wales Press

Procter N.G., Newman L. and Dudley M. (2013) Seeking asylum in Australia: immigration detention, human rights and mental health care. *Australasian Psychiatry: Bulletin of the Royal Australian and New Zealand College of Psychiatrists* 21(4): 315-20

Prokhovnik R. (1998) Public and private citizenship: from gender invisibility to feminist inclusiveness. *Feminist Review* 60: 84-104

Prügl E. (2016) Neoliberalism with a feminist face: crafting a new hegemony at the World Bank. *Feminist Economics* 23(1): 30-53

Qui D. and Zufferey C. (2017) Homelessness in China. In: Zufferey C and Yu N (eds) *Faces of homelessness in the Asia Pacific Region*. Oxford: Routledge, 28-47

Radford L. and Tsutsumi K. (2004) Globalization and violence against women—inequalities in risks, responsibilities and blame in the UK and Japan. *Women's Studies International Forum* 27(1): 1-12

Raphael J. (2001) Domestic violence as a welfare-to-work barrier: Research and theoretical issues. In: Renzetti C., Edleson J. and Kennedy B.R. (eds) *Sourcebook on violence against women*. California: SAGE Publications, 443-57

Reavey P. (2003) When past meets present to produce a sexual 'other'. *New feminist stories of child sexual abuse: Sexual scripts and dangerous dialogues*. London: Routledge

Reina A.S., Lohman B.J. and Maldonado M.M. (2014) 'He said they'd deport me': factors influencing domestic violence help-seeking practices among Latina immigrants. *Journal of Interpersonal Violence* 29(4): 593-615

Riessman C.K. (2008) *Narrative methods for the human sciences*. London: SAGE Publications

Rios A. (2014) *Feminism(s), politics, and domestic violence: Tensions and challenges in shifting the discourse and institutional relationships*. Temple University

Roberts H. (1981) Women and their doctors: power and powerlessness in the research process. In: Roberts H. (ed) *Doing feminist research*. London: Routledge

Rorty M. and Yager J. (1996) Histories of childhood trauma and complex post-traumatic sequelae in women with eating disorders. *Psychiatric Clinics of North America* 19(4): 773-91

Rošul-Gajic- J. (2016) Agents of change. Women's advocacy during democratization in Croatia. *Südosteuropa* 2016(4): 544-59

Rowbotham S. (1977) *Hidden from history: 300 years of women's oppression and the fight against it*. London: Pluto Press

Rowbotham S. (1989) *The past is before us: Feminism in action since the 1960s*. London: Pandora Press

Rowntree M. (2010) 'Living life with grace is my revenge': situating survivor knowledge about sexual violence. *Qualitative Social Work* 9(4): 447-60

Roychowdhury P. (2015) Victims to saviors: governmentality and the regendering of citizenship in India. *Gender & Society* 29(6): 792-816

Russ J. (1983) *How to suppress women's writing*. Texas: University of Texas Press

Ryan C., Jeffreys K. and Blozie L. (2012) Raising public awareness of domestic violence: strategic communication and movement building. In: Maney G.M., Kutz-Flamebaum R.V., Rohlinger D.A., et al. (eds) *Strategies for social change*. Minneapolis: University of Minnesota Press, 61-92

Schechter S. (1982) *Women and male violence: The visions and struggles of the battered women's movement*. Boston: South End Press

Scheffer Lindgren M. and Renck B. (2008) 'It is still so deep-seated, the fear': psychological stress reactions as consequences of intimate partner violence. *Journal of Psychiatric and Mental Health Nursing* 15(3): 219-28

Schneider E.M. (2000) *Battered women and feminist lawmaking*. New Haven: Yale University Press

Schneider E.M. (2008) Domestic violence law reform in the twenty-first century: looking back and looking forward. *Family Law Quarterly* 42(3): 353-63

Schuster J. (2013) Invisible feminists? Social media and young women's political participation. *Political Science* 65(1): 8-24

Seidman S. (1997) *Difference troubles: Queering social theory and sexual politics*. Cambridge: Cambridge University Press

Sen P. (1999) Domestic violence, deportation and women's resistance: notes on managing inter-sectionality. *Development in Practice* 9(1-2): 178-83

Sharp-Jeffs N., Kelly L. and Klein R. (2018) Long journeys toward freedom: the relationships between coercive control and space for action – measurement and emerging evidence. *Violence Against Women* 24(2): 163-85

Showalter E. (1987) *The female malady*. Virago: London

Staggs S., Long S., Mason G., et al. (2007) Intimate partner violence, social support, and employment in the post-welfare reform era. *Journal of Interpersonal Violence* 22(3): 345-67

Stanley L. (ed) (2013) *Feminist praxis: Research, theory and epistemology in feminist sociology*. London: Routledge

Stark E. (2007) *Coercive control: How men entrap women in personal life*. Oxford: Oxford University Press

Stark E. (2009) Rethinking coercive control. *Violence Against Women* 15(12): 1509-25

Stark E. (2012) Looking beyond domestic violence: policing coercive control. *Journal of Police Crisis Negotiations* 12(2): 199-217

Stoltenborgh M., Bakermans-Kranenburg M.J., Alink L.R., et al. (2012) The universality of childhood emotional abuse: a meta-analysis of worldwide prevalence. *Journal of Aggression, Maltreatment & Trauma* 21(8): 870-90

Suchland J. (2015) *Economies of violence: Transnational feminism, postsocialism, and the politics of sex trafficking.* Durham UC: Duke University Press

Summers A. (1975) *Damned whores and God's police: The colonization of women in Australia.* Ringwood, Vic. Australia: Penguin

Swanberg J. and Logan T. (2007) Intimate partner violence, employment and the workplace: an interdisciplinary perspective. *Journal of Interpersonal Violence* 22(3): 263-7

The Slap (2011) [TV] ABC1. 6 October-24 November. ABC/ Matchbox Pictures Production

Thompson E.H. and Trice-Black S. (2012) School-based group interventions for children exposed to domestic violence. *Journal of Family Violence* 27(3): 233-41

Tiemeyer P. (2013) *Plane queer: Labor, sexuality and aids in the history of male flight attendants.* Berkeley, CA: University of California Press

Torrisi C. (2017) Monsters, jealousy and 'sick love' — how the Italian media covers violence against women. *Open Democracy*, 3 May

Towns A. (2016) Civilization. In: Disch L. and Hawkesworth M. (eds) *The Oxford handbook of feminist theory.* Oxford: Oxford University Press, 79-99

Tracy S.R. (2007) Patriarchy and domestic violence: challenging common misconceptions. *Journal of the Evangelical Theological Society* 50(3): 573-94

Treagus M. (2012) Queering the mainstream: The Slap and 'middle' Australia. *Journal of the Association for the Study of Australian Literature* 12(3): 1-9

Trickett P.K., Noll J.G. and Putnam F.W. (2011) The impact of sexual abuse on female development: lessons from a multigenerational, longitudinal research study. *Development and Psychopathology* 23(2): 453-76

True J. (2012) *The political economy of violence against women.* Oxford: Oxford University Press

Tseris E.J. (2013) Trauma theory without feminism? Evaluating contemporary understandings of traumatized women. *Affilia* 28(2): 153–64

Tuana N. (2006) The speculum of ignorance: the women's health movement and epistemologies of ignorance. *Hypatia* 21(3): 1–19

Turner B.S. (1990) Outline of a theory of citizenship. *Sociology* 24(2): 189–217

Turner B.S. (1997) Citizenship studies: a general theory. *Citizenship Studies* 1(1): 5–18

Turner B.S. (2001) The erosion of citizenship. *The British Journal of Sociology* 52(2): 189–209

UN Women (2017) Ending violence against women. www.unwomen. org/en/what-we-do/ending-violence-against-women

Urban B.Y. and Wagner K.C. (2000) Domestic violence: a union issue. A workplace training resource kit for unions. San Francisco, CA: The Family Violence Prevention Fund

Urry J. (2007) *Mobilities*. Cambridge: Polity

Ussher J.M. (2010) Are we medicalizing women's misery? A critical review of women's higher rates of reported depression. *Feminism & Psychology* 20(1): 9–35

VicHealth (2017) *Annual Report 2016–17*. Melbourne: Victorian Health Promotion Foundation

Wacquant L. (2012) Three steps to a historical anthropology of actually existing neoliberalism. *Social Anthropology/Anthropologie Sociale* 20(1): 66–79

Walby S. (1990) *Theorizing patriarchy*. Oxford: Blackwell

Walby S. (1994) Is citizenship gendered? *Sociology* 28(2): 379–95

Walby S. (2009) *Globalization and inequalities: Complexity and contested modernities*. London: SAGE Publications

Walby S. and Allen J. (2004) *Domestic violence, sexual assault and stalking: Findings from the British Crime Survey*. Home Office

Walby S., Towers J. and Francis B. (2016) Is violent crime increasing or decreasing? A new methodology to measure repeat attacks making visible the significance of gender and domestic relations. *The British Journal of Criminology* 56(6): 1203–34

Warner S. (2009) *Understanding the effects of child sexual abuse: Feminist revolutions in theory, research and practice*. Oxford: Routledge

Weeks W. (1994) *Women working together. Lessons from feminist women's services*. Melbourne: Longman Cheshire

Weeks W. (2003) From a Sydney squat to sophisticated services responding to domestic and family violence: progress in crisis accommodation for women escaping violence. *Parity* 16(10): 10–14

Weingourt R., Maruyama T., Sawada I., et al. (2001) Domestic violence and women's mental health in Japan. *International Nursing Review* 48(2): 102-8

Weissman D.M. (2007) The personal is political – and economic: Rethinking domestic violence. *Brigham Young University Law Review* 2007(2): 387-450

Weissman D.M. (2016) Countering neoliberalism and aligning solidarities: rethinking domestic violence advocacy. *Southwestern Law Review* 45(4): 915-57

Welch M. (2014) Economic man and diffused sovereignty: a critique of Australia's asylum regime. *Crime, Law and Social Change* 61(1): 81-107

Weldon S.L. and Htun M. (2013) Feminist mobilisation and progressive policy change: why governments take action to combat violence against women. *Gender & Development* 21(2): 231-47

Wendt S. (2009) *Domestic violence in rural Australia*. Annandale, NSW: Federation Press

Wendt S.C. (2016) Domestic violence and feminism. In: S. Wendt and N. Moulding (eds) *Contemporary feminism in social work practice*. Abingdon: Routledge: 209-19

Wendt S. and Hornosty J. (2010) Understanding contexts of family violence in rural, farming communities: implications for rural women's health. *Rural Society* 20(1): 51-63

Wendt S. and Zannettino L. (2015) *Domestic violence in diverse contexts. A re-examination of gender*. London: Routledge

WHO (World Health Organization) (2005) *Summary report. WHO multi-country study on women's health and domestic violence against women.* Geneva: WHO. www.who.int/reproductivehealth/publications/violence/24159358X/en/

WHO (2013) *Global and regional estimates of violence against women: Prevalence and health effects of intimate partner violence and nonpartner sexual violence.* Geneva: WHO

Wirth-Cauchon J. (2001) *Women and borderline personality disorder: Symptoms and stories*. Rutgers University Press

Workplace Gender Equality Agency (2016) *Australia's gender equality scorecard: Key findings from the Workplace Gender Equality Agency's 2015-16 reporting data*. Sydney: Workplace Gender Equality Agency

Yeatman A. (1994) The personal and the political: a feminist critique. In: James P (ed) *Critical politics.* Melbourne: Arena

Young I.M. (1989) Polity and group difference: a critique of the ideal of universal citizenship. *Ethics* 99(2): 250-74

Yuval-Davis N. (1997) Women, citizenship and difference. *Feminist Review* 57: 4-27

Yuval-Davis N. and Werbner P. (1999) *Women, citizenship and difference*. London: Zed

Zoepf K. (2017) What overturning the ban on female drivers means for Saudi Arabia and the world. *The New Yorker* 12 October

Index